DATE			
FEB 0 5 1989			

Y0-BQE-135

NEW VIEWPOINTS
IN AMERICAN HISTORY

NEW VIEWPOINTS
IN AMERICAN HISTORY

BY

ARTHUR MEIER SCHLESINGER

PROFESSOR OF HISTORY IN THE UNIVERSITY OF IOWA

A comprehension of the United States of to-day, an understanding of the rise and progress of the forces which have made it what it is, demands that we should rework our history from the new points of view afforded by the present.

FREDERICK JACKSON TURNER:
Presidential Address

GREENWOOD PRESS, PUBLISHERS
WESTPORT, CONNECTICUT

Library of Congress Cataloging in Publication Data

Schlesinger, Arthur Meier, 1888-1965.
    New viewpoints in American history.

    Reprint of the ed. published by Macmillan, New York.
    Includes bibliographies and index.
    1.   United States--History--Addresses, essays,
lectures.   I.   Title.
E178.6.S327   1977   973   76-49146
ISBN 0-8371-9314-1

Copyright renewed 1950, by Arthur Meier Schlesinger

Originally published in 1922 by the Macmillan Company,
New York

Reprinted with the permission of Elizabeth B. Schlesinger

Reprinted from a copy in the collections of the Brooklyn
Public Library

Reprinted in 1977 by Greenwood Press, Inc.

Library of Congress Catalog Card Number   76-49146

ISBN 0-8371-9314-1

Printed in the United States of America

TO

O. S. S.
K. B. S.
B. S.
H. N. S.

In Memoriam

FOREWORD

Most adult Americans of today gained their knowledge of American history before the present generation of historians had made perceptible progress in their epoch-making work of reconstructing the story of our past in the light of their new studies and investigations. Signs of a renaissance of American historical writing began to be evident as early as the decade of the eighties of the last century. The new interest in historical and social phenomena was shown, for instance, in the founding of the American Historical Association, the American Economic Association, the American Statistical Association and the American Academy of Political and Social Science during that decade, followed shortly after by the formation of the American Political Science Association, the American Sociological Society and the American Society of International Law. American history, which had formerly been envisaged as a record of arid political and constitutional development, began to be enriched by the new conceptions and fresh points of view afforded by the scientific study of economics, sociology and politics. Influences from abroad also played their part, particularly the notable work of John Richard Green, *A Short History of the English People* (1874), with its revisions and enlargements. Quickened by these new impulses, historians began to view the past of America with broadened vision and to attain the power of seeing familiar facts in new relationships.

The change did not take place overnight. Historical students in the nineties made important contributions toward the new history; but it was not until the opening years of the present century that the real transformation occurred. All historical study and writing since then have been strongly colored by the new interests, viewpoints and sympathies.

Unfortunately, the product of the new school of American historians has, in very large part, been buried in the files of historical society journals, in the learned publications of the universities and in monographs privately printed at the expense of the authors. The new history was being written by historians for historians rather than for laymen; and the public generally has remained oblivious of the great revolution in our knowledge of American history wrought by the research specialists. Even the school textbooks have not until a comparatively recent time been affected by the discoveries of the specialists; and too often the newer type of textbook has suffered at the hands of teachers who, though familiar with the new facts and emphases as set forth in the textbook, have no acquaintance with the general point of view which gives to these new facts their tremendous significance.

The object of the present work is to bring together and summarize, in non-technical language, some of the results of the researches of the present era of historical study and to show their importance to a proper understanding of American history. It seems unnecessary to say that the interest aroused by the World War in Americanization work makes it important that all citizens of the republic should learn what the historians have to say about the past of their country: Americanization must begin at home. History teachers in the public schools may also find in this volume a short cut to a rather extensive literature inaccessible to most of them. It is the further hope of the author that graduate students venturing forth into the field of American history for the first time may find this volume useful in suggesting the special interests of the present generation of historians and some of the tendencies that seem likely to guide historical research for some years to come. It has not been my primary purpose to celebrate the names of the men and women who have cleared the new trails; but an effort has been made in the notes at the end of each chapter to render due acknowledgment.

The title of this volume is, in a sense, a misnomer since the viewpoints presented are not new to workers in the history field nor are *all* the new viewpoints set forth. In explanation of the omissions, the author can only plead his feeling that the points of view omitted are not as essential as those that have been included or else that the viewpoint in question has not yet been sufficiently worked out or defined to merit inclusion at this time. In the latter category fall two approaches to American history which are certain to receive more careful attention in the future, that of religious and sectarian influences in American development, and the point of view represented by the psychoanalysts. Some of the groundwork upon which a religious interpretation of American history might be based has already been laid by special students of American church history; and the possibilities of the psychological approach are suggested, for example, by the series of articles on "The American Mind", written by Harvey O'Higgins and Edward H. Reede in *McClure's,* vol. 53 (1921), Nos. 3, 4, 6 and 7. It should be added that the significant point of view presented by Herbert Eugene Bolton and Thomas Maitland Marshall in their book, *The Colonization of North America 1492-1783* (New York, 1920), is not treated here for the reason that the plan of the present volume embraces only such influences and conditions as contributed vitally to the national development of the United States.

A work of this kind can hardly hope to be free of error,

although I believe that no errors have crept in that would invalidate the general conclusions reached. Nor can I hope that I have been completely successful in eliminating the personal equation. Every teacher of history evolves a philosophy of history which will find expression in spite of all efforts at repression; and this is particularly true when the subject matter dealt with is controversial in character. Because of the scheme of treatment a certain amount of repetition in dealing with special incidents and movements has been rendered necessary. In putting my material into printed form I owe much to the interest and encouragement of certain secondary school teachers who heard much of the material in lecture form in summer school classes in the Ohio State University and the University of Iowa in 1919 and 1920. A number of my friends have helpfully read portions of the completed manuscript. In particular I am indebted to Professor F. W. Coker and Dr. Carl Wittke of the Ohio State University. To my wife Elizabeth Bancroft I am obligated for assistance rendered at every stage of the preparation of the manuscript. Chapters I, VII and XI appeared originally in somewhat altered form in the *American Journal of Sociology,* the *Political Science Quarterly* and the *Historical Outlook;* and for permission to use them again I am indebted to the editors of those journals.

A. M. S.

CONTENTS

NEW VIEWPOINTS
IN AMERICAN HISTORY

NEW VIEWPOINTS IN AMERICAN HISTORY

CHAPTER I

THE INFLUENCE OF IMMIGRATION ON AMERICAN HISTORY

The New World was discovered by a man who was trying his utmost to find an older world than the one from which he had sailed. If Columbus had known that he had failed to reach the fabled Orient, he would have died a bitterly disillusioned man. Yet, in the judgment of history, the measure of his greatness is to be found in the fact that he committed this cardinal blunder, for thereby he and the later explorers opened up to the crowded populations of Europe a means of escape from poverty and oppression for many centuries to come. The ratio between man and land became changed for the whole civilized world, and there opened up before humanity unsuspected opportunities for development and progress. On account of political disturbances in Europe and the difficulties of ocean travel, the full possibilities of this epochal change were only gradually developed; and the effects were thus distributed through the last four centuries of world-history. But the event itself stands forth as one of the tremendous facts of history. So far as the human mind can foresee, nothing of a similar nature can ever happen again.

The great *Völkerwanderungen,* set in motion by the

opening up of the Western Hemisphere, have been essentially unlike any earlier migrations in history, and in comparison with them most of the earlier movements of population were numerically insignificant. In a large sense, all American history has been the product of these migratory movements from the Old World. Since the red-skinned savage has never been a potent factor in American development, the whole history of the United States and, to a lesser degree, of the two Americas is, at bottom, the story of the successive waves of immigration and of the adaptation of the newcomers and their descendants to the new surroundings offered by the Western Hemisphere. Thus the two grand themes of American history are, properly, the influence of immigration upon American life and institutions, and the influence of the American environment, especially the frontier in the early days and the industrial integration of more recent times, upon the ever-changing composite population.

I

Columbus's first voyage of discovery was a strange foreshadowing of the later history of the American people, for, in a very real sense, his voyage may be considered an international enterprise. Acting under the authority of Spain, this Italian sailed with a crew consisting of Spaniards, one Irishman, an Englishman, and an Israelite. These nationalities were later to enter fully into the rich heritage which this voyage made possible to the world. In the next two centuries the nations of Europe, large and small, sought to stake out colonial claims in America, not with entire success from an imperialistic point of view, but with the result that cultural foundations were laid whose influence may still be traced in the legal systems, customs, and institutions of many parts of the United States today. A familiar illustration is afforded in the case of Louisiana, where the continental civil law, instead of the English common law, governs domestic relations and transfers of property as a reminder of the days when the French and the Spanish owned the land.

Contrary to a widespread belief, even the people of the thirteen English colonies were a mixture of ethnic breeds. Indeed, these colonies formed the most cosmopolitan area in the world at the time. This was due, in part, to the English conquest of colonies planted by rival European powers along the Atlantic Coast, but was the result more largely of abundant immigration from various parts of the world after the original settlements had been well established. A Colonial Dame or a Daughter of the American Revolution might conceivably have nothing but pure Hebrew blood or French or German blood in her veins. During the first century of English colonization, the seventeenth, the English race was the main contributor to the population, the Dutch and French Huguenot contributions being less important. These racial elements occupied the choice lands near the coast, and thus compelled the stream of immigration of the eighteenth century to pour into the interior, a significant development in view of the different character and great numbers of these later settlers.

While the religious motive has properly been stressed in the history of colonization, it should not be overlooked that the economic urge, operating independently or as a stiffening to religious conviction, sent countless thousands fleeing to American shores. We need not wink at the fact that the immigrants of colonial times were actuated by the same motives as the immigrants today, namely a determination to escape religious or political oppression and a desire to improve their living conditions. To make this generalization strictly applicable to immigration in our own day, one might wish to reverse the order of emphasis, although the Russian Jews and the Armenian refugees are conspicuous examples of the contrary.

The earliest English settlement, that at Jamestown, was sent out by an English trading corporation which was interested primarily in making profits for the stockholders of the company out of the industry of the settlers. In a like spirit, that canny Quaker William Penn lost no opportunity, after the first settlements were made in his dominion of Pennsylvania, to stimulate immigration artificially, for the resulting enhancement of real estate values meant an increased income for him. He advertised his lands widely throughout Europe, offering large tracts at nominal prices and portraying the political and religious advantages of residence under his rule. In anticipation of later practices, he maintained paid agents in the Rhine Valley, who were so successful that within a score of years German immigrants numbered almost one-half of the population.

Another source of "assisted immigration" was to be found in the practice of European nations to drain their almshouses and jails into their colonies; it has been estimated that as many as fifty thousand criminals were sent to the thirteen colonies by Great Britain. Due allowance must, of course, be made for a legal code which condemned offenders to death for stealing a joint of meat worth more than one shilling! Perhaps one-half of all the white immigrants during the larger part of the colonial period were unable to pay their expenses. They came "indentured" and were auctioned off for a period of service by the ship captains in payment for their transportation. Still another element of the population, perhaps one-fifth of the whole in the eighteenth century, consisted of Guinea negroes who became emigrants to the New World only through the exercise of superior force. A well-known historian is authority for the statement that probably one-third of the colonists in 1760 were born outside of America.

Men of older colonial stock viewed the more recent comers with a species of alarm that was to be repeated with each new generation of the American breed. Benjamin Franklin declared that the German immigrants pouring into Pennsylvania "are generally the most stupid of their own nation. . . . Not being used to liberty they know not how to make modest use of it." They appear at elections "in droves and carry all before them, except in one or two counties. Few of their children know English." At one time a bill was passed by the colonial legislature of Pennsylvania to restrict the immigration of the German Palatines, but it was vetoed by the governor. The familiar objections to immigration on grounds of non-assimilability, pauperism, and criminality originated during these early days, leaving for later and more congested times the development of arguments derived from the fear of economic competition.

The preponderance of English settlers in the first century of colonization served to fix governmental institutions and political ideals in an English mold and to make English speech the general language of the colonists. In the later colonial period most of New England retained its purely English character because of the Puritan policy of religious exclusiveness; but into the other colonies alien racial elements came in great numbers and left their impress on native culture and, in a less measure, on American speech. It is instructive to remember that the great English Puritan migration did not exceed twenty thousand, whereas more than one hundred and fifty thousand Scotch-Irish Presbyterians settled in the colonies in the eighteenth century.[1]

[1] These were lowland Scots who had been transplanted to Ulster early in the seventeenth century. Suffering from religious and political disabilities and afflicted with hard times, these Ulstermen sought relief through migration to the colonies.

Unlike the Puritans, the Scotch-Irish were to be found in nearly five hundred settlements scattered through all the colonies on the eve of the Revolution; and being everywhere animated with a fierce passion for liberty, they served as an amalgam to bind together all other racial elements in the population. The Germans, who numbered over 200,000 in 1776, were to be found chiefly in western New York, and particularly in the western counties of Pennsylvania, where they gave risè to the breed which we call the Pennsylvania Dutch. A recent student of the subject estimates that, at the outbreak of the War for Independence, about one-tenth of the total population was German and perhaps one-sixth Scotch-Irish.

Since the best sites near the coast were pre-empted, the Scotch-Irish and the Germans for the most part pushed into the valleys of the interior where they occupied fertile farm lands and acted as a buffer against Indian forays on the older settlements. Combining with the native whites in the back country, they quickly developed a group consciousness due to the organized efforts of the English-American minorities of the seaboard to minimize the influence of the frontier population in the colonial legislature and courts; and in the case of the abortive Regulator uprising in North Carolina, they invoked civil war to secure a redress of grievances. Eventually their struggle proved to be the decisive factor in establishing the two American principles of equality before the law and of representation upon the basis of numbers. When the disruption with Great Britain approached, the non-English strains of the back country lent great propulsive force to the movement for independence and republican government. They were probably the deciding factors in Pennsylvania and South Carolina, where the ties of loyalty binding the colonists were especially strong.

Other racial strains made a deep impress upon the history of the times. Someone has pointed out that eight of the men most prominent in the early history of New York represented eight non-English nationalities: Schuyler, of Dutch descent; Herkimer, whose parents were pure-blooded Germans from the Rhine Palatinate; John Jay, of French stock; Livingston, Scotch; Clinton, Irish; Morris, Welsh; Baron Steuben, Prussian; and Hoffman, Swedish. Of the fifty-six signers of the Declaration of Independence, eighteen were of non-English stock and, of these, eight were born outside of the colonies. Joseph Galloway, the Pennsylvania loyalist, declared before a committee of the House of Commons in 1779 that in the patriot army "there were scarcely one-fourth natives of America—about one-half Irish, the other fourth were English and Scotch." This statement fails to do justice to the other foreign-born soldiers who fought in the War for Independence.

II

Throughout the period of national independence, immigration continued to exert a profound influence on the development of American institutions, political ideals, and industrial life. Within ten years of the adoption of the Constitution, immigration received unwelcome recognition as wielding a democratizing influence on American life. The Federalist party, dominated by aristocratic sympathies, was determined to deal a death blow to the heresy known variously as "mobocracy" or "democracy"; and so it passed the Alien and Sedition Acts and the Naturalization Law in 1798 for the purpose of preventing aliens from cultivating this dangerous doctrine in the United States. The party did not survive this legislation; but its hatred of the foreigner in America continued to burn unabated. The Hartford Convention of 1814, voicing the old Federalist spirit, ascribed

the fallen state of the country partly to the fact that malcontents from Europe were permitted to hold office, and
demanded that the Constitution be amended to disqualify
immigrants, even though naturalized, from holding federal
position.   Yet, during this period, two of the foremost
statesmen of the nation were foreigners by birth: Alexander Hamilton, Washington's great Secretary of the
Treasury, a native of the West Indies; and Albert Gallatin,
Jefferson's great Secretary of the Treasury, a Swiss by
birth.   It is difficult to see how the young republic could
have been guided safely through the financial perils of these
first critical years of independence without the genius of
these two men.

Beginning with the year 1820 the numbers of foreigners
migrating into the United States each decade mounted
rapidly, passing the half-million mark during the thirties
and rising above the two and a half million mark in the
decade of the fifties.   The racial strains represented in this
migration were essentially the same as during colonial times,
the Teutonic and the Celtic.   The high-water mark in the
period before the Civil War was reached when the tide of
immigration brought to American shores, in the late forties
and early fifties, great numbers of German liberals who
had fled Germany because of the failure of the Revolution
of 1848, and huge numbers of famine-stricken peasants from
central and southern Ireland.   More than half a million
Germans sought America between 1830 and 1850, and nearly
a million more came in the next decade.   The larger portion
of these went into the Middle West.   They became pioneers
in the newer parts of Ohio and in Cincinnati; they took up
the hardwood lands of the Wisconsin counties along Lake
Michigan; they went in large numbers to Michigan, Illinois,
Indiana, Missouri and the river towns of Iowa.   This
German influx contained an exceptionally large proportion

of educated and forceful leaders, men and women who contributed powerfully to . the spiritual and educational development of the communities in which they settled and whose liberal social customs were at interesting variance with the inherited Puritan austerity of the settlers of New England extraction. Virtually all the western states perceived the advantages of immigration as an agency for developing their resources; and emulating the example of William Penn they were not backward in appropriating money and establishing agents in Europe to furnish prospective emigrants with all possible information as to the soil, climate, and general conditions of the country. Colonies of European peasants began to be established in many parts of the West—at one time it appeared that Wisconsin might become exclusively a German state.

The Irish immigrants, on the other hand, sought the Eastern cities or else went forth into the construction camps. These were the years during which roads, canals, and public works were being constructed upon an extensive scale and the first railroads were being projected. The hard manual labor for these enterprises was performed mainly by the Irish. The congestion of the Irish in the eastern cities led to many evils, none more startling than the increases in pauperism, intemperance and illiteracy. In 1838 it was estimated that more than one-half of the paupers in the country were of foreign birth. A committee of the city of Boston reported in 1849 on the "wretched, dirty and unhealthy condition of a great number of the dwelling houses occupied by the Irish population," showing that each room from cellar to garret was likely to contain one or more families. Such conditions gave great impetus to the numerous movements for humanitarian reform which characterized the thirties and forties. Better housing conditions, a more humane legal code, prohibition, better schools, labor reform—

all these demands received increased emphasis because of the social conditions under which the immigrants, and particularly the Irish, lived in the Eastern cities.

As a result of the heavy immigration of the forties and fifties, political corruption became an important factor in American politics for the first time. The newly arrived foreigner fell an easy prey to the unscrupulous native politician in the cities; and fraudulent naturalization papers, vote buying, and similar practices became so notorious that a probe committee of Congress declared in 1860: "It is well known to the American people that stupendous frauds have been perpetrated in the election of 1856, in Pennsylvania, by means of forged and fictitious naturalization papers." President Buchanan wrote that "we never heard until within a recent period of the employment of money to carry elections." Much of the immigrant labor came in under contract to private corporations, and the decade of the fifties saw the first effective employment of arguments against immigration based upon the plea that the lower standard of living of the foreigners made it impossible for native laborers to compete with them.

The jealousy and ill feeling engendered by the above causes were increased by religious differences. The Irish were mostly Catholics; and it was not long before Catholic churches began to rise throughout southern New England and the Middle Atlantic States, and convents and parochial schools competed with the public schools, which were coming to be looked upon as the true basis of democracy. The outcome was the growth of a powerful movement against immigration, which is without parallel in American history. Calling themselves Native Americans, political parties were formed in New York and other eastern cities to prevent the election of foreign-born citizens to office; and ten years later, in 1845, a national organization was effected with more than one hundred thousand members. In 1850 the movement assumed the guise of a secret organization under the name, known only to the initiate, of The Supreme Order of the Star-Spangled Banner. Outsiders lost no time in dubbing the members "Know Nothings," since the rank and file, when asked regarding the mysteries of the order, invariably replied: "We know nothing." Due perhaps to the disturbed state of politics in the fall of 1854 and the hesitancy of many citizens to take a definite stand on the slavery question as reopened by the Kansas-Nebraska Act, the party enjoyed phenomenal success, carrying six states and failing in seven others only by a narrow margin. But two years later, with a presidential ticket in the field, the party showed little strength, having succumbed to the growing popular absorption in the slavery controversy. Several attempts were made after the Civil War by secret societies and minor parties to revive nativist feeling but with a notable lack of success, although, as we shall see presently, non-partisan political agitation during the same period has resulted in the passage of certain restrictive measures by the federal government.

In the period prior to the Civil War the stream of immigration had been turned from the South by the Mason and Dixon line, for the free laborers of Europe could not profitably compete with the slave laborers of the South. Nearly all the immigrant guidebooks published before the Civil War warned Europeans against the presence of slavery and the strongly intrenched caste system in that section. This avoidance had serious results for the South, as some economists of that section foresaw, for it practically precluded that diversification of industry which a plentiful supply of cheap white labor would have rendered possible. Thus the economic system of the South came to rest more and more exclusively upon a single prop, and the control of southern policy fell into the ambitious hands of the cotton planters. Furthermore, the native southern stock, left to itself, interbred, and the mass of the whites were deprived of the liberalizing influences of contact with persons and ideas from other parts of the world. The first federal law restricting immigration was passed during this period when the act of 1807 forbade the future introduction of negro slaves; but this law came too late to avert the evil consequences flowing from the earlier unrestricted importation of blacks.

Meanwhile, the European peasants and workingmen, predisposed against slavery by temperament and economic interest, had massed themselves in the North and helped to stiffen the sentiment of that section against an institution that was an anachronism in Europe. It is but a slight indication of the attitude of the German Americans to note that, when additional federal territory was opened to possible slave settlement by the Kansas-Nebraska Act, eighty German newspapers out of eighty-eight were decidedly opposed to the measure. Who can estimate of what vital consequence it was to the future of a united country that, in the eventful decade prior to the outbreak of the Civil War, the foreign population of the United States increased eighty-four per cent? It was William H. Seward, campaigning in Missouri in 1860 for the election of Lincoln, who congratulated the state upon its "onward striving, freedom loving German inhabitants" and declared that "Missouri must be Germanized in order to be free." In the actual fighting, foreign-born soldiers played a notable part, although many of them had fled Europe to escape compulsory military service. It is perhaps generally known that the militia companies formed among the Germans in Missouri, especially in St. Louis, were pivotal in saving that state for the Union in the early months of the war; but it

is not so well known that both the Germans and the Irish
furnished more troops to the federal armies in proportion
to their numbers than did the native-born northerners.

III

Immigration entered a new phase in tne years following
the Civil War. Prior to this time the immigrants had been
of racial strains very closely related to the original settlers
of the country. Indeed, from one point of view, the
American people in the *ante bellum* period were merely a
making-over, in a new environment, of the old English race
out of the same elements which had entered into its compo-
sition from the beginning in England. But with the great
industrial expansion in America after the war and the
opening of many steamship lines between the Mediterranean
ports and the United States, new streams of immigration
began to set in from Southern and Eastern Europe; and
this new invasion with its lower standards of living caused
a reduction in the old Teutonic and Celtic immigration from
Western Europe. The change began to be apparent about
1885, but it was not until 1896 that the three currents from
Austria-Hungary, Italy, and Russia exceeded in volume the
contributions of the United Kingdom, Germany, and Scan-
dinavia.

On the Pacific Coast a new situation also arose, due to
the first coming of thousands of Chinese laborers in the
fifties and sixties. California became transformed into a
battleground for a determination of the issue whether the
immigrant from the Orient or from the Occident should
perform the manual work of the Pacific Coast. In this connection it is suggestive that the notorious Dennis Kearney,
arch-agitator of the Sand Lots against the Chinese immigrant, was himself a native of the County Cork. The victory ultimately fell to the European immigrant and his

American offspring in this conflict as well as in the later and more familiar one with the Japanese immigrant; and by one means or another the yellow race has been excluded from further entrance into the United States. The considered judgment of Americans of European origin seems to be that no Asiatic strain shall enter into the composite American stock or make its first-hand contribution to American culture.

Far more important than this problem has been the effect of the latter-day influx from Europe upon American development and ideals. Since 1870 twenty-five million Europeans have come to the United States as compared with possibly one-third of that number in the entire earlier period of independent national existence. Professor Ripley pointed out in the *Atlantic Monthly* in 1908 that the newcomers of the period since 1900 would, if properly distributed over the newer parts of the country, serve to populate no less than nineteen states of the Union. These immigrants have contributed powerfully to the rapid exploitation of the country's natural resources and to the establishment of modern industrialism in America. The German and Scandinavian elements among the immigrants continued to seek the land, and were rushed out to the prairies by immigrant trains to fill the remaining spaces in the older states of the Middle West. But the majority of the latter-day immigrants avoided agriculture and bore the brunt of the manual labor of building the railroads as well as of most of the unskilled work in the mines and the great basic industries of the country.

A characteristic of the more recent immigration has been the fact that approximately one-third of the newcomers have returned to their places of origin. This has created a restless, migratory, "bird of passage" class of laborers, lacking every interest in the permanent advance of the American working class and always competing on a single-standard basis. The swarming of foreigners into the great industries occurred at considerable cost to the native workingmen, for the latter struggled in vain for higher wages or better conditions as long as the employers could command the services of an inexhaustible supply of foreign laborers. Thus, the new immigration has made it easier for the few to amass enormous fortunes at the expense of the many and has helped to create in this country for the first time yawning inequalities of wealth.

Most sociologists believe that the addition of hordes of foreigners to the population of the United States has caused a decline in the birth-rate of the old American stock, for the native laborer has been forced to avoid large families in order to be in a position to meet the growing severity of the economic competition forced upon him by the immigrant. This condition, coupled with the tendency of immigrant laborers to crowd the native Americans farther and farther from the industrial centers of the country, has caused the great communities and commonwealths of the Atlantic seaboard, about whose names cluster the heroic traditions of revolutionary times, to change completely their original characters. According to the census of 1910, Puritan New England is today the home of a population of whom two-thirds were born in foreign lands or else had parents who were. Boston is as cosmopolitan a city as Chicago; and Faneuil Hall is an anachronism, a curiosity of bygone days left stranded on the shores of the Italian quarter. In fifteen of the largest cities of the United States the foreign immigrants and their children outnumber the native whites; and by the same token alien racial elements are in the majority in thirteen of the states of the Union. When President Wilson was at the Peace Conference, he reminded the Italian delegates that there were more of their countrymen in New York than in any Italian city; and it is not beside the point to add here that New York is also the greatest Irish city in the world and the largest Jewish city.

Whatever of history may be made in the future in these parts of the country will not be the result primarily of an "Anglo-Saxon" heritage but will be the product of the interaction of these more recent racial elements upon each other and their joint reaction to the American scene. Unless the unanticipated should intervene, the stewardship of American ideals and culture is destined to pass to a new composite American type now in the process of making.

Politically the immigration of the last half-century has borne good fruit as well as evil. The intelligent thoughtful immigrant lacked the inherited prejudices of the native voter and was less likely to respond to ancient catchwords or be stirred by the revival of Civil War issues. The practice of "waving the bloody shirt" was abandoned by the politicians largely because of the growing strength of the naturalized voters, of which group Carl Schurz was, of course, the archtype. In place of this practice arose a new one, equally as reprehensible, by which the major parties used their political patronage and their platform promises to angle for the support of naturalized groups among the voters. No racial group has been as assiduously courted by the politicians as the Irish; and it was early discovered that the easiest way to gain Irish favor was to feed their hatred of England. "Twisting the lion's tail" became a recognized and successful political device, as, for instance, Alexander Mackay observed in his travels in the United States as early as 1846-1847; and incidentally much of the long-standing resentment of Americans against Great Britain may be ascribed to the uncalculated effect of this practice upon the public generally. In 1884 James G. Blaine, the Republican candidate for president, had good reason to believe that he would win the Irish vote when an indiscreet supporter lost the election for him by prominently identifying his name with opposition to "Rum, Romanism and Rebellion." In the next two presidential elections both parties found it expedient to insert in their platforms forthright declarations in favor of home rule for Ireland!

Generally speaking, racial influences have been most strongly felt in state and local politics although national parties have found it necessary to print their campaign literature in as many as sixteen different languages. The so-called "hyphenated American" has become a familiar figure in the last few years merely because the World War has made native-born citizens take serious cognizance of the polyglot political situation; and the activity of the German-American Alliance in the campaign of 1916 is an illustration of how dangerous to the national welfare the meddling of racial groups among the voters may become.

To the immigrant must also be assigned the responsibility for the accelerated growth of political and industrial radicalism in this country. While most of the newcomers quietly accepted their humble place in American society, a minority of the immigrants consisted of political refugees and other extremists, embittered by their experiences in European countries and suspicious of constituted authority under whatever guise. These men represented the Left Wing in their revolt against political authority in Europe just as three centuries earlier the Pilgrims comprised the Left Wing in their struggle against ecclesiastical authority.

Since radicalism is a cloak covering a multitude of dissents and affirmations, the influence of these men may be traced in a wide variety of programs of social reconstruction and movements for humanitarian reform. The first Socialist parties in the United States were organized by German Americans in the years following the Civil War; and political Socialism, in its type of organization, terminology, and methods of discipline, can hardly yet be said to be fully acclimated to the New World. Violence and anarchism were first introduced into the American labor movement in the eighties by Johann Most and his associates, the greater number of whom, like Most himself, were of alien birth; and the contemporaneous I.W.W. movement finds its chief strength in the support of the migratory foreign-born laborer. Even the Non-partisan League may not be hailed, though some would so have it, as a product of an indigenous American Socialism, for this organization originated and has enjoyed its most spectacular successes in a western commonwealth in which 70 per cent of the people were natives of Europe or are the children of foreign-born parents.

The new immigration from Southern and Eastern Europe, with its lower standard of living and characteristic racial differences, has intensified many existing social problems and created a number of new ones, particularly in the centers of population. The modern programs for organized and scientific philanthropy had their origin very largely in the effort to cure these spreading social sores. Out of this situation has also grown a new anti-immigration or nativist movement, unrelated to similar movements of earlier times and indeed regarding with approval the very racial groups against which the earlier agitation had been directed. This new movement has functioned most effectively through nonpartisan channels, particularly through that of organized labor, and has commanded strong support in both parties. Whereas immigrants had virtually all been admitted without let or hindrance down to 1875, a number of laws have been passed since then with the primary purpose of removing the worst evils of indiscriminate immigration, the severest restriction being the literacy test affixed in 1917.[1] This contemporary nativism cannot justify its existence by reason

---

[1] In 1921 a law was passed, professedly to meet a temporary situation, restricting the annual immigration from any country to three per cent of the number of aliens of that country in the United States in 1910.

of the large proportion of aliens as compared with the native population, for, as Professor Max Farrand has recently shown, immigration was on a proportionately larger scale in colonial times than during the last fifty years. It owes its being, doubtless, to the tendency of the latter-day immigrants to settle in portions of the country that are already thickly populated and to the fact that the Americans of older stock can no longer find relief from industrial competition by taking up government land in the West.

IV

No modern people is compounded of such heterogeneous ingredients as the American. That American manners and culture owe much to this admixture there can be little doubt though such influences are pervasive and intangible and their value not easy to assess. Of the older racial strains, the irrepressible good humor and executive qualities of the Irish, the solidity and thoroughness of the German, the tenacity and highmindedness of the Scotch-Irish, the law-abiding qualities of the English, and the sobriety and industry of the Scandinavian have undoubtedly made important contributions to our national character.

The fine arts in America have been developed largely by men of mixed blood. One critic (Mencken) would even have us believe that the "low caste Anglo-Saxons" who formed the vast proportion of the English migration to America were incapable of producing original ideas, thus leaving intellectual experimentation necessarily to immigrants of different antecedents. Although this assertion is an exaggeration, Mencken is able to marshal an imposing array of novelists, artists and poets in support of his contention—Walt Whitman who was half Dutch, James with an Irish grandfather, Poe who was partly German, Howells who was largely German and Irish, etc.

Foreign cultural influences, which in any case would

have been reflected in the artistic strivings of a new country like America, were reinvigorated by the presence in our population of the representatives of many different foreign nationalities. As Mencken again points out, our music is almost wholly German or Italian; our painting is French; our literature may be anything from English to Russian; our architecture is likely to be a phantasmagoria of borrowings. The American educational system from kindergarten to university has been patterned upon German models. "Even so elemental an art as that of cookery shows no native development" for "any decent restaurant that one blunders upon in the land is likely to be French, and if not French, then Italian or German or Chinese."

It is not fantastic to believe that, during three centuries of history, the immigrant elements in our population have not only profoundly influenced the cultural, institutional, and material development of the United States, but have also been largely responsible for distilling that precious essence which we call American idealism. The bold man falters when asked to define American idealism, but four of its affirmative attributes are assuredly a deep abiding faith in the common man, the right of equality of opportunity, toleration of all creeds and opinions, and a high regard for the rights of weaker nations. The great mass of immigrants came to the New World to attest their devotion to one or all of these ideals—they came as protestants against tyranny, injustice, intolerance, militarism, as well as against economic oppression. Nor is more concrete evidence lacking to show that neither they nor their sons rested until these great principles were firmly woven into the fabric of American thought and political practice.

During the last five years the United States has risen to a position of world leadership in a sense never realized by any other country in history. Sober reflection convinces

THE INFLUENCE OF IMMIGRATION

one that this was not an accident due to one man's personality: it grew out of the inevitable logic of a situation which found the United States an amalgam of all the peoples at war. Although the old stocks continued belligerent and apart in Europe, the warring nations instinctively turned for leadership to that western land where the same racial breeds met and mingled and dwelt in harmony with each other. Observers in Europe during the war testified to the willingness with which all classes of people in the various countries were ready to hearken to and follow the country whose liberal spirit they knew from the letters of their friends in America or from their own experiences there. In the great world-drama President Wilson played a predestined part; by reason of his position as spokesman of the American people he was the historic embodiment of the many national traditions inherent in a nation formed of many nations. This would seem to foreshadow the rôle which, for good or ill, the United States is fated to play in the future. Those who, in the discussions over the League of Nations, have advocated that the United States should occupy a position of isolation and irresponsibility have failed to grasp this great fundamental truth.

BIBLIOGRAPHICAL NOTE

There is a vast literature on immigration in the form of books, magazine articles and reports of the federal and state governments. Practically all these writers have studied immigration as a social problem and have given little or no attention to immigration as a dynamic factor in American development. Readers interested in the latter phase may, however, find relevant material in the following works: Henry Pratt Fairchild's *Immigration* (New York, 1917), chaps. ii-vi; Max Farrand's "Immigration in the Light of History" in the *New Republic*, December 2, 9, 16, 23, 1916; Frank Julian Warne's *The Tide of Immigration* (New York, 1916), chaps. xii, xx; and Samuel P. Orth's *Our Foreigners* (in the *Chronicles of America Series*, vol. 35; New Haven, 1920). Scattered through the eight volumes of John Bach McMaster's *History of the People of the United States* (New York, 1883-1913) may be found many references to immigration from 1783 to the Civil War.

Notwithstanding these fragmentary discussions, this vital approach to an understanding of American history has been neglected by the historians generally. No field is more fruitful and many years of devoted research will be required to exploit fully its possibilities.

There is a valuable and growing literature dealing historically with separate racial elements in the United States. Many of these works have to be used with caution because of the temptation of the author to give undue importance to the nationality with which he is dealing. Of these works some of the more valuable are: Rasmus B. Anderson's *The First Chapter of Norwegian Immigration (1821-1840)* (Madison, 1896); Kendric C. Babcock's *The Scandinavian Element in the United States* (Urbana, 1914); Emily Greene Balch's *Our Slavic Fellow Citizens* (New York, 1910); Charles S. Bernheimer's *The Russian Jew in America* (Philadelphia, 1905); Ernest Bruncken's *German Political Refugees in the United States during the Period from 1815-1860* (Chicago, 1904); Thomas Burgess's *Greeks in America* (Boston, 1913); Thomas Capek's *The Czechs in America* (Boston, 1920); Mary Roberts Coolidge's *Chinese Immigration* (New York, 1909); J. G. Craighead's *Scotch and Irish Seeds in American Soil* (Philadelphia, 1879); Henry Pratt Fairchild's *Greek Immigration to the United States* (New Haven, 1911); Albert B. Faust's *The German Element in the United States* (2 v.; Boston, 1909); George T. Flom's *A History of Norwegian Immigration to the United States* (Iowa City, 1909); Henry Jones Ford's *The Scotch-Irish in America* (Princeton, 1915); Charles A. Hanna's *The Scotch-Irish* (2 v.; New York, 1902); George Ford Huizinga's *What the Dutch Have Done in the West of the United States* (Philadelphia, 1909); Amandus Johnson's *The Swedes in America, 1638-1900* (Philadelphia, 1914); Stanley C. Johnson's *A History of Emigration from the United Kingdom to North America 1763-1912* (London, 1913); Eliot Lord, J. J. D. Trenor and Samuel J. Barrows's *The Italian in America* (New York, 1905); John Francis Maguire's *The Irish in America* (London, 1868); Thomas D'Arcy McGee's *A History of the Irish Settlers in North America* (Boston, 1850); H. A. Millis's *The Japanese Problem in the United States* (New York, 1915); O. N. Nelson's *History of the Scandinavians and Successful Scandinavians in the United States* (2 v.; Minneapolis, 1904); Madison C. Peters's *The Jews in America* (Philadelphia, 1905); Ruth Putnam's "The Dutch Element in the United States" in the *Annual Report* of the American Historical Association for 1909, pp. 205-218; Peter Ross's *The Scot in America* (New York, 1896); Benjamin Brawley's *A Social History of the American Negro* (New York, 1921).

A suggestive biographical approach to the historical influence of immigration is Joseph Husband's *Americans by Adoption* (Boston, 1920), a volume in which the lives of nine eminent Americans of foreign birth are dealt with, among them Agassiz, Schurz, Carnegie, St. Gaudens and Jacob A. Riis.

CHAPTER II

"Man can no more be scientifically studied apart from the ground which he tills, or the lands over which he travels, or the sea over which he trades, than polar bear or desert cactus can be understood apart from its habitat. . . . Man has been so noisy about the way he has 'conquered Nature,' and Nature has been so silent in her persistent influence over man, that the geographic factor in the equation of human development has been overlooked." That the geographic factor has played an important part in shaping the history of the American people no thoughtful person can deny. The conformation of the Atlantic coast, the mountains and plains and virgin forests of the interior, the frequency of water courses and the variations of climate and soil have all left their impress upon the manner and quality of American development. In a strict sense of the term, geographic influences are to be regarded as those influences exerted on man by the exterior physical features of the earth; but, for all practical purposes, variations in temperature and moisture may be included as a part of the physical conditions because of the close connection between physiography and climate.

In American history two features of the geographic situation have been of commanding importance: the sheer distance of the New World from the Old; and the physiographical peculiarities of the North American continent. Although, of course, these two aspects of American geography were parts of an inseparable whole and constantly interacted upon each other, their historical consequences will be examined separately for purposes of the present discussion.

I

So real was the physical isolation of the New World that the Christian era was fifteen hundred years old before the existence of the western hemisphere was known to educated Europe. European peoples emerged from barbarism, great empires arose and fell, religious conflicts devastated the fair fields of the continent, while the New World remained undiscovered—a tremendous reserve of land with resources practically untouched by its primitive inhabitants. Even Columbus's voyage might not have led to the rapid opening up of the New World had he not been favored by Nature in the selection of his place of embarkation and the presence of favorable trade winds. Due to these fortunate circumstances, he chanced to discover a portion of the western land that utterly charmed a South European with its tropical climate, luxuriant vegetation and promise of trading possibilities. If, like John and Sebastian Cabot, he had touched upon a bleak and barren coast, the subsequent development of the Americas would have proceeded at a much slower pace.

As colonies came to be planted in the western hemisphere by rival European powers, their American settlements found themselves drawn into wars that were the outgrowth of purely European causes and in which they had only a secondary interest. Geographic remoteness did not serve in this instance as a means of insulation; but the preoccupation of the European monarchs with international politics combined with the distant situation of the colonies to invite an attitude of inattention and laxness on the part of the mother countries toward matters of routine colonial administration. This affected the colonial development of the settlements of different countries in different ways. While the Spanish and French colonists found themselves placed at the mercy of tyrannous and incompetent local officials, the English colonies possessing liberal charters made the most of their opportunity to work out a system of colonial home rule untroubled by active interference from the mother country. Indeed, the English settlers cherished governmental ideals and enjoyed political rights which far exceeded those of their kinsmen in England.

As new generations grew up in the thirteen colonies who had themselves never seen England, it was inevitable that the colonists should unconsciously begin to think of themselves as a people possessing interests apart from the mother country and deserving recognition and protection from her. The psychology of the colonists in 1765 was, in an important degree, the imperceptible outgrowth of many years of geographic separation. Such a people very naturally regarded the new plan of imperial control, inaugurated by Grenville in 1764-1765, as the unjustifiable interference of an "alien" government. An extreme though not unrepresentative expression of this attitude may be found in the resolutions of the town of Windham, Massachusetts, in 1774, to the effect that "neither the Parliament of Britain nor the Parliament of France nor any other Parliament but that which sits supreme in our Province has a Right to lay any Taxes on us for the purpose of Raising a Revenue."

The success of the Americans in the War for Independence was closely related to the geographic conditions of warfare. Fighting on their own ground, the little American armies utilized their familiarity with the topography to launch attacks and effect strategic retreats which left the slow-moving British armies at a loss. The powerful British aggregations were forced to rely upon water transport and were never able to penetrate into the back-country sufficiently to destroy the American forces.

Far-seeing statesmen in the early years of our national independence fully appreciated the safety afforded by our physical aloofness from Europe and sought to make this fact the cornerstone of American foreign policy. "Our detached and distant situation," wrote Washington in his Farewell Address, "invites and enables us to pursue a different course" from that of Europe with her never-ceasing international embroilments. "Why forego the advantages of so peculiar a situation? Why quit our own to stand upon foreign ground? Why, by interweaving our destiny with that of any part of Europe, entangle our peace and prosperity in the toils of European ambition, rivalship, interest, humor, or caprice?"

Events of the next twenty-five years caused the same thought to be repeated with increasing emphasis by Jefferson and later presidents. In the period from 1793 to 1815, we know that geographic remoteness alone protected America from the devastating blows of Napoleonic ambition showered so freely upon the continental countries of Europe. It seems safe to conjecture that, if the new American republic had been situated closer to the hotbed of European politics and intrigue, her course would have been beset with peril at every turn, a danger not to be lightly regarded at a time when men like Alexander Hamilton viewed the Constitution as "a frail and worthless fabric" and republican government in general as a doubtful experiment. As it was, the United States became involved in a quarrel over her neutral rights on the high seas with both Great Britain and France, a controversy that yielded a naval conflict with France in 1798 and a second war with Great Britain in 1812. Thus, it was from a purpose to capitalize our favored geographic situation that there originated that well-established practice of American foreign policy, which is summed up in the familiar phrase: no entangling alliances.

Another great principle of American diplomacy owed its origin largely to geographical considerations. The width of the Atlantic and the physical proximity of the Spanish American colonies were controlling factors in the formulation of the Monroe Doctrine. A series of revolutions had swept through these colonies beginning about 1810; and in 1822 it appeared that the so-called Holy Alliance of European despotisms would take active steps to reconquer them. The remoteness of Europe from these colonies emboldened the United States solemnly to warn the powers against intervention, an action which the actual military strength of the United States in no sense justified. The interests of the United States were directly involved in the situation, for the success of European intervention would have led to the re-establishment of a principle of government, near our boundaries, which Americans regarded as a menace to national security. Hence, while sympathy with the spread of republican ideas was instinct in President Monroe's message, he explicitly emphasized the thought: "It is impossible that the allied powers should extend their political system to any portion of either [American] continent without endangering our peace and happiness. . . . It is equally impossible, therefore, that we should behold such interposition, in any form, with indifference."

Generally speaking, the history of American foreign relations has been marked by enlightened views of international right adopted in advance of the leading European powers. "From the beginning of its political history," says John W. Foster, the United States has "made itself the champion of a freer commerce, of a sincere and genuine neutrality, of respect for private property in war, of the most advanced ideas of natural rights and justice; and in its brief existence of a century, by its example and persistent diplomatic advocacy, it has exerted a greater influence in the recognition of these elevated principles than any other nation of the world." Here again geographic situation coincided with enlightened diplomatic statesmanship, for, being a country remote from the storm center of the world's wars, the interests of the United States were usually those of a nation at peace, and her object has been to secure for her citizens rights and privileges as nearly approximating those of peacetime as possible. The liberal views of American statesmen on such questions as contraband of war, definition of a blockade and the inviolability of neutral vessels from search were, to a large extent, inspired by the unique geographic position of the United States and by the peculiar commercial advantages inherent in such a position.

Since the Civil War much of the physical isolation of the United States has disappeared and the foreign policy of the nation has tended to change correspondingly. The steamship and the cable, the wireless and the airplane have all helped to cause the earth to shrink and to bring North America closer to the shores of Europe. After all, distance is not a matter of miles but, in terms of human relationships, it consists in the length of time required to travel from one place to another. In stage-coach days Boston and Charleston, South Carolina, were farther removed, for all practical purposes, than are New York and Havre in this age of steam and electricity; and the distance between Philadelphia and New York was greater than an aerial flight from Newfoundland to England today.

When the republics of the western hemisphere, led by the United States, became participants in the World War, their action signalized the final crumbling of the barrier of distance before the onslaughts of modern science; and an irrecoverable blow was inflicted on an illusion of isolation which had, in fact, ceased to exist. The peoples of the earth were shocked into a realization of a new world of contracted dimensions, a world that had become a neighborhood. A scheme for world peace through international organization was the natural concomitant of such a situation.

Many Americans deplore the passing of "splendid isolation"; but it should always be remembered that isolation was of greatest importance to the United States when the republic was small and weak, when, as Washington phrased it in his Farewell Address, it was necessary "to gain time to our country to settle and mature its yet recent institutions, and to progress without interruption to that degree of strength and consistency . . . necessary to give it . . . the command of its own fortunes." With the geographic barriers down, America stands face to face with new international duties and responsibilities.

II

Not only were the interrelations of Europe and the western hemisphere affected by geographic conditions but, from first to last, the internal development of America was strongly modified by the same influences. The advance of European discovery and exploration was determined largely by the sinuosities of the coastline and the conformation of the interior. The rapidity with which the New World was opened to European colonization was likewise dependent upon accidents of physiography. And, as we shall see, the dispersion of the later settlers throughout the vast hinterland of the continent was subject to a similar control. The discoverers and pioneers sometimes found Nature a harsh taskmaster, but more often they were likely to find in her a lavish patron.

Columbus's voyages had been prompted by a desire to

discover a direct western route to the Far East; and when the truth was in time made known to the world that, instead of discovering the Orient, he had in reality found a great continental barrier blocking the route, the minds of discoverers became obsessed with a new idea, the possibility of finding a water passage through the American continents. Every promising inlet or gulf along the shoreline now became the object of exploration. Cartier, Newport, Hudson, Verrazano, Magellan, Champlain and a host of other adventurers, representing many different nations, took part in the fascinating game—and their efforts vastly broadened European knowledge of the topography and economic resources of the New World.

After a time the quest for a transcontinental waterway became of secondary consideration, for the interest of the discoverers and explorers had become captured by the alluring possibilities of America itself. Indeed, such an interest had been in evidence from the beginning; but it did not become the dominant motive of exploration until half a century or more had elapsed after Columbus's first voyage. It was a fortunate circumstance that, unlike the Pacific coast, the Atlantic shoreline of North America presented an inviting front to European seekers, offering so many open doors to the venturesome newcomers in its numerous rivers and indentations and in its spacious Gulf of Mexico. In those primitive days of travel the location and frequency of navigable waters were the controlling factors in directing the progress of exploration.

The Spaniards were for many years the most active in investigating the mysteries of the New World. Following the route of Columbus into the Gulf of Mexico, the Spanish explorers and *conquistadores* fell under the spell of that great inland sea, not unlike their own Mediterranean; and using it as their base of operations, they launched a series

of explorations and conquests, to the north and the west and
the south, which yielded them almost the whole of South
America and a goodly portion of North America as their
reward.

The course of French exploration, almost a century later,
was determined very largely by the fact that, as an outgrowth
of the discoveries of Cartier and Champlain, France had
fallen heir to a string of inland seas, the Great Lakes,
tapped by the mighty St. Lawrence. Utilizing this natural
advantage, as the Spaniards had the Gulf of Mexico, French
missionaries and traders found their way into the very
heart of the continent. They came upon the great central
river of North America with its huge tributaries, followed
the Father of Waters southward to the Spanish Gulf of
Mexico, and established their claim to the imperial inland
domain known as Louisiana.

When the English undertook actively the work of explor-
ing and colonizing in North America, they found themselves
at a serious disadvantage since the Spaniards had pre-
empted the lands to the south and French discovery and
settlement were placing limits to their expansion northward
and westward. Only the Atlantic coast south of the St.
Lawrence and north of Florida seemed to offer them the
possibilities they desired. Unfortunately, as it seemed, the
great streams flowing into the Atlantic, discovered or
claimed by the English, had their origin in the mountain
ranges paralleling the coast, and therefore no very convinc-
ing claim could be made by the English, under the international law of the time, to the extensive interior of the continent. Even along the Atlantic seaboard the English found
interlopers in the Dutch and Swedish settlements, but these
feeble enterprises were summarily disposed of by conquest.

In the long run, the contracted dimensions of the area
settled by the English proved to be a blessing in disguise.

The vast spaces embraced by the Spanish and French dependencies made necessary widely scattered settlements, thin populations, and the development of hunting, trading and mining as the chief occupations of the colonists. The consequence was a rapid exploitation of the country's superficial resources and the building up of communities that were organically unstable. The English settlers, on the other hand, found themselves hemmed in on the west by an almost unbroken mountain wall covered with a heavy mantle of primeval forest. By a decree of Nature they were confined to a narrow strip of tidewater area, sufficiently isolated to afford that protection and cohesion which a well-ordered colonial life requires, sufficiently large to permit of conservative growth, and possessing that extended sea frontage so necessary for the development of a maritime people.

In the century of conflict between the French and the English colonies, time was the strongest ally of the English, for time meant a more compact population, greater material resources, and a wider knowledge of the topography of the interior. Massachusetts and Virginia were longer established as colonies than the United States is today as a nation before the English had gained any exact knowledge of the great transmontane empire that lay to the west of the Alleghanies; and their interest was then provoked by the attempt of the French to enforce their claims to the Ohio valley by a system of stockades commanding the strategic approaches from the English settlements. In this final great trial of strength, the French and Indian War, the English colonists availed themselves of the geographic peculiarities of their situation, planning their campaigns so as to take advantage of the routes through the mountains of western Virginia and Pennsylvania formed by river and portage, and of the deep natural depression in the mountains formed by the Hudson-Mohawk river system of western New York.

Handicapped by distance from their base of operations, difficulties of transportation and inferior numbers, the French lost the war and, with it, were forced to surrender their empire in North America by the treaty of 1763.

III

From first to last, the natural conditions which the European settlers found in America had a formative influence on their character and outlook. This was particularly true of the English colonists who, unlike the Spanish and French, emigrated to the New World without let or hindrance from the Crown. In the first place, the precarious voyage across the Atlantic discouraged all but the stouthearted and ambitious from undertaking the adventure. Further than this, the dangers and hardships of living in the virgin wilds served to accentuate all the characteristics in which the original colonists had differed from their own stock in the Old World. The metamorphosis that occurred in the character and mental make-up of the early settlers marked the appearance of something new in the world. The impact of frontier life, with its generous economic opportunities, upon the European mind produced a complex of reactions which, for lack of a better term, we must call "American."

From the standpoint of Englishmen, the earliest American frontier was the seaboard itself, consisting of small isolated communities scattered along the inlets and river mouths of the extensive coastline. As we see it now, it was, in truth, a frontier very European in its traits with a society consciously modeled on European patterns and only unconsciously modified by the changed conditions of the American environment. By 1700 the outposts of white civilization had left the tidewater and made contact with the foothills of the Appalachians, forming what may be called the second American frontier. This new frontier was as different from the original zone of settlement as the latter had been from Europe; and there were quickly evoked those differences of sympathy and interest which differentiate newer settlements from old established communities. By the middle of the eighteenth century the mountains themselves had been reached, and pioneer settlement was to be found up and down the longitudinal valleys cutting across colonial boundaries in a northeasterly and southwesterly direction.

The influence of physical conditions upon man can no place be better studied than in these successive frontiers, for there Nature held unmitigated sway and man was subjected to the severest tests. Cut off from the conventions of older communities, and tempered by the hazards and difficulties of wilderness life, men were counted successful for what they did, not for what their ancestors may have done. Like the castaways in Barrie's delightful play "The Admirable Crichton," the pioneers forgot those artificial distinctions which had no validity in the stark facts of their daily existence; for, in the presence of primeval Nature, a family tree is infinitely less important than the ability to make a forest clearing.

Such conditions were productive of a race of men, sturdy in their individualism, impatient of restraint, and impetuous and resourceful in action. The fusing powers of the back-country were evidenced by the fact that its population represented a wide mingling of ethnic strains, who lived together in harmony and shared the same general outlook on life. The character of the pioneer was rounded out and sealed by the economic conditions under which he lived: the abundance of land and the equality of material possessions. Such a diffusion of property inevitably begot the ideal of political democracy.

The physical background of colonial life, however, was not, in other respects, such as to promote a sentiment of unity among the people. In each colony there existed bitter political antagonism between the settlers of the older and those of the newer frontier because of their different needs and aspirations. While these differences were chiefly economic in character, they were deepened and perpetuated by the geographic aloofness of the two sections of the population. Intercolonial unity also suffered from geographic conditions. In the seventeenth century, colonial settlements were feeble and far apart, each living in a world by itself, surrounded by forests that were difficult to traverse and confronted with dangers from wild beasts and the Indians. Rivers and coast waters were the customary highways of travel; and, except along certain beaten paths, few men were venturesome enough to pass by land from one colony to another. Within its own environment each colony was engaged in working out its own salvation with little regard for the others. Each had its own problems to solve, which absorbed the time and attention of its people and tended to promote strong sentiments of individualism and particularism.

These sentiments were strengthened by intercolonial rivalries, among which boundary controversies occupied a large place. Boundary difficulties began with the granting of charters to Maryland and Pennsylvania and continued to create friction among the colonies for more than a century. Hardly a colony but had at least one serious dispute over boundaries. Maryland was at odds with Virginia and with Pennsylvania, New York with Pennsylvania and the New England colonies, Massachusetts with New Hampshire, Rhode Island and Connecticut, Virginia with North Carolina. Other causes also contributed to intercolonial misunderstanding, with the result that the people of one colony were inclined to look on those of another with distrust and even dislike. In 1736 Colonel William Byrd of Virginia wrote sarcastically of the "Saints of New England" with their "dexterity at palliating a perjury so well as to leave no taste of it in the mouth"; and so late as the Continental Congress of 1774, John Adams, one of the leading members, had to act cautiously and secretly in order to avoid arousing the antagonism of the southern delegates because of his New England connections.

These centrifugal tendencies were eventually overcome only by forces which broke down the barriers of isolation. Facilities of travel and communication gradually improved. Whereas the first settlers had followed buffalo tracks and Indian trails, ferries began to be provided, fords discovered, bridges built, morasses filled in or covered with corduroy. Within the settled area of the coast, passable roads were built, more rapidly in the north than in the south, although it was not until the middle of the eighteenth century that a continuous journey from Portsmouth to Philadelphia was made possible. The increase of population, and the filling in of the unoccupied areas between the settlements, also gave opportunities for more frequent intercourse and consequent understanding.

Another mighty factor toward the promotion of inter-colonial unity was the migration and mingling of the settlers of the back-country of the several colonies. Many Germans of western New York moved into Pennsylvania and on to the mountain valleys of Maryland and Virginia. The French immigrants occupied the hinterland of both South Carolina and Virginia. The Ulstermen from Ireland, who came in such huge numbers, penetrated to the frontier district of New England, moved westward into the backwoods of New York, entered Pennsylvania by way of Chester county, and pushed back toward the center of the province.

From there many went southward, following the foothills into Maryland and Virginia and even going as far as the Waxhaws of South Carolina. These wayfarers brought with them no narrow attachment to a locality and became, in a sense, the denizens of a larger country.

On the foundations of this growing physical cohesion it was possible to erect a superstructure of political unity. When confronted with serious dangers from without, such as Indian wars or attacks from the French colonists, temporary unions of groups of colonies were formed. And finally, when the colonies faced what they considered the gravest menace of all, the plan of the mother country for colonial subordination, they were able to act together in the Stamp Act Congress (1765) and, most effectively of all, in the First and Second Continental Congresses (1774-1781).

IV

The process by which waves of humanity rippled westward, paused, and began its movement again, did not cease with the conclusion of the colonial period, but proved to be a recurrent one which came to rest only in the closing years of the nineteenth century. There has been not one frontier in American history but, before the movement of population reached its final equipoise, a succession of frontiers, each hurling back its challenge to those who dared to brave the perils of an unbroken and obdurate wilderness. Each time a new weeding-out process occurred, by which the young and courageous spirits, together with those whose criminal conduct made them seek a refuge from justice, became the pioneers of the new zone of settlement. Thus the Americanizing process was a progressive one, each new frontier producing a psychology and a type of living less like the previous one and more decidedly "American" in its characteristics.

Coincident with the winning of national independence, a new frontier was already beginning to be established in the Ohio valley; and by the opening years of the nineteenth century, the vanguard of American settlement had reached the Mississippi river. The great flow of population into the heart of the continent was controlled by geographic conditions, for the settlers naturally followed the lines of least resistance offered by waterways, mountain passes and valleys. One great stream of settlement passed through Cumberland Gap and down the Kanawha valley into the Ohio river or, when it was completed, followed the Cumberland road. In the south picturesque caravans of planters with their slaves sought fresh tracts for cultivation by going around the southern end of the Appalachian system or by directing their westward way through mountain passes into Georgia, Alabama and Tennessee. New Englanders found their natural passageway into the Middle West by means of the Mohawk valley and the Lakes and, after the Erie Canal was opened, they migrated in greatly increased numbers. Generally speaking, the currents of population from the older sections of the country moved in roughly parallel lines from their places of origin. So great was the movement of population that eight territories—Tennessee, Kentucky, Ohio, Indiana, Illinois, Missouri, Mississippi and Alabama—quickly became so populous that they were admitted as states, the last five between the years 1816 and 1821.

As in the case of the colonial frontiers, the problems connected with conquering the wilderness and vanquishing the Indian served to cause a rebirth of American society and to rejuvenate the spirit of American democracy. Society found itself once more without the conveniences and the conventions of the older settled portions, and once more forced to find a solution for such typical frontier problems as those of transportation and communication with the East, of rights of land ownership, rights of self-government and educational facilities. One of the significant contributions of the Middle Western spirit to American history came to be a strong attachment to the sentiment of nationalism. The settlers were emigrants from all parts of the United States and from many parts of Europe; but the great central valley of the continent made them all part of the same physiographic province. Moreover, they owed their enlarged opportunities to the gift of the federal government; and their allegiance went forth naturally to the government of all the states rather than to that of any individual state.

Their exultant nationalism, their boastful speech and their chauvinistic spirit, all in harmony with the vast open spaces in which they dwelt, made them the butt of the ill-natured criticisms of Charles Dickens and other English travelers, who thought in terms of the cramped dimensions and congested populations of Europe and failed to see beneath the rugged exteriors of the western people. An anecdote told by Alexis de Tocqueville, a sympathetic French observer, illustrates the boisterous spirit of the time. In a crowded meeting certain officials were trying to force a way through to the platform. "Make way there," they cried; "we are the representatives of the people." "Make way yourselves," came the quick retort. "We are the people." It was the young Warhawks of this western country, unaccustomed to parley in their dealings with the Indians and impatient of the cautious diplomacy of the elder statesmen of the seaboard, who rushed the country into the War of 1812. It was, in large measure, the irrepressible nationalism of the Middle West, which led the men of that section, time and again, to settle beyond the borders of the United States, and then to embroil the government in territorial disputes with the inevitable outcome of annexation and expansion.

No political leader ever raised the cry of territorial expansion without finding a warm-hearted response in this west, whether the object was Florida, Louisiana, Texas or Oregon.

It may be noted, in passing, that the star of empire was guided in its movements by the law of geographic gravity. Every addition of territory to the original domain of 1783 was made in response to a desire to procure natural boundaries for the area we already possessed. Jefferson's original interest in the vast Louisiana territory was merely to secure American ownership of the east bank of the Mississippi at its mouth in order to assure American control of river navigation to the Gulf; but the exigencies of European politics gave us the whole hide in return for our interest in the tail. Even before this transaction was completed, Senator Jackson of Georgia announced in Congress: "God and nature have destined New Orleans and the Floridas to belong to this great and rising Empire." In a geographic sense the senator knew whereof he was speaking. In the absence of a physical boundary, Florida was proving an intolerably bad neighbor in the hands of Spain. Moreover, some important streams draining the interior of Mississippi, Alabama and Georgia had their ocean outlets in Spanish West Florida. By the treaty of 1819 all of the Spanish territory east of the Mississippi river passed into the hands of the United States; and the national boundaries stood flush with the Atlantic and the Gulf.

A few years later the sentiment for Texas was increased, in a somewhat similar fashion, by the feeling of Americans that the Rio Grande formed the boundary which Nature had intended for the United States in the southwest. After the annexation of Texas, "Manifest Destiny" seemed to demand the extension of American suzerainty to the Pacific ocean, though the peaks of the Rockies might have been considered a natural divide; and soon came such accretions of territory as Oregon, California, and enough of the interior country to join Texas solidly with California. With these additions the continental mass of the United States seemed to reach an equilibrium geographically, and no additions of any importance have been made from contiguous territory since then.

The democratic fervor which characterized the Middle West was produced rathei by the equality of worldly possessions that prevailed than by the physical environment. Nevertheless it should be noted that the physical hardships of life on the frontier had attracted into the Mississippi valley a type of man naturally venturesome and unconventional in his outlook in life. Such men seemed predestined to come to grips with the new and the untried; and when they came to frame their new state constitutions, it seemed natural and inevitable that they should defy the experience of the seaboard states by inserting provisions for universal manhood suffrage.

Geographic situation was an important element in the growth of sectionalism that occurred between 1800 and 1860. The prevalence of similar climatic and soil conditions throughout the Gulf states supplied the physical basis for the great cotton-growing industry and consequently for the attachment of the South to the institution of slavery. The great central trough of North America, continental in its dimensions, made the Northwest and the Southwest a part of the same physiographic area and foreshadowed a political combination of the Northwest and the South which should exclude New England and the Middle Atlantic states from the councils of the nation. If this were to be averted, it appeared that the very face of Nature must be altered.

In a resolute effort to accomplish this, Henry Clay advocated the construction of internal improvements at national expense, planning by this means to vanquish the Alleghany barricade and join the seaboard North and the Northwest through frequent intercourse and economic exchanges. His policy never won complete acceptance by Congress; but the efforts of the federal government were ably supplemented by the appropriations of New York and other states for canals and highways. The union of the two northern sections was finally accomplished by the construction of railroads in the forties and the fifties. Thus the North rose superior to natural obstacles; and, partly due to this fact, it was able to present a united front to the South in 1860.

The campaigns of the Civil War, like those of every other war in which the United States has taken part, were determined, to a very great extent, by physiographic considerations. The subject is too large for treatment here. The great strategic objectives of the armies of both sides were mountain passes, railroad centers, and the control of the waterways. The tremendous importance of rivers in the conduct of the war is reflected in the names of the Union armies: the Army of the Potomac, the Army of the James, the Army of the Cumberland and the Army of the Tennessee. Although railroads were more important than in any previous war, the lengthening lines of communication of the advancing federal forces made rivers more effective routes than the iron highways which could be easily destroyed by enemy raiders.

v

Before 1860 the frontier had already passed beyond the Mississippi river to the margin of the arid belt and, leaping the Great Plains and the Rockies, had firmly established itself on the Pacific seaboard. By 1890 the last of the fertile public lands had been transferred to private owners and the frontier, in an official sense, disappeared, although the last two territories of the Far West, New Mexico and

Arizona, were not admitted into the Union until 1912. Perhaps the most remarkable feature of this last continental wilderness of the United States was the unprecedented speed with which it was peopled. The age of steam and steel had arrived; and a few tons of coal applied to rail locomotion conquered distances and physical barriers in this new age that would have halted the progress of settlement for many years in the earlier stages of American history.

The rapid subjugation of the trans-Mississippi frontier created vexatious industrial and social problems, new in degree and form but old as the frontier itself in kind. These problems grew out of the distance of the western producer from the market, the excessive cost of transportation, the consequent high prices of manufactured articles, and the low prices received for farm products. These conditions, partly geographic in origin, formed the substratum of a period of agrarian unrest which found successive manifestation in the Granger movement, the greenback agitation, the movement for "free silver," and the more recent agitation against monopolies and "Big Business."

The contact of American society at its fringes with conditions of primitive democracy gave a fresh impulse to the development of American equalitarian thought and practice. The thinly populated frontier states and communities served anew their function as laboratories of political experiment and social adaptation, making their greatest contribution to modern American democracy in the origination of the doctrine of equal suffrage regardless of sex. Out of these states, also, came many new political devices designed to insure the control of the people over their government, such as direct nominations, the initiative and referendum, the recall, and the popular election of United States senators.

The passing of the frontier has had important economic consequences, for with the exhaustion of this great public-land reservoir the poor man can no longer receive a helping hand from the government to make a new start in life. Hardly less important is the fact that throughout American history the frontier has served as the zone of most rapid and thorough Americanization. In the crucible of the frontier men of all races were melted down and fused into a new race, English in speech but American in nationality. Therein lay the secret of the "melting pot," which has constituted one of the marvels of modern times. Under the new conditions the imperative problem is to furnish a substitute to perform the work which the frontier accomplished for us, and in spite of us, in the past. The present-day Americanization movement, in its various aspects, is a groping toward a solution of this difficulty. Whether the answer be found in new restrictions on immigration or a broader program of education, no question of our time merits more serious consideration and honest thought.

In all probability the influence of natural conditions on American national development will be less important in the future than it has been in the past. The age of steam and electricity has neutralized many of the effects which proved vital determinants of political and social progress in the past. Mountains have been conquered by the railroad and the telegraph; unproductive soils have yielded to irrigation and fertilization; rivers have been rendered navigable and their courses changed. The long contest between man and Nature in America has been decided in favor of man; and for the future, man seems determined to create the kind of physical environment which is best adapted to his fullest development.

BIBLIOGRAPHICAL NOTE

The publication of the *History of Civilization in England* (2 v.; London, 1857-1861) by the English historian, Henry Thomas Buckle, did much to open the eyes of historians all over the world to the vital relationship between natural conditions and human develop‑ ment. A generation passed before students of American history made any constructive application of Buckle's ideas. The first systematic attempt to apply a geographic interpretation to American history was made by Nathaniel Southgate Shaler, who in 1884 con‑ tributed a brief section on "Physiography of North America" to Justin Winsor's *Narrative and Critical History of America* (8 v.; Boston, 1884-1889), vol. iv, pp. i-xxx, and later elaborated his ideas in his book entitled *Nature and Man in America* (New York, 1891). Approaching the subject from the standpoint of a geologist, he first traced in this volume the effects of terrestrial changes upon the fauna and flora of North America, and then devoted several notable chapters (vi-viii) to setting forth, in a large way, the influence of geographic variations upon the history of man in America from pre-Columbian days to the present.

In 1892 the Englishman Edward John Payne published the first volume of his notable work, *History of the New World Called America* (2 v.; Oxford, 1892-1899). This work, which has never been completed, sought to explain the conditions of life among the American aborigines as the result of natural conditions, especially the nature of the food supply and the lack of useful domestic animals.

In 1893 Frederick Jackson Turner read his epoch-making address to the American Historical Association on "The Significance of the Frontier in American History," later published in the *Annual Report* of the American Historical Association for 1893, pp. 197-227, and also in his *The Frontier in American History* (New York, 1920), pp. 1-38. Professor Turner's thesis, that "The existence of free land, the continuous recession, the advance of American settlement westward explain American development," is almost too well known to require re-statement here. Although Professor Turner phrased his thought in this and his other studies very largely in the terminology of the physiographer, the frontier is to him "a form of society rather than an area," and his chief importance to American historical thinking has, in last analysis, been his elucidation of the part played by economic group conflicts in our history. See pp. 69-70 of the present volume.

The fullest statements we have of the importance of physical influences in American history appeared in two books, published in 1903, which had been worked out independently of each other. Albert Perry Brigham's *Geographic Influences in American History* (Boston) marked no important advance beyond what Professor Shaler had set forth in 1891. Ellen Churchill Semple's *American History and its Geographic Conditions* (Boston), couched in English of unusual charm, continues to be the best manual that has been written on the subject.

A number of monographic studies along the lines suggested by these works have been carried out since 1903. A notable series has been written by Archer Butler Hulbert under the general title *Historic Highways of America* (16 v.; Cleveland, 1902-1905). In 1907 a notable Conference on the Relation of Geography to

History, presided over by Professor Turner, was held in conjunction with the meeting of the American Historical Association at Madison. The principal papers were presented by Miss Semple and Orin Grant Libby. See report of this conference in the *Bulletin* of the American Geographic Society, vol. xl, pp. 1-17.

Students interested in this field should be acquainted with Professor Hulbert's article entitled, "The Increasing Debt of History to Science" in the *Proceedings* of the American Antiquarian Society, vol. xxix (1919), pp. 29-42, wherein he summarizes the results that have been achieved from the application of a physiographical explanation to American history and suggests that further clarification might be brought about by utilizing the information made available by the climatologist, botanist, geologist, ornithologist and hydrographer. Teachers of American history should be familiar with Dixon Ryan Fox's essay, "American History and the Map," introducing his carefully-prepared map studies in *Harper's Atlas of American History* (New York, 1920).

CHAPTER III

I

By the term "economic interpretation of history" is meant that view of the past which maintains that economic influences have been the preponderant factors in the history of mankind. Although traces of this theory may be found in writings prior to his time, Karl Marx, the father of modern Socialism, is rightly regarded as the great formulator of the doctrine. Undoubtedly the association of Marx's name with the theory of economic determinism has caused many people to regard this point of view with considerable distrust; and even the historians, particularly those in the United States, have been cautious about admitting themselves to be adherents of the doctrine. During the excitement of the World War, the avowal by a New York school teacher of his belief in the economic interpretation of history was regarded by certain members of the Board of Education as sufficient grounds for his expulsion. Perhaps the feeling of the ordinary man is best expressed by the witticism of a learned historian in an address delivered before the American Historical Association, to the effect that the members of this school of historical interpretation were responsible for putting the "hiss" into history.

As a matter of fact there is no necessary connection between a belief in the predominance of economic influences in history and the doctrine of Socialism. Most historians who have subscribed to the former view are not Socialists;

47

and, on the other hand, it is probable that few Socialists outside of the small circle of the *intelligentzia* know anything about this special theory of historical development. The economic interpretation of history merely represents an effort to explain, from the viewpoint of economic tendencies, the deep-flowing currents moving underneath the surface of the past. Socialism, on the other hand, is a prediction, one of a number of possible predictions, as to the direction, velocity, and goal of these currents at some time in the future.

Because of the popular confusion of the theory of economic determinism with Socialism, the student of American history may prefer to ignore the Marxian origin of the doctrine and claim for it an earlier and purely American authorship. Certainly the thought underlying the theory has seldom been better expressed than by James Madison, the "Father of the Constitution," in No. 10 of the *Federalist Papers*, which were written in 1787 and 1788 to win popular support for the federal Constitution then pending before the state ratifying conventions. After pointing out that mankind has constantly been influenced and divided by differences over religion and government or by attachment to outstanding leaders, Madison added: "But the most common and durable source of factions has been the various and unequal distribution of property. Those who hold and those who are without property have ever formed distinct interests in society. Those who are creditors, and those who are debtors, fall under a like discrimination. A landed interest, a manufacturing interest, a mercantile interest, a moneyed interest, with many lesser interests, grow up of necessity in civilized nations, and divide them into different classes, actuated by different sentiments and views." Here is an explicit avowal that, in the long run, history is the resultant of the interplay of social energies produced by differences in the amount and kind of material possessions held by the several sections of the population.

In attempting to apply the principle of economic interpretation to American history, one is at once confronted with the necessity of distinguishing between geographic or environmental influences, on the one hand, and the purely economic basis of American development, on the other. The fact is that the two classes of influences are sometimes so blended that it is impossible, or at least undesirable, to separate them. As has already been pointed out in this volume, the geographic background of history includes such elements as the contour of the earth's surface, the distribution of land and water, relationships of the size and distance of natural objects and, in the larger meaning of the term, climatic conditions. Economic influences arise from the possession of property by man, or from the desire for such possession, or from the use of such property as a lever of political or social power. A mountain range might, as a geographic condition, obstruct the movement of population; with the discovery of gold, it becomes an economic influence which draws people irresistibly.

II

Historians have generally treated the discovery of America as being the inevitable outcome of the economic plight in which Europe found herself because of the blocking of the Oriental trade routes by the Turks after the fall of Constantinople in 1453. That view now requires correction, for Professor Lybyer has shown, from a study of contemporary documents and of the curve of prices of Oriental commodities in Europe, that the main routes of Oriental trade through the Levant were not obstructed by the Turks until some years after Columbus's voyage of discovery. While this revelation disposes of the traditional view, it also serves to bring into sharper relief the commercial rivalry of the Atlantic countries, Portugal and Spain, as a factor in the situation.

The merchants of the Mediterranean cities, Genoa and Venice, had been the chief beneficiaries of the old routes of trade; these cities had waxed wealthy as termini and distributing centers of Far Eastern commerce. The aspiring monarchs on the Atlantic saw an opportunity to seize this trade, with all the profits accruing therefrom, if they could discover a water-passage to the Orient by way of the Atlantic. Thus Portugal, after some experimental voyages of discovery, put forth heroic efforts in the quest of a passage around Africa, finally achieving her goal in the voyage of Vasco da Gama in 1498; and the Spanish Court, with grave misgivings, backed the scheme of the Italian visionary, Cristoforo Colombo, for a due western passage. In view of the opposition of economic interests involved, it is not surprising that Columbus should have been forced to leave Genoa in order to obtain assistance for a venture which promised the commercial eclipse of his native city. Had Columbus not appeared on the scene at the psychological time, there can be no doubt that, with the economic situation as it was, the discovery would have been made at about the same time by some other mariner. Indeed, there is absolute proof of this conjecture in the fact that the coast of Brazil was accidentally discovered in the year 1500 by a Portuguese captain who was blown out of his course by unfavorable winds while attempting to follow Vasco da Gama's route around Africa.

The economic motive played a large part in the colonization of the New World. The main incentive to the establishment of colonies was the desire of European monarchs to secure new sources of national revenue, to which must be added, in the case of the English colonists, the desire of the settlers to improve their living conditions. Spain was richly rewarded with great stores of gold and silver. The French and the Dutch found the fur trade a never-ending source of wealth. In the case of the English colonists, as Professor Andrews has pointed out, the first efforts at planting colonies, made by romantic Elizabethan adventurers, were failures; and the beginnings of effective colonization grew out of the commercial ambitions of noblemen, merchants and capitalists in the Stuart period. They saw in the New World great opportunities for wealth, such as earlier Englishmen had seen in the Mediterranean and the Baltic. With few exceptions the British colonies in North America were founded as business ventures; and even where the original motive was religious or philanthropic, there was, in most instances, also a commercial aspect.

Two forms of promoting colonization were widely employed by the English: the trading company, and the proprietary grant. The trading company differed in no essential respect from a modern business corporation. The money necessary for fitting out a colonial expedition—for transporting settlers and providing their food and clothing and implements during the initial years—was obtained through the sale of stock; and the stockholders expected dividends on their investment in the shape of furs or some agricultural or mineral product that could be marketed in Europe. Fortunately, these companies proved unsuccessful financially in Virginia and elsewhere; otherwise the English settlements might not have developed beyond mere trading posts. The proprietary grant, on the other hand, was feudal in character. The proprietor to whom the land had been granted undertook the planting of a colony as one might set about the cultivation of a distant estate. He met the expenses of shiploads of laborers sent out to develop its resources, and expected returns on his investment from the rental and sale of lands, tariff duties, and receipts from mines.

While the latter scheme was more profitable to the promoters than the trading corporation (as witness the instances of Pennsylvania and Maryland), the historical importance of both forms of colonial promotion lay in the fact that they mapped out domains, and paved the way, for a spontaneous migration of Europeans who were animated, first and foremost, by the prospect of their personal material betterment. Indeed, the original backers of colonization projects became discouraged as to their financial returns after a generation, in the case of most of the colonies; and the stockholders and heirs of the original grants were generally willing to sell out their rights to the Crown for a modest remuneration. One of the significant movements of the colonial period was the transition of most of the thirteen colonies from their original condition of private ownership and control to royal provinces possessing representative government. This trend was conditioned, in large degree, by the desire of both the English government and the colonials to participate in the vested interests possessed by the original promoters and enterprisers.

The history of each one of the English colonies was marked by political antagonism between the people living in the coast towns and the settlers of the interior. Racial and religious differences, and intervening distance, contributed to this antipathy; but the real contention between tidewater and back-country was an economic one. The men of the cities were merchants and capitalists, and the people of the backwoods, possessed of slender means, were generally in debt to them. This tended to divide the population of each colony on all questions of public policy arising in the provincial legislature, especially those involving the economic welfare of the one group or the other. Moreover, the people of the interior were likely to be radical democrats, for on the frontier the small farm was the unit of economic life, and the terms of virtual economic equality on which the people lived taught them to believe that all men were entitled to equal treatment politically.

Two of the prolific causes of contention in the domestic politics of the colonies had to do with fiat money and the apportionment of taxes. The back-county where specie was scarce had greater need of paper currency than did the creditor and merchant class living in the older settlements; and the eastern members of the legislature endeavored to prevent that body from granting any relief. Likewise in the matter of taxation the inland farmers believed that they were being discriminated against by their tidewater brethren and forced to raise an undue proportion of the public revenues. In such contests the older settlements, even when numerically inferior, were usually able to maintain the upper hand because of the system of apportionment whereby they were over-represented in the colonial legislature. When the inequities of their situation became unendurable, the frontiersmen did not hesitate to take up arms in vindication of their rights. Some notable examples of this are to be found in Bacon's rebellion in Virginia, the Regulators' uprising in North Carolina in 1770 and, during the Confederation period, Shays' rebellion in Massachusetts.

The prosperity and progress of the colonies depended upon their commercial connections with the rest of the world. As newly-settled farming and fishing communities, they could not with any wisdom develop their own manufactures, nor could they find a market for their surplus products without access to British or foreign markets. But they were under the wing of the greatest manufacturing and commercial nation of the earth; and in the world as it then was, fenced off into exclusive trading monopolies, this connection with

England undoubtedly redounded to the economic advantage of the colonies. Recent researches have shown that, contrary to a long-held opinion, the colonists suffered no real hardship from the regulation of their commerce and industry by Parliament prior to 1763 and, indeed, that they enjoyed some substantial benefits in the subsidizing of certain industries (like indigo culture and timber production) and in the protection against foreign competition extended to shipbuilding. There is no reason to believe that the people during most of the colonial period were not as contented under British rule as the people of Canada are today. But a radical change in British colonial policy about 1763 threatened the economic welfare of the colonists and created such widespread protest and unrest in America that within a dozen years the colonists were engaged in launching a war for separation. As this matter is discussed at some length in a later chapter, nothing further need be said here about it.[1]

The winning of independence brought with it a loss of the commercial advantages which the colonists had enjoyed by reason of their membership in the British Empire. Since the federal government established under the Articles of Confederation lacked the power and energy to place American business and commerce upon a stable footing, men of substance and national vision began a campaign of agitation for replacing the existing government with a new one possessing authority to protect property rights, and to establish national credit at home and abroad. "I conceive, sir," declared Fisher Ames of Massachusetts, "that the present Constitution was dictated by commercial necessity more than any other cause."[2] After the new government was once established under the Constitution, the efforts of our diplomacy were very largely motivated by economic considera-

[1] Chapter vii.
[2] The economic phases of the movement for the federal Constitution are discussed in some detail in chapter viii.

tions: the desire to recover old markets or to acquire new ones for our commerce, and the necessity of protecting our neutral trade from the encroachments of Great Britain and France during the Napoleonic wars. A notable series of treaties testify to the degree of success attained by these efforts.

III

The political history of the United States affords abundant evidence of the direct relationship between self-conscious economic groups in the population and political parties. Many illustrations might be cited; but, for present purposes, the original alignment of parties between Federalists and Republicans in the first quarter of a century under the Constitution will suffice. The Federalists were, in the main, the same group who had carried the movement for the Constitution against heavy odds; they were interested in translating into effective statutes those clauses of that instrument which promised the establishment of the national credit, the security of property and contracts, and the protection of commerce and manufactures. In other words, the effective nucleus of the Federalist party consisted of merchants, money-lenders and capitalists.

Alexander Hamilton's monumental financial plan, providing for the funding of the debt, assumption of the state debts, a United States Bank, etc., reduced their ideas to a definite code, and undoubtedly served to anchor the young republic at a time when blustering winds threatened to drive it on the rocks. And it is to be noted that while Hamilton used the nation to buttress wealth, he also reversed the process and used wealth to buttress the nation. This is nowhere shown better than in his project to have the debts contracted by the states during the Revolutionary War paid off, or assumed, by the federal government, an object which, it may be noted, he attained only by means of a political deal with his enemy, Thomas Jefferson, whereby he agreed to a Potomac site for the national capital in return for southern votes for assumption. By this assumption measure Hamilton aimed to consolidate behind the new national government the support of all the men who in past years had invested their money in the securities of the state governments. The measure formed, in the language of Henry Cabot Lodge, an important link in Hamilton's system "to create a strong and . . . permanent class all over the country, without regard to existing political affiliations, but bound to the government as a government, by the strongest of all ties, immediate and personal pecuniary interest."

Since the merchant and moneyed class formed only a small minority of the population, we find in this circumstance the economic basis for the philosophical and constitutional doctrines of the Federalist party. In order to protect their peculiar economic interests in the presence of an overwhelmingly agricultural population, they became strong exponents of the aristocratic ideal of government—government by the few or the well-born. Their economic situation further necessitated a belief in a government strongly centralized and made of them upholders of a broad construction of the Constitution and of a military establishment. Likewise their foreign policy was susceptible of an economic explanation. Toward Great Britain they were consistently friendly, even to the point of agreeing to such an unfavorable treaty as the Jay treaty of 1794, for in the establishment of closer relations with Great Britain lay their great hope of recovering their commercial prosperity. For France the Federalists felt only distrust and hostility, for that country since 1789 had become the abode of social unrest and doctrinaire radicalism.

On the other side of the political fence, the Jeffersonian

Republicans as faithfully represented the interests and aspirations of their rural constituency. The abundance of good farm land and the consequent ease of acquiring a livelihood relieved the farmers and planters of the need of governmental tariffs and other financial assistance in their economic life, and caused them to envisage government merely as a sublimated policeman whose sole function was to preserve peace and good order. Hamilton's ingenious scheme of a national bank, tariff system, and complete financial reorganization seemed to them pure class legislation, officious intrusions into a domain of interests wherein private citizens could best work out their own salvation. As they watched the Federalists at work, they became embittered against a government which appeared to be working in the interests of a strongly-organized minority; they devised a doctrine of state rights as their strongest bulwark against federal encroachments; and, confident in their numerical superiority, they exalted democracy—control by the majority—as the only proper government for a free people. Their attacks on the entrenched moneyed interests brought to their support the workingmen of the towns, as yet an unimportant though growing element of the population. Without the prestige of Washington and the disorganized state of the opposition party, it is doubtful if the Federalists could have retained power as long as they did. With his death they quickly succumbed to the democratic tide and passed out of power forever.

It seems unnecessary to dwell further in any detailed way upon the relation between political parties and economic group conflicts. In a general way, the National Republicans of 1828, the dominant element in the Whig party, and the *post bellum* Republicans have in turn represented the interests of the manufacturing and financial class. The economic basis of the Democratic party has been more complicated in character but, except for a period of about twenty years before the Civil War, the Democrats have generally represented the interests of poorer and less fortunate classes of society.

IV

The political events of the "Middle Period" of American history (1800-1860) find their explanation very largely in the sectionalization of American life which, during this period, divided the nation into three distinct economic areas, a broad western zone of independent small farmers, a northern seaboard section in which manufacturing was becoming the dominant interest, and a southern seaboard area wedded to cotton culture and slave labor.

In the preceding chapter the movement of settlers across the Alleghanies into the heart of the continent was sketched with particular attention to the geographical conditions affecting the migration. It remains here to point out, more specifically than in the earlier discussion, that the vast majority of the pioneers who journeyed westward,

> Some to endure, and many to fail,
> Some to conquer, and many to quail,
> Toiling over the Wilderness Trail,

were moved by economic considerations. As the East became more populous and economic competition grew keener, ambitious workingmen in the cities saw an opportunity for improved living conditions in the cheap lands of the Ohio valley; and farmers working the smaller and less fertile farms saw larger holdings and greater prosperity in the West also. The same attraction was felt by the people of the seaboard South, by the better class of the "poor whites" who saw in Kentucky and the free Northwest a means of escape from the degrading position they held in southern society, and by planters desirous of abandoning their worn-out lands for new estates in the black alluvial belt of the Gulf coast. Other economic incentives were at work as well. Let us analyze the successive waves of migration into the frontier as they have been so often pictured for us by writers on the subject. The desire for hunting and fur-trading animated the first comers. Then hard-by followed the land speculators. Next came men seeking new lands for cultivation or cattle grazing. As homes began to multiply, opportunities were opened up for business enterprise in commerce and transportation. So swiftly did one group follow another that sometimes they became an almost indistinguishable mass.

The transfer of population from east to west occurred with amazing rapidity. In these early years, frontier conditions prevailed throughout the Mississippi valley, south of the Ohio river as well as north. Much the same difficulties confronted the pioneer in Mississippi and Alabama as in Indiana and Illinois and tended to give to the West a similarity of outlook. Great commonwealths were founded and admitted into the Union; and a new and threatening influence, the outgrowth largely of the economic conditions of wilderness life, made its appearance in national politics.

The West was totally unlike the older East in its sympathies, ideals and needs. The abundance of cheap lands promoted individualism, economic equality and a lyric enthusiasm for government by the people. The major problems of the people had to do with the paucity of transportation facilities, and the lack of capital for the proper development of the region. With some direct connection through the mountains with the eastern markets, the western farmers might dispose of their surplus crops to much greater advantage and receive in return those manufactured articles which added so greatly to the comfort of living. With a greater abundance of fluid capital, local improvements of all kinds might be made, economic enterprise stimulated, and the region more rapidly developed. The national policies which the westerners favored were, as we shall see, the resultant of their democratic idealism and economic needs.

New England and the Middle Atlantic states formed another fairly homogeneous economic unit. Throughout the colonial period and during the first decades of national independence, the economic life of New England had been centered in shipbuilding and the carrying trade. But the adoption of the embargo and other restrictive trade measures by Jefferson and Madison, followed by the War of 1812, led to a stagnation of New England commerce, though it created conditions ideally fitted for the stimulation of American manufacturing. While New Englanders who could see their future only in their past became disgruntled with the federal government and began a campaign of disaffection and protest that culminated in the Hartford Convention of 1814, other men of the region, shrewder to seize a new opportunity, turned their capital from shipping to manufacturing. They saw that their section possessed an almost unexploited source of wealth in the abundant water power furnished by its swift rivers, and that, with the proper application of human energy, the wheels of industry might soon be made to turn. Hence, already by 1815, 500,000 spindles and 76,000 persons were employed in the manufacture of cotton, chiefly in New England, and the annual output of woolens was estimated to be worth nineteen millions of dollars. In the Middle Atlantic states—New York, New Jersey and Pennsylvania—manufacturing had already become a principal industry; and their economic interests thus tended to unite them politically with New England.

The new factories of the seaboard North produced so much more than had the old domestic processes that markets for the disposal of their output were needed in those parts of the country in which no manufacturing was to be found.

But to bring this about, two obstacles had to be surmounted. The difficulties of trade with the West and the South were immense owing to the lack of proper means of transportation. Moreover, in these markets the eastern manufacturers and merchants found themselves in competition with English manufacturers who could undersell them because of their lower cost of production. So here, too, as in the case of the frontier states, was a combination of conditions that were productive of definite national policies.

The third area that stood cemented by common economic ties was the South or, to be more exact in speaking of the early years of the Middle Period, the South Atlantic states. Since the invention of Eli Whitney's cotton gin in 1793, the attention of this section had become increasingly absorbed in the development of cotton culture. From a crop of negligible importance the total product leaped in 1800 to about thirty-five million pounds, of which a little more than half was sent abroad, and in 1820 arose to one hundred and sixty million pounds, of which more than three-fourths were exported. The rapid growth of the cotton industry was as important in one of its indirect results as it was in its direct effect, for it caused a rejuvenation of the institution of negro slavery.

It is a truism of the historians that slavery was, at bottom, a geographic and economic question. Slavery had existed throughout the thirteen colonies at the start, but before long it had begun to show signs of thinning out in the northern section where slaves had no useful part to play in the prevailing system of economic life—small farms and mercantile establishments. Even in the South slavery appeared to perform no vital economic function in colonial times except possibly in the rice fields of South Carolina and Georgia. During the high emotional excitement aroused by the Revolutionary War, steps were taken for the abolition of slavery in all the states north of Maryland. At the time of the federal Constitutional Convention a general expectation was shared alike by southerners and northerners that the institution of slavery was destined to gradual extinction in the course of the next generation or so.

But the vast expansion of cotton culture due to Whitney's invention put the matter in a new light. Cotton culture was peculiarly adapted to the employment of slave labor. Its simple requirements, not involving the use of expensive machinery, gave systematic employment for most of the year and permitted the use of women and children as well as adult men. Cotton growing was so profitable that there was no incentive to a diversification of industry, for which slave labor would have been unsuited. The low cotton plants, moreover, allowed the overseer to superintend a large gang of workers. The new importance of slaves was reflected in their rising market value. The prohibition of slave importation in 1808 at the same time that the demand was increasing made this rise unusually sharp. The average value of a good field hand about the time of the invention of the cotton gin was $200.00; by 1815 it was $250.00, by 1836 $600.00, and in 1850 $1000.00. By 1850 the value of the slave property in the entire South amounted, at a conservative computation, to more than one and one-quarter billions of dollars. Corresponding with this new background of southern economic life, we find the teachers and religious leaders of that section at first palliating the institution and then, later, roundly defending it on moral, biblical and ethnic grounds.

Having developed an economic system based upon agriculture and centering in cotton culture, the public men of the South Atlantic seaboard became increasingly interested in political measures that would contribute to their sectional prosperity. From early colonial times the population had relied upon Great Britain for cloth and tools and luxuries; and with the development of English cotton manufactures, they found their most profitable market for raw cotton in that country. They were therefore opposed to any measures of the federal government which might interfere with this natural and mutually profitable exchange of goods. In the northern proposal of a protective tariff they saw only higher prices for the goods they consumed with no corresponding benefits for themselves.

The period from 1800 to 1830 was a time of economic transition and change in the case of all three sections; and it was not until the latter date that the distinctive economic character of each was definitely fixed and the section had become politically self-conscious. The real inwardness of the history of the United States to the Civil War cannot be understood without constant reference to these cross-currents and countercurrents of sectional interest. It is possible here to consider only a few of the more important aspects of the history of that time.

The West did not speak with undivided voice. One important element, led by Henry Clay of Kentucky and representing the nascent industrial interests of the region, were ardent advocates of internal improvements at national expense, and held, furthermore, that the United States government should assist the states financially by a distribution of the proceeds of the sales of public lands. The majority of the backwoodsmen were probably better represented by Andrew Jackson of Tennessee and Thomas H. Benton of Missouri, who had a simple and hearty belief that the difficulties of the masses would be removed when officers trusted by the common people were placed in charge of the government. This element, when forced to define their views further, revealed an inbred suspicion of governmental interference in the affairs of the people; and, convinced that banks had hindered rather than helped western development through irresponsible issues of paper money, they favored the disestablishment of the Second United States Bank and the use of "hard money" as the standard circulating medium. They believed that the federal government should hand over to each state the unsold public lands within its borders; and as for the transportation problem, they would solve it by having the states appropriate the proceeds of land sales to that purpose and also through the initiative of private enterprise.

The major political interest of the northern seaboard states was focused on an adequate protective tariff system for the encouragement of domestic manufactures. As tributary to this central idea, the business class of that section were strong friends of the United States Bank, which made for stable money conditions, and of national aid to internal improvements, which would facilitate the marketing of their wares. The political acumen, and the economic substratum, of Henry Clay's much vaunted "American System" may now be apparent. By joining in political wedlock the two principles of protection and national internal improvements, he hoped to bind the Northeast and the West in a political alliance solidified by the consciousness of mutual economic advantage.

There were, to be sure, other elements in the population of the northern seaboard section who felt that their interests were not served by the legislation advocated by the business and manufacturing classes—the mechanics in the cities and the small farmers. They were best represented in the politics of the time by Martin Van Buren and, in general, their outlook on politics resembled that of Jackson's followers in the West.

The people of the South Atlantic seaboard states were mainly interested in preserving or establishing conditions of free trade, an attitude and purpose which brought them at once into collision with the tariff demands of the northern manufacturers. They were not averse to the United States Bank, and only by gradual stages were they adopting pronounced views against national aid for internal improvements. Although they were watchful for any interference with the slavery system, the militant abolition movement was just getting under way in the decade of the thirties and, as yet, they had little to fear. South Carolina was still the chief cotton state, and John C. Calhoun was her prophet and statesman.

It is now possible to follow these sectional economic needs and aspirations into the hurly-burly of actual politics. The John Quincy Adams administration, which came into office in 1825, represented a combination of New England with the Clay element of the West; and the laws enacted during the four-year period testified eloquently to the zeal of those two leaders in promoting the interests of their sections. More than twice as much was appropriated for roads and harbors as in the whole previous history of the country; and the tariff was increased from an average of thirty-three per cent under the act of 1824 to a general level of forty-nine per cent (1828).

The election of Jackson in 1828 came as the result of an alliance of the planters of the seaboard South and the Jackson western element, assisted by Van Buren's followers in the Northeast. Under President Jackson, national appropriations for internal improvements were checked, the United States Bank destroyed, the Specie Circular issued, the Indians ejected from Georgia; and in lieu of the surrender of the unsold public lands to the several states, the surplus revenue was distributed among them. Not long after the beginning of Jackson's term the flimsy character of the political combination that elected him became apparent.

South Carolina decided to take a stand against the protective system, even to the extremity of nullification, if necessary; but the leaders of that state discovered, to their dismay, that the president was inclined to be indifferent to their needs and determined at all odds to prevent any steps toward disunion. The South Carolina group, followed by many individual Democrats in other parts of the Southeast, thereupon abandoned the party until a time should come when the evil Jackson influence had waned and the party might be made to stand for southern interests.

Toward this culmination time was indeed working in behalf of the cotton planters. As the initial difficulties of pioneer life in Alabama, Mississippi and Tennessee were overcome, the plantation system of cotton growing was rapidly extended throughout that region. This westward spread of large scale cotton culture soon broke down the contrast between Southeast and Southwest. It is an economic fact of great political import that, whereas in 1824 the annual cotton production of the South Atlantic states was almost double that of the Gulf states, this ratio was reversed in 1841. By the latter date it was beginning to be possible to speak of the South from the Atlantic to the Mississippi and beyond as a compact political entity.

The Cotton South proceeded to organize itself to dominate the federal government and decided to use the Democratic party as its special instrument for that purpose. The leaders of the South were constantly kept acutely conscious of the peculiar economic situation of their section by the increasing severity of the anti-slavery agitation in the North. A powerful and pervasive influence began to be felt in national politics, the "Slave Power" or the "Slavocracy," in its operations not unlike the "Money Power" or the "Plutocracy" in the period since the Civil War. So successful was this new political force that from 1844 to the Civil War every presidentiai candidate of the Democratic party was a southerner or a northerner with southern views. The basic political objects of the "Slave Power," other than the lowering of the tariff, were the extension of slavery into the federal territories, and the annexation of foreign soil suitable for the peculiar system of labor. These were two aspects of the same economic need since the prevailing system of cotton culture brought about the rapid exhaustion of the soil and necessitated expansion into undeveloped lands wherever they might be found. Moreover, the building up of new slave commonwealths enabled the South to maintain its equality in the United States Senate with the rapidly growing North.

To be successful in national politics the cotton interests must add to their own voting strength the support of the pioneer farmers of the Northwest. How this was done is a record of shrewd political strategy that can be only lightly touched on here. In the campaign of 1844 the South won the support of the Northwest for the annexation of Texas by bracketing this demand with a demand for Oregon. Shortly after, when the question arose as to slavery in the Mexican cessions following the peace of Guadaloupe Hidalgo (1848), the southerners were willing to concede the principle of popular sovereignty for its solution, a device having a peculiar appeal to the pioneer Northwest with its predilections for local self-government. The same device was applied dramatically in 1854 when the Missouri Compromise line of 36° 30′ was abolished and the territories of Kansas and Nebraska were opened to possible slave settlement.

But in this last manœuvre the southern Democrats and their northern allies overshot themselves. The territories in question formed a part of the public domain which the northern farmers and workingmen, and the European peasants who had immigrated into the North, regarded as peculiarly their own for settlement. The people of the Northwest thus became acutely aware of a fundamental antagonism of interest between the slavery system and free labor, and thereafter they were ready to join themselves with the anti-slavery idealists of the North in a battle to the death with the "Slave Power." From this combination of circumstances arose the Republican party, "a purely sectional party," as Stephen A. Douglas said, "with a platform that cannot cross the Ohio river." Henceforth the political alignment of the nation was distinctively one of North against South. When the Republicans proved successful in the election of Lincoln in 1860, the dominant leadership of the cotton states believed that the only hope of safeguarding their future prosperity lay in the establishment of a southern slave republic. The economic antagonism of the sections, exacerbated, of course, by personal, political, ethical and psychological differences, thus plunged the nation into the great Civil War.

v

It is hardly necessary here to advert to the fact that the superior economic resources of the North were the decisive factor in determining the issue of the war favorably to the Union. The South paid the penalty of having confined its productive efforts practically to the growing of one staple crop. From the moment that the federal blockade became effective, the doom of the South was sealed unless some military victory might miraculously turn the tide of events. The Confederacy hoped anxiously for recognition from Great Britain because of the dependence of British textile manufacturers upon southern cotton; but the British situation in that respect was somewhat relieved by the importation of cotton from Egypt and India, and crop failures during 1860, 1861 and 1862 made the British people more anxious for northern wheat than southern cotton.

The close of the Civil War was followed by an epoch of tremendous economic and industrial development which transformed the whole fabric of American life and raised far-reaching questions of political and economic policy. These matters are discussed at some length elsewhere in this volume,[1] and indeed form a part of the common stock of knowledge of our times. Suffice it to say here that our thinking today is perhaps more distinctively in economic terms than ever before. Any list of campaign issues will at once reveal this—such questions, for instance, as the tariff, the merchant marine, the currency, the railroads, trust regulation. Or any survey of newspaper editorials on domestic affairs—covering topics like the "open shop," co-operation, immigration, farmers' grievances, the high cost of living and profiteering—leads to the same conclusion.

Although economic influences are probably no more potent in American life than earlier, they are more frankly accepted than ever before. Present-day politics is very largely the resultant of a complex of economic and social forces, working frequently at cross purposes with each other; and the "principal task of modern legislation" continues to be, in the classic language of James Madison, "the regulation of these various and interfering interests."

BIBLIOGRAPHICAL NOTE

John Bach McMaster broke new ground in 1883 when he published the first volume of his monumental work, *A History of the People of the United States* (8 v.; New York, 1883-1913), for it was his purpose to recount the history of the United States from a social point of view. Garnering his facts very largely from the files of old newspapers and setting them forth with photographic fidelity, he portrayed the life of the masses with a profuseness of detail that gave new realism to the old story.

But Professor McMaster was concerned rather with reconstructing a human chronicle than with accounting for the mainsprings of social conduct. The first historian who perceived the importance of economic influences in American history was Frederick Jackson Turner, who first expounded his views publicly in his address, "The

[1] Chapter xi.

Significance of the Frontier in American History," printed in the *Annual Report* of the American Historical Association for 1893, pp. 199-227. Compare p. 45 of the present volume. Professor Turner's main interest, in this and many later papers, was to trace the influence of frontier conditions, particularly the abundance of cheap lands, upon our historical development. The most important of these essays may be found in convenient form in his *The Frontier in American History* (New York, 1920). Although Professor Turner had reached his conclusions independently, it is a matter of interest that his main thesis had been set forth as early as January, 1865, by Ernest Lawrence Godkin in his article entitled "Aristocratic Opinions of Democracy" in the *North American Review* (reprinted in his *Problems of Modern Democracy*, New York, 1896).

Under Professor Turner's influence, a new direction was given to American historical research; and many articles and books have been written by students who sought to apply his viewpoint to particular periods or aspects of American history. A bibliography of these writings would be too extensive for inclusion here; but the mention of a few of the names of the authors will suggest the scope and character of the work that has been done: Reuben Gold Thwaites, Clarence W. Alvord, Solon J. Buck, Clarence E. Carter, Isaac J. Cox, Archibald Henderson, Homer C. Hockett, Frederic L. Paxson, Louis Pelzer and Milo M. Quaife. The Turner point of view is most felicitously presented in his own volume of essays, already cited; but excellent restatements may be found in Woodrow Wilson's "The Making of the Nation" in the *Atlantic Monthly*, vol. 80, pp. 1-14; Archibald Henderson's *The Conquest of the Old Southwest* (New York, 1920), pp. ix-xix; and Frederic L. Paxson's *The Last American Frontier* (New York, 1910), chap. i.

The Turner school of historians has tended to discuss American development in geographic terms and has generally avoided the expression, "economic interpretation of history"; it has, on the whole, paid little attention to the rôle of industrial capitalism and the wage system in American history. Indeed it was not until the early years of the twentieth century that students of history began, frankly and comprehensively, to apply an economic analysis to American history. A strong impulse in this direction was furnished by the manuals prepared by several economists interested in delineating the economic and industrial history of the country. Not counting the earlier work done by J. L. Bishop and A. S. Bolles, there appeared in a short space of years Carroll D. Wright's *The Industrial Evolution of the United States* (New York, 1895); Horace White's *Money and Banking Illustrated by American History* (Boston, 1895); Davis Rich Dewey's *Financial History of the United States* (New York, 1902); Katharine Coman's *The Industrial History of the United States* (New York, 1905); Ernest Ludlow Bogart's *The Economic History of the United States* (New York, 1907); and Guy Stevens Callender's *Selections from the Economic History of the United States, 1765-1860, with Introductory Essays* (Boston, 1909).

A number of Socialist writers now came forward as avowed

economic determinists and set themselves the task of justifying the Marxian view of historical development. A. M. Simons's *Class Struggles in America* (Chicago, 1903) and his *Social Forces in American History* (New York, 1912), Austin Lewis's *The Rise of the American Proletarian* (Chicago, 1907), James Oneal's *The Workers in American History* (New York, 1910; revised and enlarged in 1912 and in 1921), and Gustavus Myers's *History of the Supreme Court of the United States* (Chicago, 1912) are richly suggestive, though untrustworthy, surveys written from the standpoint of Marxian exegesis.

Not until 1913 did an American student of scholarly standing and scientific historical training undertake to apply the concept of economic interpretation to American history with careful documentation and infinite detailed analysis. In that year appeared Charles A. Beard's *An Economic Interpretation of the Constitution of the United States* (New York), the first of a series of volumes under the general title *An Economic Interpretation of American Politics*, of which the second appeared two years later, *Economic Origins of Jeffersonian Democracy* (New York, 1915).

From this account it is not to be thought that other historians of our day have been unaware of the economic influence in American history, for most members of the modern school have recognized its existence in a greater or less degree. Charles McLean Andrews, for example, following in the footsteps of W. B. Weeden, P. A. Bruce and G. L. Beer, has gone a long way toward rewriting colonial history from an economic point of view; and delvers in the later periods of American history are constantly making greater use of an economic explanation of events and movements. Nevertheless, it is a significant fact that the standard *Cyclopedia of American Government* (3 v. edited by Andrew Cunningham McLaughlin and Albert Bushnell Hart; New York, 1913) does not include the economic interpretation of history among the subjects for treatment.

Advocates of the theory of economic determinism do not usually deny the existence of geographic, moral, religious and other forces in history nor the contributions made by great men. But, following Engels, Marx's collaborator, they hold that even the ideas and ethical code of any age are influenced, and in the long run controlled, by its economic background, although the acceptance of new standards may be delayed by the transmitted conceptions of a former age, which in turn had been the product of economic conditions once prevailing. As for the superman in history, they assert that, while his appearance at a particular crisis may seem to be a matter of chance, he is able to influence society only when society is ready for him. If conditions are not ripe, he is called, not a great man, but a mad man or a visionary. The best critique by an American of the economic theory of historical development is Edwin R. A. Seligman's *The Economic Interpretation of History* (2d ed., revised, New York, 1917).

CHAPTER IV

Aristocracy is something more than a form of govern‧
mental organization. It is an outlook on life that infuses its
peculiar spirit of exclusiveness and superiority, of self-pride
and special privilege, into all phases of human relationship.
It is mirrored in the manners and morals of a people, in
their religious organization and beliefs, in their provisions
for education, in their language and their literature, in their
labor system, and in the relations of the sexes to each other,
as well as in their system of government and law. To
Americans of today the most inspiring theme in American
history is the story of the successive advances of the common
man into rights and powers and opportunities previously
monopolized by an exclusive class; we call it the rise of
democracy. But to our anxious ancestors watching with
deep misgivings the restless stirrings and recurrent upheavals
of the nether strata of society, the changes that occurred
appeared not as the working out of a beneficent destiny but
as the degradation of all that seemed good and stable in the
world. In their eyes each new victory won by the masses,
whether in government or education or in some other department of life, signified the yielding of aristocracy to the combined forces of ignorance, avarice and mobocracy.

The story of the struggle of aristocracy against democracy
is a complex one, touching the life of the past generations
of American society at many vital points and throwing much
light upon the processes of human progress. In the sketch

that follows it is only possible to dwell upon some of the outstanding phases of this long conflict.

I

Judged by our present-day standards, the aristocratic idea was firmly enthroned in the life of the people in colonial times. At the apex of the social pyramid stood the colonial governor with the official class that surrounded him, constituting a caste that looked to England not only for its governmental authority but also for its models and standards of social conduct. Life at the governor's court was gay and extravagant, and frequently brilliant; to become members of the charmed circle was the aspiration, and sometimes the despair, of the colonial aristocracy which ranked next in the social scale.

In every province such a native aristocratic class had developed irrespective of the lowly European antecedents of the original settlers. Social and political leadership in New England belonged as a matter of custom to the "well-born"—the clergy, the professional classes, and the wealthier merchants. Seats in the meeting-houses, places at the table and in processions, were regulated with a nice regard for social differentiation. Even at Harvard College students were seated according to social rank, whereby John Adams found himself fourteenth in a class of twenty-four. In New York, pre-eminence belonged to the landed gentry, living in feudal elegance on their great estates along the Hudson, and dominating the affairs of the province by the aid of their connections, through business or marriage, with the wealthy merchant families of New York city. In the neighboring province of Pennsylvania a similar position was occupied by a compact group of rich Quaker families dwelling in the eastern counties of the province.

Class distinctions were even more rigidly maintained in

the provinces to the south. In those parts was to be found an aristocracy of birth and manners which more nearly approached its counterpart in England than anything else to be found in America. Composed of the owners of great plantations and resting on a vital distinction between slave labor and gentlemanly leisure, the members of this exclusive order lived a life of luxurious ease, educated their sons abroad, and prided themselves on keeping abreast the modish fashions of London society.

As befitted their social position, the aristocratic class in all the colonies occupied the seats of power in provincial politics. In order to insure their control they did not rely solely upon a popular acceptance of their superior qualifications, for they entertained no exalted notions as to the mental acuteness of the average man. Hence the right to vote was nowhere bestowed upon all men, only on such white adult men as possessed a stated amount of property; and in most provinces they must in addition subscribe to certain religious tenets. For fear that the ease of acquiring land might render some of these restrictions nugatory in the outlying districts, the ruling class employed certain additional devices to safeguard their privileged position. A favorite method was to postpone the political organization of the new communities as long as possible, and then to allow them a disproportionately small representation in the provincial legislature. As a result of such practices, the mass of the population in every province was excluded from participation in the government, to the great glory of the aristocracy.

Traces of the aristocratic principle were likewise to be found in education and religion. In Massachusetts and Connecticut alone was a system of public education established; and in Pennsylvania and Virginia, several free elementary schools for the poor had been founded under private auspices. It was in large degree true elsewhere that schools of any kind were rare; and "higher education" was the prerogative of the wealthy few. In four of the southern provinces the Church of England was the established church, supported out of public funds, and in Virginia no one could be legally married except by a minister of the established church. Throughout the colonial period the Congregational Church occupied a similarly privileged position in Massachusetts and Connecticut.

The distinction between "gentle folk" and "simple men" was maintained everywhere throughout the colonies, not merely as a badge of social distinction but also as a deterrent to the political, educational and social advancement of those of ungentle rearing. The periwig and knee breeches were the outward token of the inner superiority of the gentleman. The mean-born accepted as their meed the bobwig and plain baggy waistcoats or even the unlovely pantaloons. The line of cleavage was unmistakable and of obvious convenience; and one can readily understand the wrath with which that fine old aristocrat, Governor Hutchinson of Massachusetts, charged that in one of the Stamp Act riots "there were fifty gentlemen, actors in this scene, disguised with trousers and jackets on." The inferior class were numerically in the great majority; they were the small farmers, the shopkeepers, the sailors, the artisans, and mechanics—the plain people of the time. They were saved from being the base of the social pyramid only by the fact that below them, separated by an infinite gulf, were the enslaved negroes.

As the colonial period approached its close, there began to appear signs that the long-established security of the privileged order was being threatened. The fact that land was abundant and easily obtainable by those who were willing to undergo the hardships of frontier life made it impossible to build up a rigid and enduring caste system such as existed in the countries of the Old World. The backcountrymen always proved to be a source of equalitarian feeling; and their "leveling spirit" was undoubtedly accentuated by the addition of groups of immigrants unfamiliar with and disregardful of petty class distinctions in the New World. The period of agitation preceding the Revolutionary War added fuel to the flames of anti-aristocratic feeling, for the great tidewater leaders and pamphleteers, seeking to place the controversy with the mother country on a dignified philosophical plane, unintentionally aroused the plain people to a high degree of excitement and self-assertion, through their constant employment of such expressions as "the natural rights of men" and "no taxation without representation." In particular the artisans and mechanics of the towns were galvanized into group-consciousness and, notwithstanding their legal exclusion from the franchise, they insisted upon playing an equal part with the well-to-do in the mass-meetings and informal conventions that characterized the period. "The mob begin to think and to reason," was the acute observation of Gouverneur Morris in 1774, himself an aristocrat. "Poor reptiles! it is with them a vernal morning; they are struggling to cast off their winter's slough, they bask in the sunshine, and ere noon they will bite, depend upon it. The gentry begin to fear this."

In the face of this alarming situation, the security of the aristocracy depended upon presenting a united front to the pretensions of the unprivileged orders; but the nature of the controversy with the British government was such as to render this impossible. The colonial aristocracy found itself of two minds. The wealthier merchants and many of the distinguished leaders in colonial politics (like Thomas Hutchinson, Joseph Galloway and Daniel Dulany) were impelled by every influence of tradition and social connection to ally themselves with the British side notwithstanding their strong colonial sympathies. "If I must be devoured," declared one of their number, "let me be devoured by the jaws of a lion, and not gnawed to death by rats and vermin." When the armed conflict came, thousands of men and women, bearing the stigma of "Tory," were forced to flee their native land, many of them settling in Canada where they became the Pilgrim Fathers of that great dominion. Their estates and fortunes were confiscated by the revolutionary state governments; and decrees of proscription were issued against their possible return. This expatriation was likened by a contemporary to the expulsion of the Huguenots upon the revocation of the Edict of Nantes. But other members of the upper class, like the landed gentry of the South and some of the great Quaker merchants, cast their fate with the revolutionists, although many of them seriously disapproved of the extremist doctrines advocated by the popular leaders. This branch of the aristocracy, though seriously weakened by the defection of the loyalists, was eventually to be instrumental in restoring the caste idea in American life.

II

The first great official denunciation of aristocratic rule that we have in American history was contained in the Declaration of Independence, adopted July 4, 1776. This document was written under a high pressure of excitement, phrased by a revolutionist of a visionary turn of mind, and designed to rally to the American cause the liberals of America and Europe. It has therefore not erroneously been called a political platform. Its preamble is the most eloquent and succinct defense of the rights of the masses and of popular rule that can be found anywhere in the English language. Every foe of aristocracy the world over has pondered its glowing periods and adapted them to his own uses. "We hold these truths to be self-evident," read the immortal words, "that all men are created equal, that they are endowed by their Creator with certain unalienable Rights, that among these are Life, Liberty and the pursuit of Happiness. That to secure these rights, Governments are instituted among Men, deriving their just powers from the consent of the governed. That whenever any form of Government becomes destructive of these ends, it is the Right of the People to alter or to abolish it, and to institute new Government, laying its foundation on such principles and organizing its powers in such form, as to them shall seem most likely to effect their Safety and Happiness."

But it was one thing to hurl these exalted sentiments against the King of England and the colonial representatives of his prerogative, and another to apply the bold precepts to the conditions under which people actually lived in America. The members of the aristocratic class who had joined the revolutionary movement had no intention of surrendering their own special privileges in government and society simply because they had joined with the unlettered masses in repudiating all political connection with royal Britain. What the phrase in the Declaration respecting equality of birth meant to the signers, it is difficult to say; but it is certain that they had no notion of setting forth a program of domestic reform. Neither at that time nor for many years later were all persons in America equal before the law or in the making of the law.

The actual conditions have already been touched on and may be summed up as follows: One-sixth of the population, woolly-haired and of dusky hue, were held in slavery. Of the remainder of the people, one sex, notwithstanding its white skin, was regarded as politically and legally inferior to the other sex. White men were ordinarily regarded as possessing equal civil rights, but the great majority of them were excluded from political participation and from educational advantages. To be sure, aristocracy in America lacked one important sanction of the upper class in Europe since it did not possess hereditary titles; but it might well have taken pride in the fact that it retained its privileged position amidst a race of people who, notwithstanding the fetters and handicaps that have been mentioned, possessed at that time greater freedom than any other people in the world.

The era of *post bellum* reconstruction, known as the Confederation period, undoubtedly gave the aristocracy its moments of fear and consternation. Its prerogatives were seriously jeopardized by the social ferment of the times; but the net result, as we shall see, was a vindication of the well-born to the positions of leadership and public trust. The first state constitutions adopted by the colonies shortly after the beginning of the war had continued the traditional political distinctions between class and mass and were based upon the principle—the Declaration of Independence to the contrary notwithstanding—that governments derive their just powers from the men of property and tax-payers. Only men possessing a property stake were permitted to vote, and the right to hold office was further restricted to those who owned a larger amount of property than the ordinary voter. Religious restrictions also remained substantially as before. The chief manifestation of anti-aristocratic feeling in these first constitutions appeared in the introduction of new rules regarding the inheritance of estates when the owner died intestate. Primogeniture, which existed in colonial New York and the southern provinces, and the assignment of double portions to the eldest son, which was the practice in certain other provinces, were done away with. Likewise, entails were abolished in four states. Thus the American aristocracy was deprived of these important Old World props to the maintenance of a landed gentry.[1]

[1] The same principle was extended a few years later to the public domain northwest of the Ohio river by the Ordinance of 1787.

A more serious threat to the ascendant position of the aristocracy resulted from the disorganization of the life of the people by the impact of the war. Intense popular opposition greeted the formation of the Society of the Cincinnati, organized by veterans of the Revolutionary War, because of the fear that the public liberties would be endangered by a secret military organization in which membership was to be perpetuated by hereditary grant. In a number of states the party of the masses gained control of the government and assailed wealth by the issuance of fiat money and the passage of laws for postponing the payment of debts; elsewhere, as in New Hampshire and Massachusetts, the waning respect for constituted authority was shown in mob demonstrations and armed uprisings. County conventions in Massachusetts in 1784 and 1785 declared that the state senate should be abolished and that property should be owned in common.

No events could have better demonstrated to the satisfaction of the aristocracy the incapacity of the masses for self-government; and with a zeal animated by despair, it turned every energy to recovering its lost ascendancy in public affairs. The leaders of the federal Constitutional Convention, which assembled in 1787, were brutally frank in passing judgment on the merits of government by the people. Elbridge Gerry, confessing that he "had been too republican heretofore," declared that "the evils we experience flow from the excess of democracy." Alexander Hamilton denounced the masses as "turbulent and changing; they seldom judge or determine right," and ventured the opinion that the British form of government was "the best in the world." Like Gerry, Edmund Randolph believed that the evils of the country had their origin "in the turbulence and follies of democracy." Gouverneur Morris held that there was no more reason to entrust the vote to "the ignorant &

the dependent" than to children. Roger Sherman thought that the people directly "should have as little to do as may be about the government."

The Constitution as it was framed by the Convention was well calculated to keep the plain people in a subordinate place and to assure political power to the men of substance and quality. Only one branch of the federal government was made directly elective by the people—and the separate states were permitted to continue to restrict the franchise as they chose. The more powerful branch of Congress, the Senate, was to be chosen by the state legislatures acting in behalf of the people. The president was to be selected by a special group of men in each state, who were presumably wiser than ordinary men and who should be chosen in any manner that the state legislature might specify. This meant, in states where the legislatures themselves assumed the duty of appointing the presidential electors, that the chief executive of the nation was three removes from direct popular election. It was further provided that the members of the federal judiciary should be appointed by the two branches of the government that had no immediate contact with the voters, the President and the Senate, and that the appointment should be virtually for life. Arthur Lee, among others, confidently predicted that from such a system "an oligarchy" would arise and govern the country to its will.

The influential leaders who came into power under the new instrument were bent upon giving a distinctively aristo-cratic cast to the government that was thus set in motion. The guiding genius of the new régime, Alexander Hamilton, freely admitted to his intimates that the Constitution was imperfect to the extent that it fell short of a constitutional monarchy but that he intended to do what he could "to prop the frail and worthless fabric." Jefferson tells us that when he arrived at the capital in 1790 from France to take his post as Secretary of State, "I found a state of things, in the general society of the place, which I could not have supposed possible. Being a stranger there, I was feasted from table to table, at large set dinners, the parties generally from twenty to thirty. The revolution I had left, and that we had just gone through in the recent change of our government, being the common topics of conversation, I was astonished to find the general prevalence of monarchical sentiments, insomuch that in maintaining those of republicanism, I had always the whole company on my hands, never scarcely finding among them a single co-advocate in that argument. . . . The furthest that any one would go, in support of the republican features of our new government, would be to say, 'the present Constitution is well as a beginning, and may be allowed a fair trial; but it is, in fact, only a stepping-stone to something better.' "

One of the early concerns of the Hamiltonian group was to attempt to invest the president with the trappings and ceremonials of European monarchy. The Senate labored painstakingly at the task of discovering an appropriate title for the chief executive, deciding at one time on "Elective Majesty" and again on "His Highness, the President of the United States of America, and Protector of their Liberties." Only the obduracy of the popular branch prevented the official adoption of a title; and subsequent efforts took on more subtle forms perforce. Thus, Hamilton's newspaper organ, the *Gazette of the United States,* was in the habit of treating official functions after this style: "The principal ladies of the city have with the earliest attention and respect paid their *devoirs* to the amiable consort of our beloved president, namely, the Lady of his Excellency the Governor, Lady Stirling, Lady Mary Watts, Lady Kitty Duer, La Marchioness de Brehan, the ladies of the Most Honorable Mr. Layton, the Most Honorable Mr. Dalton, the Mayoress, Mrs.

Livingston of Clermont, Lady Temple . . . and a large number of other respectable characters." After the fashion of European monarchs, the president gave formal weekly levees to an invited list of guests; and it is said that when Mrs. Washington found a trace of dirt on her wall after one of the receptions, she exclaimed angrily: "It was no Federalist; none but a filthy Democrat would mark a place on the wall with his good-for-nothing head in that manner."

The democratic spirit of revolutionary times was subdued but, as events were to show, not conquered. Indeed, while the Federalists were still in the full sway of their power, aristocracy was being insidiously attacked in some of its supports through changes in state constitutions decreeing the separation of church and state. The Anglican Church had been disestablished in Virginia as early as 1778. During the Federalist régime, most of the states abolished religious qualifications for voting and office-holding. In national politics a political party was being formed by Jefferson and Madison who made all possible capital out of the aristocratic tendencies of the Federalists, calling them "monocrats," "monarchists" and "Anglomaniacs." The latter retaliated by calling the opposition party by the opprobrious name of "democrats."

The government of wealth and intelligence, as carried on by the Federalists, bore fruit in an unparalleled crop of constructive legislation under Washington and Adams; but the general opinion that many of these laws were despotic and designed primarily for the welfare of the ruling class aroused a popular clamor that made inevitable their dismissal from the seats of authority.

III

In 1801 a new period opened in the history of aristocracy in America with the accession of the Jeffersonian Republicans to power. The event was hailed by the Republicans as a return to the principles for which the War for Independence had been fought. "The Revolution of 1776 is complete" was their exultant cry. But the Federalists stood aghast at the disaster which they believed had befallen their country. Theodore Dwight of Connecticut asserted in a Fourth of July oration that the great object of democracy was "to destroy every trace of civilization in the world, and force mankind back into a savage state. . . . We have a country governed by blockheads and knaves; the ties of marriage with all its felicities are severed and destroyed; our wives and daughters are thrown into the stews; our children are cast into the world from the breast and are forgotten. . . . Can the imagination paint anything more dreadful this side of hell?" Cabot, a Massachusetts leader, declared that by democracy was meant "the government of the worst." Both Hamilton and Rufus King apprehended "a bloody anarchy" as the consequence of the leveling tendencies of the times; and Henry Cabot Lodge tells us in his biography of the former that the reason Hamilton accepted Burr's challenge to the fatal duel was because he desired to keep himself available for military leadership in the struggle for the establishment of law and order, which he regarded as the inevitable outcome of government by Jefferson's rabble.

But Jeffersonian democracy did not, as a matter of fact, cause the doom of the caste principle in American society and government. On the contrary, it perpetuated it in a more enlightened and less offensive form. In the retrospect of history it is clear that political power had shifted from a mercantile aristocracy built on English models to a landed aristocracy fully acclimated to the American environment. The great planters of the South supplied the atmosphere of gentility in which the federal administration at Washington moved and had its being; and the presidency for six administrations fell, almost as a matter of right, to a line of succession known as the "Virginia Dynasty." From the viewpoint of subsequent progress toward democracy, "Jeffersonian aristocracy" seems the appropriate term to employ, for the mass of the people still continued very largely as spectators of events.

The philosophical outlook of the new aristocracy was, to be sure, quite different from the old. Where the latter had regarded itself as fashioning public policy in the interests of the superior class, the former prided itself as functioning as the guardian and protector of the masses. Yet, whatever its professions may have been, the new aristocracy was moved rather by a lofty spirit of public service and a sense of *noblesse oblige* than by an unfaltering acceptance of democratic dogma. Thus, while subscribing to the theory of manhood suffrage and of free, public education, Jefferson and his friends took no very energetic part in hastening their adoption. They did indeed introduce a more democratic spirit into the system provided for electing the president, by seeing to it that the presidential electors merely registered the will of the voters; but they deliberately ignored the opportunity of dispensing with the electoral system in its entirety when they adopted the twelfth amendment (1804).

On the other hand, the Jeffersonian aristocracy discarded much of the formalism and ostentation of the Federalist régime, and with it went the cynical contempt of the innate capacity of the people to govern themselves. "Jeffersonian simplicity" became a byword and a rule of conduct. The new president refused to avail himself of the customary coach and four and walked quietly from his boarding-house to the capitol to take the oath of office. He dispensed with the official rules of etiquette, which Hamilton had drawn up, and introduced the custom of public receptions open to anyone who might wish to attend. The House of Representatives granted better facilities for newspaper reporters; and the Senate began to hold public sessions and employed a stenographer to record its debates.

Thus "Jeffersonian democracy," as a term descriptive of American social ideals during the period from 1801 to the defeat of John Quincy Adams in 1828, meant no panacea for the people who had hitherto been excluded from the full enjoyment of the opportunities of American life. The mass of the white population in the East discovered little change for the better in their political and civil status although federal policy was molded chiefly with an eye to their good, and the abundance of good lands in the interior continued to insure their material well-being. However, in the northern half of the country, negro serfdom was being abolished by provisions for gradual emancipation; and in the Northwest, the foundations were being laid for a free elementary school system.

IV

This genial aristocracy was not long to hold its place unchallenged by the less fortunate classes. While its members were yet engaged in passing about the higher offices of the land among themselves, fundamental changes beneath the surface of American life were beginning to undermine their position. In the West, the frontier states were displaying a hearty disrespect for the wisdom of their betters by granting universal white manhood suffrage and abolishing special qualifications for office-holding. In the newly-established factory centers of New England and the Middle states, the workingmen were rebelling against the hampering and unsanitary conditions under which they were obliged to labor, and were insistently demanding equal political rights and the establishment of a public school system. Everywhere immigrants from the Old World joined their voices in the

swelling chorus for the diminution of aristocratic privilege.
A movement of irresistible momentum got under way for
the extension of political rights to all white men regardless of
their fitness or their property rating; so that by 1821, fifteen
of the twenty-four commonwealths possessed white manhood
suffrage, absolute or virtual.

Confronted with the realistic results of Jefferson's theoretical attachment to manhood suffrage, the fine old person-
ages, many of whom had been young men when Jefferson
entered the presidency, condemned and opposed with utmost
bitterness the impending vulgarization of politics.   Daniel
Webster and Justice Story united with the venerable John
Adams in resisting the change in Massachusetts.   In New
York the justly renowned Chancellor Kent declared to the
state constitutional convention that "Universal suffrage
jeopardizes property and puts it into the power of the poor
and the profligate to control the affluent.   Shall every department of the government be at the disposal of those who
are ignorant of the importance and nature of the right they
are authorized to assume?   The poor man's interest is always
in opposition to his duty, and it is too much to expect of
human nature that interest will not be consulted."   In Virginia, the contest for equal political rights for white men
was only partially successful (1830) because of the opposition of John Marshall, James Madison and John Randolph,
three ancient antagonists in politics who now made common
cause for their order and succeeded in excluding fifty
thousand white men from the franchise for a period of
twenty years more.   So stubborn in Rhode Island was the
resistance of those who wished to maintain the *status quo*
that, after twenty years of wrangling, Dorr's rebellion was
necessary to effect a liberalization of the suffrage.

The control of the federal government could not long
remain in the accustomed hands when leveling tendencies

were sweeping aside the barriers of suffrage. Portents of the impending subversion were all too apparent to the decorous gentlemen of the age. Salmon P. Chase, then a young law student in Washington, relates that the bi-weekly levees of President John Quincy Adams were always crowded to excess, and that at the New Year's reception, 1827, the guests became so unruly in their eagerness to secure refreshments that they pushed the attendant over. On the same occasion, a hat belonging to a Delaware Congressman was stolen, which caused Chase to remark laconically: "Something of this kind almost always occurs and those who attend would do well to wear the poorest articles they have, that their value may not tempt the honesty of others." Even more disturbing to polite society at the capital, so Chase reported, was the news that the brother-in-law of one of the president's sons had married his sister's serving-maid!

The elevation of the backwoodsman Andrew Jackson to the presidency in 1829 was a dramatic symbol of the success of the disintegrating forces of the time. The men of quality and wealth who had dominated the public service for so many years were left with no alternative but to execute as dignified a retreat as possible. "As they cannot occupy in public a position equivalent to what they hold in private life," observed the Frenchman, Alexis de Tocqueville, who visited America at this time, "they abandon the former, and give themselves up to the latter; and they constitute a private society in the state, which has its own tastes and pleasures." The seats of the government became, for the first time, filled with men whom the people had elected, not because the officials were superior to the multitude but because they were so like them. The taint of aristocracy now became as definite an obstacle to political preferment as a suspicion of democratic sympathies once had been. The fact that Martin

Van Buren used goldware and had installed a billiard-table in the White House was a serious campaign issue in 1840; and the object of every astute candidate was to convince the voters that he was only a plain and democratic citizen. Daniel Webster apologized publicly because he had not been born in a log-cabin but eagerly claimed that distinction for his elder brother and sisters. "If ever I am ashamed of it," he solemnly averred, "may my name and the name of my posterity be blotted from the memory of mankind!"

The overthrow of the forces of aristocracy in the arena of politics was accompanied by attacks on their prerogative in other fields hitherto monopolized by them. It is extremely significant that all class distinctions in matters of dress disappeared at this time. All men began to wear the homely garb and short-cropped hair that had been the distinguishing mark of servants and day-laborers in colonial times. James Monroe had been the last president to affect the stately colonial costume; and in Connecticut it was observed that after the democratic victory in 1818 public officials ceased to wear the formal attire of earlier times. Elsewhere the courtly dress of colonial days had survived longer.

The exclusive position of the aristocratic class was challenged at another point: a concerted effort was made in the second quarter of the century to drag down education to the level of the crowd. The principle of free education supported by public taxation had long been recognized in New England and the Northwest although the practice had fallen sadly short of the theory; but in the few other places where free schools were maintained, they were regarded as charitable institutions for pauper children, the instruction offered being extremely rudimentary. The demand for equal education at the government's expense grew out of labor agitation in New York and Pennsylvania in the twenties and the thirties; and it aroused the same feelings of disapproval and indignation in the ranks of the aristocracy as did the agitation for manhood suffrage. The *National Gazette* of Philadelphia denounced the scheme as "virtually Agrarianism. It would be a compulsory application of the means of the richer for the direct use of the poorer classes; and so far an arbitrary division of property among them." The editor further pointed out that "The peasant must labor during those hours of the day which his wealthy neighbor can give to abstract culture of his mind; otherwise, the earth would not yield enough for the subsistence of all: the mechanic cannot abandon the operations of his trade, for general studies; if he should, most of the conveniences of life . . . would be wanting; languor, decay, poverty, discontent would soon be visible among all classes."

But the tide of popular demand was not to be stemmed. By the decade of the forties, free public schools were common throughout the North, and the notion that the common people needed merely the elements of education was abandoned for the ideal of equal educational opportunities for all classes. Only in the South were the landed gentry successful in maintaining the monopoly of educational advantages that their wealth and social position assured to them.

Notwithstanding the irreparable losses suffered by the aristocracy as a result of the upheavals from below, the caste idea founded sources of rejuvenation in certain other aspects of American development before the Civil War. On the broad basis of African slavery the southerners had already in colonial times perfected a semi-feudal order of exclusive manners comparable to the age-long aristocracies of Europe. The vast expansion of cotton culture from 1800 to 1830 gave a new dignity and importance to this high-toned gentry. The few thousands of "first families," who lived upon the incomes of plantations and formed the upper-crust of southern society, spent their winters in New Orleans, their springs in Charleston and their summers at the Virginia springs. Every gentleman had his valet, every lady her maid; tutors were employed to train their children. The personal ideal of this aristocracy was summed up in the term "chivalry," an expression denoting the virtues of gallantry toward women, courtesy to inferiors, a mettlesome sense of honor, and a lavish hospitality. On all appropriate occasions the southerners openly declared the failure of democratic government and were at one with the renowned Chancellor Harper of South Carolina in scorning the glittering generalities of the Declaration of Independence.

Forming the governing class of the South—for Jacksonian democracy had never disturbed their seats of power within the borders of their own states—they looked upon themselves as prepared by training, temperament and interest to guide the destinies of the federal government. Their cultivation of the arts of leisure gave them a decided advantage in the science of statecraft over the rough-and-ready political organizers of the North. Yet the circumstances of the times were such that no southern aristocrat could ever expect to occupy the presidency again; and the planting class had to employ as their instruments in the presidency and many other high offices men of the democratic North whom they could in no measure accept as their social equals. Their direct personal participation was confined to membership in the House and the Senate and to various appointive offices.

In the North at the same time a pretentious aristocracy was rapidly establishing itself socially, confined largely to the great cities of the Atlantic seaboard. Men of that section who had made money out of land speculation and the nascent manufacturing industries were beginning to coalesce into a special caste although as yet there were few millionaires to be found among their number outside of the Astors, the Girards and the Longworthys. Distinguished visitors in

America became aware of the growing importance of social distinctions. The English historian, Harriet Martineau, was told much about the "first people" of Boston, New York and Philadelphia when she visited the United States in the thirties; and in the last named city she discovered a sharp social cleavage between the ladies of Arch Street whose fathers had made their own fortunes and the social leaders of Chestnut Street who owed their wealth to their grandfathers. Compared with the corresponding social class in the South, the upper stratum of northern society constituted an upstart aristocracy, based upon fluid capital rather than upon land, and destitute of traditions or culture or negro vassals. Contemned by the southern patricians as *nouveaux riches,* this aspiring group were destined to be the forerunners of the class that was to supplant the southern aristocracy in the period after the Civil War and become the modern conservators of the aristocratic tradition.

Thus, by the middle of the nineteenth century, the well-born in America had lost their proprietorship of the government, they had in large degree lost their monopoly of education, and, finally, they had even lost their clothes. As if the cup of humiliation were not already running over, a new blow was being prepared for the subversion of the securely-established aristocracy of the South. The story is a familiar one and need not be retold here. The ownership of slaves was an unmistakable badge of social superiority and presumably the pillar upon which southern wealth and culture rested. Chancellor Harper was but expressing the common opinion of the southern gentry when he declared that without slavery "there can be no accumulation of property, no providence for the future, no tastes for comfort or elegancies, which are the characteristics and essentials of civilization," and that opposition to the institution came from men "whose precipitate and ignorant zeal would overturn the fundamental institutions of society, uproar its peace and endanger its security, in pursuit of a distant and shadowy good . . . ." Therefore when the party of "precipitate and ignorant zeal" elected their candidate, Abraham Lincoln, president of the United States in 1860, separation from such an unhallowed association seemed to be the only reasonable course to adopt.

The Civil War dealt a body blow to the most exclusive aristocracy our country has ever known. The former master class issued from the conflict with the stigma of unsuccessful revolutionists; they had lost the flower of their manhood and most of their wealth; they had lost their slaves and, for a space of time, their political equality in the Union. The slaves emerged from the conflict at first as freedmen possessing undefined rights, then as citizens with all the legal rights of whites, and quickly thereafter the male negroes were endowed with the right of suffrage. But the aristocracy of the old South, which had played so large a part in the history of the nation and had produced many of its greatest men, was annihilated, to live no more except as a splendid and romantic memory of the days "before the war."

v

By 1870 the impartial historian must record that aristocracy in America appeared to have reached the nadir of its decline. The confident assurance of the Fathers of 1776 that "all men are created equal" had at last become embodied in the law of the land, if by the word "men" were understood "males." The principle of equality had been introduced into political participation, into religion, into education, and into social relationships generally. The Homestead Act of 1862 had opened the public lands upon more generous terms than ever before; and hence political equality for men was coupled with a virtual equality of economic opportunity. The women formed the only element of the population whose rights and privileges were distinctly inferior to those of the rest of the people.

But devotees of the aristocratic tradition had no real occasion for despair. As a social institution, aristocracy has chameleon-like qualities and takes its color and form from each new situation in which it may find itself. Though individual aristocrats may lose prestige and position, the caste idea never fails to find new sources of sustenance. An era of dynamic development occurred in the United States following the Civil War, which manifested itself in every field of economic endeavor. The energetic captains of the new age found opportunities for the accumulation of wealth on every hand—in railway enterprises, in all sorts of manufacturing enterprises, in unappropriated natural resources and public utilities, in stock manipulation. The epoch of colossal fortunes dawned upon the country; and soon people began to speak of "coal barons," "steel kings," "railroad magnates," "cattle kings," and "Napoleons of finance." The master minds of the new order used their personal prestige and economic power to establish their control over the state and national governments. The political policies of the period from 1870 to 1900 were, in great degree, fashioned to augment and fortify the position of this new power in American life through tariffs, land grants, liberal charters and franchises, and a *laissez faire* attitude of the government.

"It is useless for us to protest that we are democratic . . . ," wrote Josiah Strong in 1885. "There is among us an aristocracy of recognized power, and that aristocracy is one of wealth. No heraldry offends our republican prejudices. Our ensigns armorial are the trademark. Our laws and customs recognize no noble titles; but men can forego the husk of a title who possess the fat ears of power." The new aristocracy was dubbed by its critics as "the plutocracy" since its authority was based upon wealth rather than upon the heritage of birth. Its exalted position was enhanced by the wide gulf dividing it from the great wage-earning class which made its appearance simultaneously with the rise of the new aristocracy. Nothing quite like this toiling class had been known in American history before either in numbers or circumstances. The massing of immigrants on our shores, and the growing scarcity and eventual disappearance of free lands in the West, gave an unprecedented fierceness to the problem of making a living and tended to drive the workingmen onto a plane of living where life became a drab existence. For such men the forms of political democracy remained as before; but the substantial equality of wealth and economic opportunity of the earlier days was fast disappearing.

The finest spirits of the new aristocracy regarded themselves as pioneers of a new kind, impelled by the creative fever in their blood to carry on the old work of developing the natural resources of the nation under modern conditions; and they believed that the prosperity of the few would eventually penetrate the nether strata of society. Arising out of the ranks of the people, the members of this new order lacked the culture and traditions and tastes of a long-established aristocracy—but they believed that all these refinements might be bought for a price. Occupied themselves with the sterner realities of wealth-production, the men good-humoredly left to their womenfolk the responsibility of creating a fitting social atmosphere to gild the new order.

To this end no stone was left unturned or dollar unspent. In the generation following the Civil War, playgrounds of the rich began to appear overnight along the Atlantic seaboard; international marriages became the goal of ambitious mothers; palatial mansions and liveried retinues were recognized as the accustomed symbols of the new superiority. As the first generation grew older and the second generation began to come of age, the new régime began to feel its social position firmly established, its newness worn off; and its efforts at ostentation, though no less carefully sustained, became less frantic. Thus it happened that the second and the third generations were able to found a genuine leisure class with the prodigality and profligacy that attends such a mode of existence. Natural refinements began to grace the life of the "exclusive set"; and with the development of a sense of *richesse oblige,* men of wealth became the patrons of libraries, art galleries, scientific organizations, and impoverished colleges.

But the new order of things did not remain without opposition from the less fortunate classes. To be sure, the social pre-eminence of the plutocracy could not, with any degree of effectiveness, be disputed or prevented, but the sources of its economic and political predominance presented vulnerable points of attack. Disgruntled groups of the plain people, farmers in the West and workingmen in the cities, began to make their voices heard in protest against what they called "Special Privilege" and "Vested Interests," and to urge that the government use its power to demolish the foundations of the superstructure upon which Plutocracy rested. The monied aristocracy was no more inclined to yield to leveling tendencies than had been its prototypes in the earlier days of the republic. "This country has been developed by a wonderful people, flush with enthusiasm, imagination and speculation bent . . ." declared E. H. Harriman, the organizing genius of twenty thousand miles of railroad. "Stifle that enthusiasm, deaden that imagination and prohibit that speculation by restrictive and cramping conservative law, and you tend to produce a moribund and conservative people and country." In a more exalted strain George F. Baer, president of the Philadelphia and Reading Railroad, entered his classic defense of the ascendant class as "the Christian men to whom God, in His infinite wisdom, has given the control of the property interests of the country."

Meantime, the popular movement against plutocratic control continued to gain in volume and volubility; and by 1900 the people generally were aroused to the point of taking swift and drastic measures. Since that time their chief energy has been directed toward restoring that equality of opportunity which had characterized the days of the undeveloped frontier and without which they regarded political democracy as devoid of meaning. Proposing to destroy the alliance of political bosses and the plutocracy, the popular leaders prevailed upon the state legislatures to pass corrupt practices laws, to establish systems of direct nominations and to insure popular sanction of legislation through the initiative and referendum. These measures were followed in 1913 by the establishment of a new method of electing United States senators—by direct vote of the people. The impracticable and dangerous character of all these proposals were eloquently portrayed by the men of wealth and position, but to no avail. The national government was also forced to yield to the popular clamor; and, in conjunction with the state governments, laws were passed to regulate the business practices of railroads and industrial corporations, to conserve our natural resources, and to improve the conditions of the laboring class. The unequal distribution of wealth was another subject for legislation; and acts have been passed for imposing graduated taxes on large incomes, inheritances and excess business profits.

These laws, disconcerting and disrupting as they are in the judgment of the aristocracy, do not involve a complete annihilation of its special privileges, for many of these privileges were granted in terms and under circumstances that make their revocation an impossibility. The most fundamental menace to the continuance of the privileged class is found in the increasing self-consciousness and self-assertion of the laboring class. The great labor organizations are seeking, by means of collective bargaining and the strike, to introduce the principles of political democracy into the management of industry. Their aspiration has received high sanction in a message of President Wilson, who declared on May 20, 1919, his endorsement of a "genuine democratization of industry based upon a full recognition of the right of those who work . . . to participate in some organic way in every decision which directly affects their welfare or the part they are to play in industry." Should this tendency work out to its logical conclusion, industrial magnates will find themselves forced to yield control over their own business enterprises and be reduced to the status of partners, perhaps silent ones, with their own employees. A remoter peril is held forth in the equalitarian program of those radical laborites who maintain that private profits should be abolished, and that all industry should be "socialized" with complete control in the hands of the workers.

The warfare against aristocracy during the years since the Civil War concerned itself also with the inferior position which woman occupied in American society. The chief contenders for the abolition of artificial sex distinctions were members of the subordinate class; and each decade saw new inroads made on the exclusive position held from time immemorial by the male members of society. Susan B. Anthony, the great leader in the movement for sex equality, made the issue clear in 1873 when she said that, for women, "this government is not a democracy. It is not a republic. It is an odious aristocracy. . . . Surely this oligarchy of sex, which makes the men of every household sovereigns, masters . . . can not be endured." The leaders of the privileged sex repeatedly pointed out the dangers which any lowering of the sex barriers would involve—that woman would lose her charm and forfeit the respect of man, that equalization of the sexes would lead to the breaking-up of family life, that the feminine mentality was unfitted to cope with public questions. Behind these arguments lay the deep-seated conviction of the men, so a member of the New York constitutional convention of 1867 averred, that "The right of self-government upon which our whole superstructure is based is in the man. It has been written by the finger of God himself upon the mental constitution of every human being and in such unmistakable characters that it is impossible for us to misunderstand, misinterpret, or mistranslate them." The failure of women to be silenced by these arguments seemed to constitute added proof of their irrational and emotional nature. Nevertheless, sex bars fell one by one until finally, in 1920, the women of the nation were admitted as political partners with the men by an amendment to the federal Constitution.

In this veracious chronicle of aristocracy in America, it would be unfair not to record one positive advance that the forces of privilege have made in recent years. The status of legal equality which, in a moment of high exaltation, had been thrust upon the southern negro by the federal government has been quietly disregarded by the superior race of that section; and in the period since southern reconstruction, the negro has been reduced to a special plane of his own, destitute of the vote, deprived of equal educational advantages and restrained by class discriminations from enjoying equal rights in public carriers and places of assemblage.

In conclusion, it may fairly be asked: what lesson is to be learned from the history of aristocracy in the United States? Those who are protagonists of the democratic ideal may draw their own moral. For them the fact of outstanding significance must doubtless be the steady advance and eventual conquest of democracy over all forms and traditions of aristocracy. But, however impressive this thought may be, the confirmed aristocrat need not lose heart. He may always expect the common people to think with Thomas Jefferson that "the mass of mankind has not been born with saddles on their backs, nor a favored few booted and spurred, ready to ride them legitimately, by the grace of God"; but if history has shown anything, it has demonstrated that the multitude tend to grow careless of their liberties and to think in terms of their own generation rather than with an eye to the future. New conditions and altered circumstances of society have, in the past, rendered possible the creation of new privileges and pretensions for those who were energetic and alert. In the shortcomings of democratic society, therefore, lies the hope of the future for the perpetuation of the aristocratic tradition in America.

BIBLIOGRAPHICAL NOTE

The development and interrelations of aristocracy and democracy in the United States have since colonial times excited the intense interest of countless numbers of foreign travelers in this country. This is not surprising since the United States was for many years the great laboratory of democratic social and political experimentation for the world. These foreign observers were not merely interested in democracy in the restricted sense of political self-government but also in its broader social manifestations. When due allowance is made for the motives which brought the travelers to our shores and for their social and political predispositions, this class of literature, distinguished by such names as the Marquis de Chastellux, Alexis de Tocqueville, Harriet Martineau, James Bryce and Edward A. Freeman, contains the most penetrating observations that may be found anywhere of the conflict of aristocratic and democratic ideas in American life at the various stages of our history. A useful index to this extensive literature for the period prior to the date of its publication is Henry T. Tuckerman's *America and her Commentators* (New York, 1864).

Native Americans of the early days of the republic seldom viewed these contrasting institutions objectively or, if they did, it was with some ulterior political purpose in mind. Nevertheless, such essays as the following, notwithstanding their polemic purpose, shed considerable light upon the contemporary conceptions of aristocracy and democracy in American history: John Adams's *A Defence of the Constitutions of Government of the United States* (1787-1788) and his *Discourses on Davila* (1790); John Taylor's *An Enquiry into the Principles and Policy of the Government of the United States* (1814); and John C. Calhoun's *A Disquisition on Government* and his *A Discourse on the Constitution and Government of the United States* (published posthumously). C. Edward Merriam's *A History of American Political Theories* (New York, 1910) offers incidentally an excellent sketch of the growth of democratic ideals in the writings of American statesmen and political philosophers.

It was not until a quarter of a century ago that American students began to single out democracy as a theme for special study and treatment, although it is perhaps true to say that no history of the United States has ever been written which is not, however unconsciously and inadequately, a running commentary upon the expansion of political democracy. In 1898, three works appeared which were concerned with isolating the democratic trend in American history and studying it: Frederick A. Cleveland's *The Growth of Democracy in the United States* (Chicago), Francis Newton Thorpe's *Constitutional History of the American People, 1776-1850* (2 v., New York); and Bernard Moses's *Democracy and Social Growth in the United States* (New York). The first two of these works were occupied very largely in setting forth the enlargement of popular rights in government and law; and since then a number of other studies have been carried out along the same lines, among which may be mentioned: J. Allen Smith's *The Spirit of American Government* (New York, 1907); Kirk H. Porter's *A History of Suffrage in the United States* (Chicago, 1918); Dixon Ryan Fox's *The Decline of Aristocracy in the Politics of New York* (New York, 1919); and Andrew Cunningham McLaughlin's *Steps in the Development of American Democracy* (New York, 1920). The volume by Professor Moses paid relatively more attention to the social and economic conditions of democratic development; and this point of view has since then received fuller treatment in such studies as John Bach McMaster's *The Acquisition of the Political, Social and Industrial Rights of Man in America* (Cleveland, 1903); Frederick Jackson Turner's "Contributions of the West to American Democracy" in the *Atlantic Monthly*, vol. xci (1903), pp. 83-96, reprinted in his *The Frontier in American History* (New York, 1920); Robert Tudor Hill's *The Public Domain and Democracy* (New York, 1910); and Frederick C. Howe's *Privilege and Democracy in America* (New York, 1910).

An adequate history of aristocracy and democracy in America is yet to be written, for, as the foregoing sketch has indicated, these social ideals have been mirrored not only in government and politic but also in the manners and customs, religion and education, eco nomic organization, literature and thought of the people. The materials for compiling a comprehensive account of the decline of aristocracy will be supplied only when a genuine social history of the United States is written. Important contributions toward such a history have been made by a host of writers, among whom may be mentioned John Bach McMaster, Philip A. Bruce, Alice M. Earle, Henry Adams, E. D. Fite, William E. Dodd, Arthur W. Calhoun, John R. Commons, and the special writers on American religious history and the history of literature and education in the United States. A handy compendium is the book entitled *Social and Economic Forces in American History* (New York, 1913), composed of chapters selected from the volumes of *The American Nation: a History* (New York, 1905-1918). Very suggestive is Albert Bushnell Hart's volume *National Ideals Historically Traced* (in *The American Nation: a History*, vol. 26; New York, 1907).

CHAPTER V

I

The heated discussion conducted in recent years by press and platform on the merits and demerits of radicalism and conservatism causes the student of American history to search his mind concerning the effects of these opposing types of thought on the past history of the United States. In such an inquiry, an initial difficulty presents itself: what do the terms, "conservative" and "radical," mean? Popular usage has tended to rob these expressions of exact meaning and to convert them into epithets of opprobrium and adulation which are used as the bias or interest of the person may dictate. The conservative, having mapped out the confines of truth to his own satisfaction, judges the depravity and errors of the radical by the extent of his departure from the boundaries thus established. Likewise the radical, from his vantage-point of truth, measures the knavery and infirmities of his opponents by the distance they have yet to travel to reach his goal. Neither conservative nor radical regards the other with judicial calm or "sweet reasonableness." Neither is willing to admit that the other has a useful function to perform in the progress of society. Each regards the other with deep feeling as the enemy of everything that is fundamentally good in government and society.

In seeking a workable definition of these terms, the philosophic insight of Thomas Jefferson is a beacon light to the inquirer. When Jefferson withdrew from active political life at the close of his presidency in 1809, he left behind him the heat and smoke of partisan strife and retired to a contemplative life on his Virginia estate, where his fellow-countrymen learned to revere him as the "Sage of Monticello." The voluminous correspondence of these twilight years of his life is full of instruction for the student of history and politics. His tremendous curiosity caused him to find an unfailing source of speculation in the proclivity of mankind to separate into contrasting schools of opinion. In one luminous passage, representative of the bent of his thought, he declared: "Men, according to their constitutions, and the circumstances in which they are placed, differ honestly in opinion. Some are Whigs, Liberals, Democrats, call them what you please. Others are Tories, Serviles, Aristocrats, etc. The latter fear the people, and wish to transfer all power to the higher classes of society; the former consider the people as the safest depository of power in the last resort; they cherish them, therefore, and wish to leave in them all the powers to the exercise of which they are competent."

In this passage Jefferson does not use the expressions "conservative" and "radical"—indeed, those words had no place in the American political vocabulary until Civil War times—but his penetrating analysis throws a flood of light on the significance of those terms nevertheless. The Tory who fears the people and the Whig who trusts them are equivalent to our own categories of "conservative" and "radical." Thus Jefferson finds the vital distinction between the two schools of opinion in their respective attitudes toward popular government.

But before accepting Jefferson's classification as correct, what shall we do with the common notion that the conservative is a person who opposes change and that the ear-mark of the radical is his liking for innovation? This does not seem

to be a fundamental distinction. If a difference of opinion
concerning the need of change were the basic difference
between the two, then Americans who advocate a limitation
of the suffrage to male property-owners may properly be
regarded as radicals, for they advocate an alteration in the
established order; and French patriots of today opposing the
re-establishment of the Orleanist monarchy are to be classed
as conservatives, for they would keep things unchanged.
Few people would be willing to follow the logic of their
premises to such conclusions. On the other hand, it cannot
be denied that history has generally shown the radical in the
rôle of an active proponent of change and has cast the conservative for the part of the stalwart defender of things as
they are. Is such evidence to be dismissed as a coincidence
oft-repeated, or has there been behind the actions of both
radical and conservative some self-interested purpose which
has determined their respective attitudes toward the established order?

The very question perhaps suggests the answer. Broadly
speaking, all history has been an intermittent contest on the
part of the more numerous section of society to wrest power
and privilege from the minority which had hitherto possessed
it. The group which at any period favored broader popular
rights and liberties was therefore likely to find itself as a con-
tender for the new and untried, leaving to its antagonists the
comfortable repute of being the conservators of the *status
quo* and the foes of change. But, though the historical
conditions influenced the character of the contest, such
conditions were, after all, merely the stage setting of the
struggle. Advocacy of change should, under such circumstances, be regarded merely as the means employed to attain
an end and, in no sense, as an end in itself. Recurring now
to Jefferson's definition, the goal sought by each group—
whether it be in the direction of greater or less democracy—

would appear to constitute the real difference between the two.

It should be clear, then, that the radical is a person who, in contrast to the conservative, favors a larger participation of the people in the control of government and society and in the benefits accruing from such control. To attain his ideal the radical may become a protagonist of change; he usually has been one, as a matter of history, but this fact is a mere incident to, and not the touchstone of, his radicalism. The temperament of the radical is sanguine. He can say with Jefferson: "I steer my bark with Hope in the head, leaving Fear astern. My hopes, indeed, sometimes fail; but not oftener than the forebodings of the gloomy." The conservative, on the other hand, is skeptical of the capacity of the mass of the people to protect their own interests intelligently; and believing that social progress in the past has always come from the leadership of wealth and ability, he is the consistent opponent of the unsettling plans of the radical. If the old saw is true that a pessimist is the wife of an optimist, perhaps the cynicism of the conservative is amply accounted for by his enforced association with the radical. The radical regards himself as a man of vision; but the conservative sees him only as a visionary. The radical as a type is likely to be broad-minded and shallow-minded; the disinterested conservative is inclined to be high-minded and narrow-minded.

Of course, the expressions "radical" and "conservative" are relative terms, for at any given time the lines are drawn by the opposing forces upon the basis of the circumstances then existing. It is a truism that the radical of today may become the conservative of tomorrow. This does not necessarily argue inconsistency. It may indicate rather that, when the specific measures which the radical has advocated have been adopted, he believes that the supreme aim of public policy has been attained and he becomes a defender of the new *status quo* against any further extensions of popular rights. This is perhaps the same as saying that the conservative of today, had he held the same opinions on political and social questions a generation ago, would have been looked upon then as a radical. The movement of history has been from radicalism to conservatism so far as the attitude of individuals is concerned, but from conservatism to radicalism so far as the trend of public policy is concerned.

Not only are the terms relative in the sense just indicated, but they are comparative as applied to variations of opinion that exist within each school of thought. In the conservative camp are to be found different degrees of distrust of popular rule, varying from the purblind reactionaries on the extreme right to the moderates on the extreme left. Similarly the radical camp has its subdivisions, comprising all grades of confidence in popular government from a left wing of ultra-radicals to a wing at the opposite extreme composed of progressives or liberals. The apostles of lawlessness— those who would accomplish their ends through a defiance of, or assault on, the law—are to be found in the exterior wings of both camps. In this sense the reactionaries who seek to gain their purposes through the corruption or intimidation of the courts are to be regarded as much the enemies of law and order as the followers of Daniel Shays in 1786 when they tried to disperse the courts with violence. On the other hand, the moderates of the conservative camp tend to fraternize with the liberals of the radical camp without, however, completely merging their identity because of deep-grained prepossessions and habits of thought. It is in this middle zone or "No Man's Land" between the camps that there occurs the only true meeting of minds; and in democratic countries, advances can be made, under legal forms and proper safeguards, only through the temporary union of these groups for common purposes.

No attempt need be made here to idealize or glorify either

the radical or the conservative. Adherents of each are constantly engaged in constructing traditions which would ascribe superhuman attributes to the great leaders and spokesmen of their respective schools of opinion in the past. In this myth-making process the radicals inevitably suffer a serious handicap, for the audacious reformer of a century ago is likely to appear today as a man of orthodox ideas, and latter-day conservatives, without any appreciation of the earlier clash of ideas, are likely to claim him as their very own. For example, the average American citizen who values property rights as superior to human rights easily imagines himself in the forefront of the riot that led to the Boston Massacre, for through the mellow haze of time he forgets the real character of that street brawl with its raucous mob of blatant, missile-hurling roughs and halfbreeds.[1]

Whatever may be said in praise of either the conservative or the radical, both find themselves in bad company, for each makes his appeal to some of the basest as well as to some of the most ennobling qualities of human nature. The thinking conservative finds his chief allies in the self-complacency of comfortable mediocrity, in the apathy and stupidity of the toil-worn multitudes, and in the aggressive self-interest of the privileged classes. All those who dread uncertainty either because of timidity or from conventional-mindedness or for fear of material loss are enlisted under the conservative standard. The honest radical draws much of his support from self-seeking demagogues and reckless experimenters, from people who want the world changed because they cannot get along in it as it is, from *poseurs* and *dilettanti,* and from malcontents who love disturbance for its own sake. The two schools have more in common than either would admit; both have their doctrinaires and dogmatists; both

---

[1] The reader, of a conservative turn of mind, should not fail to read A. P. Peabody's article, "Boston Mobs before the Revolution" in the *Atlantic Monthly,* vol. lxii, pp. 321-333.

tend toward a stiffening of intellectual creeds; and who can deny that each has its share of mental defectives and the criminal-minded?

II

There are special reasons why radical thought and aspiration should have attained fertile growth in American soil. From our earliest history a process of social selection has been going on which has served to separate the radical from the conservative elements of the population and has given to the former unique opportunities for impressing their philosophy upon the population in general. As Professor Van Tyne has pointed out in a notable passage, the tendency of colonization was to stock the American colonies with radicals and dissenters and to leave behind in England the conservatives and conformists, thereby rendering inevitable sharp contrasts in temperament and outlook between the colonists and the mother country. This process has repeated itself with endless variation in the later history of our country. The incoming tides of foreign immigration have deposited upon our shores many of the restless and rebellious spirits of the Old World civilizations. The periodic flow of westward settlement in this country has tended to carry the adventurous and the discontented forward into new lands of opportunity, leaving the older settlements to the control of timid and conservative people. Thus the radical spirit has constantly been fed and refreshed by contributions from abroad; and in our own land the processes of social integration have tended to segregate the radical-minded geographically and to permit them to develop without the restraining influences of a long-established conservative class.

Under such favoring circumstances radicalism might have been expected to attain its most extreme expression in America. The result, however, has been neither a reign of overbearing individualism nor the establishment of a co-operative commonwealth, although both forms of social organization had their advocates and were given sporadic trial. The acquisition of property on easy terms in the newer parts of the country made the settlers quickly forget the bitter injustices and oppressions of the older civilizations and, without sapping their interest in democratic progress, gave them a personal stake in the orderly advance of the community. Indeed, the very freedom which they enjoyed to experiment as they wished with their own lives and property exercised a moderating influence on their conduct. So it has happened that, while progress along liberal lines has been rapid in the newer parts of America, it has been accomplished through the acts of legislatures and the amending of constitutions. In the older sections such advances have been made slowly and have often been attended by severe political struggles, sometimes culminating in armed conflict, as in the case of the Dorr Rebellion in Rhode Island in 1842-1843.

It is not surprising that, as a result of this continuing process of social differentiation, one of the outstanding characteristics of American national development should be the constant interest of the people in movements for democratic and humanitarian reform. Every movement of radical tendency has developed through certain clearly-defined stages, as if in obedience to some immutable law of social dynamics. These phases can generally be reduced to three. At the outset there occurs a period of violent propaganda conducted by a small group of agitators. These pioneers resort to picturesque and sensational methods of propaganda in order to awaken the apathetic public to the presence of evil conditions and the need for change. They constitute a flying wedge of protest and moral indignation. The late ex-President Roosevelt referred to this vanguard when he declared in his autobiography: "Every reform movement has a lunatic fringe." It is indeed a "lunatic fringe," in the sense that these trumpeters of reform act irrationally according to the standards of the majority of the people, and must expect to suffer their ridicule or ostracism or persecution. In this advanced group may ordinarily be found the "soapboxer," the "muckraker," the idealist, the doctrinaire, the fanatic, the would-be revolutionist and, at times even in American history, the martyr. These agitators, irrespective of individual peculiarities, share a bitter disregard of existing public opinion, a passion for destructive criticism, and an emotional conviction that in their proposal is to be found a panacea for human ills.

Some movements never advance beyond this first ultra-radical stage, for they fail to gain converts outside of the group immediately engaged in furthering the cause. The second stage arrives when the pioneer reformers succeed in arousing interest and approval among the soberer elements of the population. The ideas long regarded as "queer" or "dangerous" are now on the point of gaining the sanction of respectability; and the assurance of a growing popular favor enlists the support of some of the experienced leaders of the people—the "practical statesmen." These men possess the constructive ability, the organizing genius and the knowledge of political strategy which are necessary in order to carry into execution the ideas of the agitators. Less agile of imagination and frequently less pure of purpose, they know better the temper and limitations of the average man; and under their direction the new policies and doctrines, perhaps in modified form, become the law of the land. Thus the actual achievers of the reform are the liberals or progressives, aided perhaps by those moderates of the conservative camp who favor the proposed change as the best preventive of more basic changes. If, as sometimes happens, some of the abler leaders of the first period survive into the second and are placed in positions of power by a surge of popular feeling, they usually become sobered and moderated by responsibility and experience, and their conduct is scarcely distinguishable from that of the practical statesmen.

The third and final stage of the reform is reached when the new doctrines, having lost their air of strangeness and demonstrated either their utility or harmlessness, become imbedded in the conscience and philosophy of the people at large. The public becomes adjusted to practices and policies that were altogether unacceptable a few years earlier; indeed most of the people have already forgotten that these reforms were not always a part of the commonly accepted stock of ideas. The cycle of reform has about completed itself; for public opinion hardens into a new conservatism and forms a crust that toughly resists any further efforts for change. Advocates for new advances must employ the militant and fantastic methods which mark the "lunatic fringe" of a new crusade for reform.

III

Examples of reform movements abound in American history. These have been multifarious in their objects and reflect the diversified interests and social outlook of the ages in which they flourished. Some of the most significant of these enterprises have been concerned with improving the lot of the average man or the condition of society's wards—the dependent and the criminal. From many points of view such movements would appear to merit more careful study by the youth in our schools than most reforms of a purely political type; but, the anti-slavery movement excepted, reformative movements of a humanitarian character receive little or no attention in the orthodox histories. Yet what thoughtful American can deny the superb courage and inestimable service of the men and women (unknown to most of us) whose efforts made possible religious liberty, free public education, scientific care of the deaf, the dumb and the blind, a more humane criminal code, the abolition of child labor, reformative treatment of criminals, statutory reduction of the workday, governmental protection of the public health, and the abolition of the saloon?

The reforming activities of political parties and party factions are better known. Jefferson advanced the proposition that a people should never pass legislation binding for a period longer than the lifetime of their own generation, for, as conditions change, men change, and every fresh generation should have a free opportunity to fashion its own laws and constitutions according to its special circumstances. Using certain tables compiled by M. de Buffon, he went so far as to fix the average duration of a generation at nineteen years. Looking back over the annals of the United States, we can see that the course of our national development has, in a large degree, mirrored the changing needs and interests of the procession of generations. From one point of view, American history may be regarded as a succession of eager new generations ruthlessly elbowing aside older and effete generations; and although lacking the automatic modes of expression that Jefferson would have provided, each fresh accession of leadership has wrought a transformation of party creeds, and represented new policies, practices and ethical conceptions, better adapted to the changed economic and social conditions of the time. It is scarcely necessary to set forth the history of each of these generations in detail, for the results of their labors are recorded in the achievements of the nation. Each fresh generation experienced the usual difficulties of a group advocating unaccustomed ideas; and the following sketch should yield, among other things, many illustrations of the familiar cycle by which novel ideas become acceptable maxims of policy and then are consecrated as the truisms of statesmen.

Without going back into the period of our colonial beginnings, it is plain to see that the Declaration of Independence signalized the accession of the first generation to power in our national history. No spirit of decrepit age or feeble counsel stalked through the scintillant passages of that immortal document. Strong medicine though it was for the American subjects of George III, their minds had been prepared for the event by a long period of violent propaganda conducted by such skilled masters of the art as James Otis, Patrick Henry, Samuel Adams, Alexander McDougall, Charles Thomson, Christopher Gadsden and Tom Paine. The methods of these patriot-agitators were thoroughly demagogic and sensational, characterized by unlawful assemblages and mob violence as well as by legislative memorials and pamphleteering of unusual merit; and gradually they succeeded in arousing the colonial population to a realization of the injustices which they decried. They sought radical reform, for it was their object to destroy the autocratic power of the British king and to establish in America an untried form of government based upon the principle of popular rule.

Due to the unusual conditions existing in a country torn by revolutionary conflict, the influence of the original agitators continued beyond the time when their chief usefulness had expired. Independence proclaimed, the task fell to them of establishing a federal government for the thirteen new-fledged states, a task demanding constructive genius of a high order. Their effort at a solution, offered in the form of the Articles of Confederation, precipitated the "Critical Period" of American history and revealed the poverty of their organizing ability. Under the circumstances they were compelled to surrender leadership not to a new generation but to a different element of their own generation—to men who thought less in terms of theories and emotions, and more in terms of realities, men who did not despise bargain and compromise if they might thereby gain the end they had in view. The accession of these men inaugurated a period of conservative reaction. Hamilton, John Adams, Washington, John Jay and their Federalist associates accepted the liberal philosophy of their predecessors with mental reservations; but they brought about the adoption of the Constitution and created under it a national government which not only worked successfully at the time but which stands today as one of the oldest continuous constitutional governments in the world.

When the Federalists were yet at the height of their power, the sappers and miners of a new age were passionately devoting their energies to the subversion of the existing régime. Led by such men as Jefferson, Madison, Aaron Burr, William Duane, Thomas Callender and Philip Freneau, the object of these crusaders was radical reform. They wished to replace what they considered to be a centralized government of pseudo-monarchical tendencies with a truly republican government based upon the principle of decentralization of authority. The presidential election of 1800 brought the new leaders into control, and Jefferson's inauguration may be regarded as the beginning of the second generation of American statesmanship. The new rulers consisted in part of the abler figures among the group of agitators; and the leaders of the supplanted generation formed the dwindling nucleus of an intransigeant opposition. Jefferson and his successors in the presidency, Madison and Monroe, were sobered by the responsibility of holding office and found themselves forced to modify in practice many views that had seemed unassailable in speculation. Notwithstanding a flabbiness of administration characteristic of a liberal government in power, the Jeffersonian Republicans succeeded in proving the practicability of liberal principles as the guide of public policy.

While the Jeffersonian Republicans were still holding the seats of authority, a growing discontent against their control began to find expression under the skillful direction of a younger generation of leaders aspiring for power. The pacifistic foreign policy of the elder statesmen in face of the aggressions of England and France furnished the issue upon which the new group succeeded in attaining national prominence. Henry Clay, John C. Calhoun, Richard M. Johnson, Felix Grundy, Langdon Cheves, Peter B. Porter and other "War Hawks" entered Congress in 1811 and plunged the nation into an unprofitable war contrary to the best judgment of many of the seasoned statesmen of the time. By the close of the war, the new generation had formulated their plan of legislative reform and were definitely in command of the situation, although their measures were looked on askance by Madison and Monroe and bitterly opposed by Daniel Webster, a young man of the new age still lingering under the influence of the discredited Federalist leadership. Their program of legislation, presented to Congress in 1816-1817, was essentially conservative in its tendency, containing as its main features a protective tariff, a new and greater United States Bank, the construction of internal improvements at national expense, and adequate military preparedness. Before they yielded to the onrush of the next generation most of these reforms had been passed into federal statutes; indeed, their chief policies gained such general acceptance that party lines disappeared entirely about 1820.

Shortly thereafter began the inevitable agitation which presaged the accession of a new generation to the control of public policy. The forerunners of the new leadership raised their voices in protest against the political philosophy that controlled the times—the right of the well-born to rule—rather than against any specific measures which the dominant group had enacted. The first attempt at revolt resulted in the indecisive election of 1824; but thereafter a veritable hue and cry was raised against the Adams-Clay administration and all their works and doctrines, and the forces of discontent became well organized under the direction of such men as William B. Lewis, Thomas H. Benton, Amos Kendall, Duff Green and Martin Van Buren. The inauguration of Andrew Jackson in 1829 marked the entrance of the new political generation, the fourth in order of succession, into command of the government. The practical statesmen of the new order were Jackson himself, Thomas H. Benton and Martin Van Buren, each of whom, in his own way, embodied the liberal ideals of the new time. Their principles called for increased control of the common people in all departments of government and politics; or, in other words, for the abolition of special privilege in appointments to office, in the federal banking system (the United States Bank), in internal improvements, and in the disposition of western lands. Before they were retired from power, the Jacksonian Democrats succeeded in translating their doctrines into governmental practice though challenged at every turn by the brilliant and versatile opposition of the leaders whom they had supplanted. Many of the details of their program were modified by later generations, but the basic principles of government which they established are to this day accepted as the foundations of the American democratic structure.

While the generation of Jackson was still strongly entrenched in power, the portents that foretold the oncoming of a new statesmanship were beginning to display themselves in the political heavens. The heralds of the coming era were deeply convinced that the pivotal issue in national affairs was one which the elder leaders had carefully ignored and evaded—the slavery question. To a consideration of this issue the new generation brought all the energy and arrogant assurance with which fresh generations have always approached weighty problems of public policy. Unfortunately for the orderly evolution of national institutions, the new leadership brought conflicting viewpoints to bear upon the great problem of the time, one portion of the new statesmen hailing from the South and the other portion from the free states of the North. The great conflict of the new era was not, as so often before, a contest between a superannuated statesmanship and the buoyant, resistless vanguard of a new leadership, but a struggle between men of the same generation, equally sure of themselves, equally determined to attain dominance and establish their policies in governmental practice.

With the accession of John Tyler to the presidency in 1841 the new generation assumed direction of the government with the conservative pro-slavery contingent in the ascendant, a position which they succeeded in retaining for nearly twenty years. From the outset they had to contend with the ceaseless and growing agitation of the abolitionists, led by such men as Garrison, Giddings, Wendell Phillips, Gerrit Smith and John Greenleaf Whittier; and all their guile and power availed them nothing against zealots who were inspired only to greater effort by "gag resolutions" and mob attacks. Nevertheless the mass of the people were slow to accept the teachings of the abolitionists; and in the meantime the conservative ideas of the pro-slavery group were in large part carried into force. Under the skillful guidance of men like James K. Polk, Jefferson Davis, Stephen A. Douglas and Alexander H. Stephens, half of the Republic of Mexico was annexed, the federal territories were opened to slavery, and a stricter fugitive slave law was enacted.

But gradually the anti-slavery agitation began to bear fruit. Leadership in the movement, originally held by ultra-radical abolitionists like Garrison and Phillips, passed to anti-slavery liberals like Chase and Seward and Lincoln. The propaganda of emotionalism was succeeded by appeals to reason and organized political activity culminating in the Republican party. Division within the ranks of the Democratic leaders early in 1860 gave the anti-slavery forces their opportunity; and in the presidential election of that year they elected their candidate Abraham Lincoln to the presidency on a platform pledging the party to the non-extension of slavery. The southerners believed that behind this moderate program lay the uncompromising purposes of men like Garrison and John Brown; and they chose to shift any subsequent controversy from legislative halls to the battlefield.

The processes of orderly social growth are always unsettled by military conflict; and in the case of the Civil War the high passions aroused by the struggle made it possible for the anti-slavery radicals to gain ascendency in Congress although under other circumstances their period of influence would have expired when the anti-slavery cause was taken up by the practical statesmen. Such men as Thaddeus Stevens, Charles Sumner and Ben Wade gloried in the name Radical as distinguished from Conservative or Administration Republican; and under their propulsion, abolition measures of increasing severity were enacted by Congress, and the president was given no peace until he had issued the Emancipation Proclamation. When victory crowned the Union arms, the task fell to the Radicals, unsuited to their genius, of reconstructing the South; and this they undertook with the same energy and singleness of purpose with which they had fought the war. Applying their doctrinaire preconceptions to the solution of the negro problem, they raised the slaves to the level of white citizens and conferred upon the black men the right to vote. But by these last measures the generation had over-reached itself in its radicalism; reforms enacted under such auspices and at such a juncture were not likely to be enduring in effect. Although the changes were solemnly embodied in the federal Constitution in the fourteenth and fifteenth amendments, they were so far in advance of public opinion that to this day they remain a dead letter so far as the great majority of the negroes are concerned.

The reconstruction statesmen began rapidly to pass away early in the seventies as if burnt out by the very intensity of their zeal, and their places were soon taken by new men whose minds dwelt on matters far removed from the idealistic and humanitarian interests of the earlier period. The new leaders were concerned primarily with the economic and industrial exploitation of the nation's resources and with governmental policies that would assist material development at every turn. Under their direction the energies of the government were, in the sixth generation of American politics, turned to conservative purposes—to land-grants for railroads, the protective tariff system, "sound money" finance and a policy of non-interference in the methods and management of industry. Men like Roscoe Conkling, Blaine, Garfield, Levi P. Morton, Samuel J. Randall and "Czar" Reed came into charge of public affairs. Even such spokesmen as Schurz, Curtis and Cleveland, whose voices were raised in protest against some of the more obnoxious practices of the dominant leadership, did not differ fundamentally from them in their conception of the functions of government. While this generation was in power, the United States made the transition to the modern era and the foundations were laid for the stupendous business development of the present time.

The note of dissent was early sounded against the domination of the government by the great corporate interests; but the protestants were for many years in a hopeless minority. They spent their energies, with little effect, in launching radical minor parties and in organizing radical agrarian and workingman associations. In the decade of the nineties the movement of protest against the existing order reached threatening proportions in the Populist movement and the "free silver" campaign of 1896. In the opening years of the new century the work of propaganda was taken up with missionary zeal by the "muckrakers," a group of publicists and writers whose object it was to inflame public opinion against corruption and abuses in government and "big business."

On the crest of the wave of popular resentment thus raised up, the leaders of the new generation came into power, the seventh political generation since the natal days of the republic. Unlike the elder leaders, the new statesmen were animated with liberal ideals; without regard to party affiliations they labored for "progressive" legislation and strove for the advent of a "new democracy." Under the inspiration of such men as Bryan, Roosevelt, Wilson, La Follette, Hughes and Hiram Johnson, they brought about the enactment of laws for the restraint of trusts, railroads, land-grabbing corporations and the financial interests; the working conditions of employees were greatly improved by the enactment of a wide variety of welfare legislation; and an effort was made to rejuvenate the power of the people in governmental affairs through direct nominations and direct legislation, the granting of woman suffrage and the popular election of senators. The new measures were carried through in face of the embittered opposition of the survivors of the departed epoch.

When the United States entered the World War in 1917, the signs of the times indicated that the generation had about run its course. Its program of domestic reform had been enacted; Roosevelt passed away in 1919, Wilson, La Follette and other vigorous reformers of an earlier day were beginning to show signs of physical decline; the adoption of federal suffrage for women suggested a point of departure for a new era. An unceasing criticism directed against the foundations of the existing order had been conducted by the Socialists and other radical groups and was apparently preparing the way for the transfer of power to fresh hands. New and lively issues were already looming up which had received little serious consideration by those in power, questions concerned with the application of democratic principles to industrial organization and with the relations of the United States to the world order. A leadership representative of the new day seemed slow in making its appearance, and the presidential campaign of 1920 showed the country in a condition of drift awaiting the coming of new pilots. Future events alone can supply the confirmatory evidence to show whether, as at present seems likely, we are today standing on the threshold of the eighth generation of American statesmanship.

IV

For confirmed radicals and orthodox conservatives this survey of the successive generations of American history will serve merely to reinforce their preconceptions as to the importance of their respective theories of progress to national development. The one group will find in the evidence sufficient reason for maintaining that the American people would have fared better if statesmen of the Jeffersonian school had always been at the helm. The other will discover justification for the conviction that the nation made its chief advances under the guidance of statesmen of the Hamiltonian school. The former group will be likely to stress the dynamic quality of democratic and humanitarian ideals as the motive force of national progress. The latter will point to administrative efficiency and the stimulation of economic enterprise as supplying the chief impulse to national achievement.

But to the candid student of social tendencies it is not likely that either conclusion will prove wholly acceptable. Beyond question the foregoing review yields two generalizations which would seem to be pregnant with significance. In the first place, epochs of radicalism and conservatism have followed each other in alternating order; and, secondly, with the changing of epochs, leadership in public affairs has passed from the liberals of the one division to the moderates of the other and *vice versa*, except in times of war and after-war readjustment when the extremists of the one group or the other have ordinarily been in the saddle. Whatever fallacies or losses may be apparent to the logician in such a zigzag scheme of progress, it nevertheless remains that in America social development has never followed a straight line, but, within limits, has been the result of the unconscious employment by the people of the trial-and-error method. Experimentation and opportunism, rather than preconceived theories, have been the animating spirit of American progress.

To the working out of this vital social process, both the radical and the conservative have made important and essential contributions. Their mutual criticism and vigilant antagonism have served to keep America abreast the most enlightened nations of the world without the periodic recourse to revolutionary violence characteristic of continental European countries. The functioning of these crosscurrents and countercurrents of opinion has been made possible by the solemn guarantees, in the state and federal constitutions, of free speech and a free press. If the experience of the past is a dependable guide to the future, the best assurance of the peaceful and orderly advance of the people in the future would seem to lie in a jealous regard for the right of free exchanges and comparisons of opinion.

In conclusion, this survey of the procession of generations suggests a criterion for analyzing the elusive quality of

greatness, which by general consent attaches to certain characters in American history. Restricting our inquiry to the
incumbents of the presidency, a consensus of opinion among
historians and publicists ascribes preëminence to Washington, Jefferson, Jackson and Lincoln, and, in a preliminary
way, to Roosevelt and Wilson. But what were the tests and
standards that were applied in making this selection? It is
not to be denied that this group of foremost presidents differed from each other in many conventional respects—in
education, temperament, training, personality, party affilia-
tion, and attachment to specific public policies. Furthermore, Washington as president was swayed by conservative
ideals whereas the other presidents were exponents of the
doctrines of liberalism as understood by the men of their own
generation. Evidently their title to fame is not derived
from any of the aptitudes or qualities that have been noted.

The answer to our query has perhaps been reached by this
process of elimination. These statesmen enjoyed one attri-
bute, and one only, in common: they were men of elastic
mind, sensitive to the quickening impulses of a new time,
swift to grasp a fresh vision of public duty and to present
their solution in a form capable of rallying public opinion to
its support. Their ability to marshal the energies of the
nation to meet the new situation assured them of their historic position among the great leaders of the nation. Thus
the essence of greatness, as viewed in the perspective of
history, does not consist in the ability to hold back or even
to mark time but in the capacity for adaptability to change,
in the quality of leading the nation to the acceptance of new
responsibilities and larger opportunities.

BIBLIOGRAPHICAL NOTE

No comprehensive study of the historical significance of radicalism and conservatism in the United States has ever been made
There is real need for such a study, for, in the mind of the average

man, the whole subject has been obscured by a cloud of misinformation and misrepresentation growing out of the political animosities of the last twenty years.

It is possible to find occasional passages, in the writings of publicists and historians, which discuss in an instructive way the meaning of radicalism and conservatism and of the various shades of opinion existing within each school, as well as the relation of these types of opinion to social and institutional development. Among the more luminous of such discussions, selected somewhat at random, may be cited: John Dewey's "How Reaction Helps" in the *New Republic*, vol. xxiv, pp. 21 22; A. V. Dicey's "An English View of American Conservatism" in Gustav Pollak's *Fifty Years of American Idealism. The New York Nation, 1865-1915* (Boston, 1915), pp. 309-324; Guy Emerson's essay "What Is a Liberal?" in his *The New Frontier* (New York, 1920); Ralph Waldo Emerson's "The Conservative" in his *Complete Works* (12 v.; New York, n. d.), vol. i, pp. 279-307; Henry Jones Ford's "Radicalism in American Politics" in the *Yale Review*, vol. ix, pp. 759-770; editorial entitled "In the Vein of Intimacy" in the *Freeman*, March 31, 1920; William J. Kirby's "The Natural History of a Reform Law" in the *Catholic World*, vol. 102, pp. 145-159; W. E. H. Lecky's *A History of England in the Eighteenth Century* (8 v.; New York, 1892-1893), vol. i, pp. 16-19, vol. ii, pp. 95-97; Walter Lippman's *A Preface to Politics* (New York, 1913), pp. 86-105, and his *Drift and Mastery* (New York, 1914), chaps. ix, xii-xiv, xvi; Brander Matthews' essay on "Reform and Reformers" in *The American of the Future* (New York, 1909); John Morley's *On Compromise* (London, 1896), pp. 201-265; James Harvey Robinson's *The Mind in the Making* (New York, 1921), *passim;* E. A. Ross's *Social Control* (New York, 1901), chap. xv; Bertrand Russell's "Individual Liberty and Public Control" in the *Atlantic Monthly*, vol. cxx, pp. 112-120; Mowry Saben's "Conservatism and Reform" in the *Forum*, vol. 48, pp. 35-44; Thorstein Veblen's *The Theory of the Leisure Class* (New York, 1915), p. 190 *et seq.* The foregoing discussions consider the subject from widely differing angles and do not agree in many respects with the point of view presented by the present writer. The *Cyclopedia of American Government* (3 v. edited by Andrew Cunningham McLaughlin and Albert Bushnell Hart; New York, 1913), which was intended to codify contemporary specialized thought in political science and American history, does not include radicalism or conservatism among the subjects for treatment.

CHAPTER VI

THE RÔLE OF WOMEN IN AMERICAN HISTORY

An examination of the standard histories of the United States and of the history textbooks in use in our schools raises the pertinent question whether women have ever made any contributions to American national progress that are worthy of record. If the silence of the historians is taken to mean anything, it would appear that one-half of our population have been negligible factors in our country's history.

Before accepting the truth of this assumption, the facts of our history need to be raked over from a new point of view. It should not be forgotten that all of our great historians have been men and were likely therefore to be influenced by a *sex* interpretation of history all the more potent because unconscious. Furthermore, while it is indisputable that the commanding positions in politics, diplomacy, and the army have always been held by men, it is also true that our ideas of what is important in our past have greatly changed in recent years.

If, as the following sketch seeks to show, the women of the nation have played their full part in American development, the pall of silence which historians have allowed to rest over their services and achievements may possibly constitute the chief reason why the women have been so slow in gaining equal rights with the men in this the greatest democracy in the world. The men of the nation have, perhaps not unnaturally, felt disinclined to endow with equality a class of persons who, so far as they knew, had never proved their fitness for public service and leadership in the past history of the country. Any consideration of woman's part in American history must include the protracted struggle of the sex for larger rights and opportunities, a story that in itself is one of the noblest chapters in the history of American democracy.

I

Although a queen as well as a king gave encouragement to Christopher Columbus and it was under another queen that the first English settlements in America were projected, colonization in the New World was not an unmixed blessing for the women settlers. It was theirs to share the hardships and perils of wilderness life in equal part with the men, but to them came little of the glory and none of the legal advantages which the men derived by fleeing from the Old World. In 1920 Europe and America joined in celebrating the three-hundredth anniversary of the voyage of the *Mayflower*. The courage and achievements of the Pilgrim Fathers were commemorated in detail; but very little was said about the Pilgrim Mothers, who formed thirty-two of the one hundred and twenty passengers but whose names were not permitted to appear on the civil compact which was signed by the settlers upon their arrival at Provincetown.

For the great majority of colonial women, life was much as former President Eliot has described it: "Generations of them cooked, carried water, washed and made clothes, bore children in lonely peril, and tried to bring them up safely through all sorts of physical exposure without medical or surgical help, lived themselves in terror of savages, in terror of the wilderness, and under the burden of a sad and cruel creed, and sank at last into nameless graves, without any vision of the grateful days when millions of their descendants should rise up and call them blessed."

The rapid increase of the colonial population was due, in great part, to the large families which the women brought into the world. The generosity of nature in a sparsely populated country removed any economic barrier to the rearing of a large number of children. Even in the upper levels of society girls often married when they were fifteen or sixteen; and to be without a husband at twenty-five was the certain sign of an "ancient maid." John Marshall, the later chief justice, fell in love with his wife when she was fourteen and married her at sixteen. From early marriages ordinarily came families of ten and twelve children. Anne Hutchinson was the mother of fifteen children. Sir William Phipps was one of twenty-six children by the same mother. Most of the large families were the offspring of at least two mothers, a fact that requires no further comment.

Women were sometimes to be found in business in a small way. This came about ordinarily as a result of the death of the husband or other provider. Advertisements in the colonial press show a wide range of such employments—shop-keeping, jelly-making, wax-working, embroidering, and the like. Benjamin Franklin's sister-in-law followed a familiar custom of widows in taking over her husband's newspaper business upon his death. But in general the sphere in which women might move was severely restricted and jealously guarded by the men of the age, who cherished the Old World idea of women as inferior beings. Now and then a woman sought to violate this convention only to be met by the contumely or persecution of the dominant sex. In 1638 Mistress Anne Hutchinson was brought to trial for sedition and heresy in Puritan Massachusetts because she had instructed the women of the neighborhood in religious precepts according to her own understanding. She was excommunicated from the church and banished from the colony, for she had committed two unpardonable sins: she had criticised the teachings of the men in authority, and she had set herself up to preach, the latter being forbidden by the solemn injunction of St. Paul. When she and her household were murdered by the Indians a few years later, John Winthrop, first governor of Massachusetts, wrote piously: "God's hand is the more apparently seen therein, to pick out this woful woman to make her and those belonging to her, an unheard of heavy example of their cruelty." It was not vouchsafed him to understand that she had taken up the weapons where the Puritans had laid them down to do her part in the long battle for freedom of thought and speech, for religious toleration and for a true democracy in religion.

Anne Hutchinson's experience was significant of the special ban under which women were compelled to live by law and custom during colonial times and, indeed, for many years thereafter. The principles of the English common law followed the colonists to America, fixed the legal restrictions and colored the social restraints which regulated woman's conduct. The unmarried woman was in most respects equal to a man in the eyes of the law, but custom and economic pressure forced her to marry at an early age and matrimony reduced her to a subordinate and cramped position. She was expected to embrace her husband's religion, to confine her activities to the home, and to make her husband's pleasure her guiding star. By the law her husband became her baron or lord and she ceased to have a separate existence to most intents and purposes. She lost the title to all her personal property, even though it had been acquired before her marriage, and she forfeited all personal control over her real property as long as the marriage lasted. If a wife earned money outside the home, the husband was entitled to her wages just as he was to those of a minor child. He had the right of controlling and punishing her conduct in the same degree as he did his children. The mother had no right to the custody of her own children, for the father was the sole guardian during his lifetime and could dispose of the children by will at his death. Conversely the husband was held responsible for many of the torts and crimes committed by his wife, and was entitled to collect damages for injuries inflicted upon his wife.

Under the circumstances it is not surprising that women were not expected to be educated and that ordinarily the obstacles in the way of their education were so great that most women could neither read nor write. Even such superior women as Mercy Warren, the sister of James Otis, and Abigail Adams, the spouse of John Adams, felt handicapped by the lack of early educational advantages. The few girls' schools of the time were limited to terms of a few months each, and the main subjects taught were needlework, music, dancing, and the cultivation of manners and morals. Women were practically unknown as participants in government, although it appears that some of them possessed the franchise for a period of years in colonial Massachusetts.

Notwithstanding these restraints and handicaps the mass of women were not discontented; and whenever occasion arose, they performed their full share with the men in the promotion of the public weal. Their labors were then greeted with masculine applause, for it was only when they worked for objects apart from the men or contrary to their immediate interests that they were regarded as unsexed and hideous to the dispassionate gaze. In the critical years preceding the War for Independence the women threw themselves heart and soul into the struggle for liberty, stimulating their men folks and supplementing their efforts. At the time of the Stamp Act women in all the colonies banded together in societies for the making of homespun; and in Rhode Island the maidens solemnly resolved that they would not receive the addresses of any suitors who favored the Stamp

Act. In later crises they formed anti-tea leagues and agreed to abstain from the use of imported fineries. Newspapers owned by women in Rhode Island, Maryland, Virginia and South Carolina went the whole distance with the other patriot papers in promoting radical propaganda. When a patriot convention of men in North Carolina adopted comprehensive regulations of non-importation, non-consumption and non-exportation in 1774, the ladies of Edenton signed an agreement declaring: "It is a duty that we owe not only to our near and dear relations and connexions but to ourselves, who are essentially interested in their welfare, to do everything as far as lies in our power to testify our sincere adherence to the same."

The spirit of such women is excellently reflected by a letter written shortly before the Declaration of Independence by a Philadelphia lady to a friend in the army: "I have retrenched every superfluous expense in my table and family; tea I have not drunk since last Christmas nor bought a new cap or gown since your defeat at Lexington; and what I never did before have learned to knit and am now making stockings of American wool for my servants; and this way do I throw in my mite to the public good. I know this—that as free I can die but once; but as a slave I shall not be worthy of life. I have the pleasure to assure you that these are the sentiments of all my sister Americans."

But the Declaration of Independence when it was adopted opened no new vistas to women as a sex. The statement that "all men are created equal" was understood in a strictly sex sense. Indeed, Abigail Adams, the stout-hearted spouse of John Adams, wrote to her husband, then in the Continental Congress: "I cannot say, that I think you are very generous to the ladies; for, whilst you are proclaiming peace and good-will to men, emancipating all nations, you insist upon retaining an absolute power over wives. But you must remember, . . . " she added with humorous asperity, "we have it in our power, not only to free ourselves, but to subdue our masters, and, without violence, throw both your natural and legal authority at our feet."

In the War for Independence that ensued the women made sacrifices and contributed services that were as essential to the success of the cause as the exploits of the soldiers in the field. They tilled the farms and garnered the crops while the men were away; they made munitions, using their pewter ware for bullets; they spun and wove and made uniforms and hospital supplies. Some gave their own property, others went from house to house to solicit contributions for the army. They carried supplies to the army, often at the risk of their own lives; they visited hospitals and prisons, seeking to relieve suffering and distress. Some even served in the ranks. The possibilities of organized feminine effort in relief work were for the first time shown in 1780 by the labors of the women of Philadelphia under the direction of Esther De Berdt Reed and Sarah Franklin Bache. Their object was to supply the destitute soldiers with clothing; and by dint of their efforts $7,500 in specie was collected for the purchase of materials. Throughout the war the women performed their work without any thought of recognition or reward; and when the days of peace finally returned, they quietly sank back in their places and took up the old endless routine of their existence.

II

The epic story of the westward march of population is usually related in terms of men; but no proper conception of the subjugation of the wilderness by the forces of civilization can be gained without an appreciation of the part that the women pioneers played. Women were not among the first adventurers into the wilds; they were preceded by the trappers, prospectors and cattle rangers. These soldiers of fortune introduced an unfettered and lawless mode of existence. Wherever they went saloons and gambling houses flourished; shooting affrays and lynchings were common occurrences. But as the frontier grew older, farmers began to appear with their womenkind, animated with the purpose of founding permanent homes. The West of Bret Harte began to give way to the West of Hamlin Garland. The presence of women necessitated a new order of society; civilized conduct began to take the place of frontier rowdyism and lawlessness, and peaceful and law-abiding communities developed.

The material conditions of early colonial life were reproduced with each new advance of the frontier to the west. It was necessary for every man, woman and child to work to help support the family. The women not only did the hard housework, including spinning and weaving, but most of them also assisted their husbands to erect the cabins, till the fields, and beat off attacks of the savage enemy. On them also devolved the entire task of educating the children. Large families were the rule. As one writer has said, the woman pioneer "was lonesome until she had a half-dozen children about her. She did not begin to feel crowded in the single room until the second dozen began coming." The frontier women were a picked lot physically; otherwise they could not have withstood the rigors of life in an undeveloped country.

While women were faring forth with their men folk to a precarious life on the frontier, many of their sisters who remained in the East found the conditions of their life fundamentally altered through no act of their own. In New England and the Middle Atlantic states women were beginning for the first time to enter factory work in the years following the War of 1812. The growth of textile manufacturing had created a demand for wage labor; and in order not to interfere with hired help on the farm, the mill owners looked to the women as an important source of labor supply. With our modern ideas of such things it is a surprising fact that many years before both Washington and Hamilton had anticipated such a culmination, and had expressed their full approval of the employment of women and children in factories. The working day of both women and children, like that of the men, extended from sunrise to sunset; and wages were miserably low. Generally speaking, women and girls formed from two-thirds to three-fourths of the total number of factory workers in the first half of the nineteenth century, and in some places as much as nine-tenths. Without their help it is doubtful whether the textile industry could have flourished, for it was not until after 1850 that cheap labor became plentiful in the form of European immigrants.

When women stepped from the spinning wheel at home to the spinning jenny in the mill, they did not enter a new field of work, although they were working under radically changed conditions. The break once made, new occupations and trades opened to them because of the cheapness of their hire. By 1840 women were employed in more than one hundred different occupations, although the great majority of the women outside of the factories worked as seamstresses and tailoresses, and teaching was the only field open to educated women. The age-long idea of the family, according to which the interests of the mother and children were restricted to the home, was thus in process of being undermined. Notwithstanding the miserable and discriminatory conditions under which women were obliged to work, the day of woman's economic independence of man was beginning to dawn.

In most other respects the position of women in the first

half of the nineteenth century remained as of yore. Catherine E. Beecher, sister of Henry Ward Beecher, writing about 1840, voiced the dominant opinion of the age when she wrote: "Heaven has appointed to one sex the superior, and to the other the subordinate, station. . . . It is therefore as much for the dignity as it is for the interest of females, in all respects to conform to the duties of this relation. And it is as much a duty as it is for the child to fulfill similar relations to parents, or subjects to rulers." Or as Miss Barber put it in the Madison (Georgia) *Visitor:* "It is written in the volume of inspiration as plainly as if traced in sunbeams, that man, the creature of God's own image, is superior to woman. . . ." Thus the legal status of women yielded but slowly to change, and the feminine intellect was hardly more esteemed than in colonial times. Such educational facilities as were afforded in the early decades of the century were meager, and the purpose of "female education" was to prepare the pupils to attract men and gain husbands. As an exception to the rule Emma Willard founded a seminary with government aid in New York in 1819 and sought to direct the education of women along more self-respecting lines. The usual experience was that of Susan B. Anthony, whose teachers would not instruct her in long division nor understand why a girl should insist upon wanting to learn it. Periodicals for women began to make their appearance, most of them edited by men. Their type is well illustrated by the most popular of them all, *Godey's Lady's Book,* filled with fashion pictures and stories of saccharine morality.

Notwithstanding the condition in which the mass of women found themselves, or rather because of this fact, the first organized movement for women's rights had its rise in this period. The courageous souls who inaugurated the movement had not merely to brave the fierce contempt of the men as well as most of their own sex but they stood in constant peril of physical violence at the hands of infuriated mobs. The battle of Anne Hutchison for the right to speak her mind in public had to be fought all over again. As Miss Ida Tarbell has said, "they had to fight for the right of fighting wrongs"; and St. Paul's dictum was again and again thundered at them from pulpit and press: "But I suffer not a woman to teach, nor to usurp authority over the man, but to be in silence" (I Timothy, ii, 12). It was the *penchant* of women for humanitarian reform, their interest in the cause of oppressed humanity, that launched them upon their long and stormy voyage for sex equality. The temperance question—which first aroused the reforming zeal of Susan B. Anthony—the transcendentalist movement, labor welfare, and, above all, the anti-slavery agitation, derived indispensable support from an earnest, self-sacrificing minority of women in all parts of the country.

The first impulse to this new phase of feminine activity was given by the visit of the Scotchwoman Frances Wright to this country in 1820. A girl of twenty-two, she had the distinction of being the first woman lecturer on lay subjects in this country. Her advanced ideas on slavery, theology and woman's rights gave offense to both press and ministry, but did not prevent her from returning to America several years later and giving new momentum to the cause of human betterment. In 1828 came the Grimké sisters from South Carolina, who after having emancipated their slaves betook themselves north to devote the remainder of their lives and wealth to the cause of abolition. About the same time Lucretia Mott, a Quaker of Philadelphia, began her active work in the promotion of anti-slavery, woman's rights and the other reforms of the time.

When the American Anti-Slavery Society was founded in Philadelphia in 1833 under the inspiration of William Lloyd Garrison, women took part in the meeting although they were not formally received as members. Immediately thereafter the women of the city formed the Philadelphia Female Anti-Slavery Society; and so successful did the organization prove to be that a few years later the first national convention of American anti-slavery women was held in New York City. By this time women in many parts of the North were taking active part in the anti-slavery struggle through circulating petitions, holding prayer meetings and conventions, and raising large sums of money by fairs. An effort was made to stem the tide by a pastoral letter issued by the Massachusetts Association of Congregational Ministers in 1837, which declared that "perplexed and agitating subjects" should not be forced upon any church and that the new practices threatened "the female character with widespread and permanent injury. . . . If the vine . . . thinks to assume the independent and overshadowing nature of the elm, it will not only cease to bear fruit, but fall in shame and dishonor into the dust." When the second convention of the women was being held in Philadelphia in 1838, the hall in which they met was surrounded all day by an enraged mob, and when the convention adjourned for the evening the building was plundered and burnt. The following year the women asked equality with the men in the American Anti-Slavery Society; but this request caused such a violent controversy among the masculine friends of negro rights that the society split, one wing led by Garrison merging with the women and the other organizing a new society.

In 1840 occurred an event which called dramatic attention to the unequal position of women and led directly to the organization of a militant woman's rights movement. A World's Anti-Slavery Convention was held in London, to which delegates had been invited from all anti-slavery societies. When several American women, duly accredited as delegates, sought admission, they were excluded by a large vote on account of their sex. This affront caused two of the delegates, Lucretia Mott and Elizabeth Cady Stanton, to resolve that on their return to America they would leave no stone unturned to remove all distinctions between the sexes. Several years passed before they were ready to launch their movement. Finally in 1848 they joined with Martha C. Wright and Mary Ann McClintock in issuing a call for a woman's rights convention, the first of its kind in the history of the world.

The meeting was held on July 19, 1848, at Seneca Falls, New York, and was counted a complete success by all who attended. Its concrete outcome was an impressive declaration of sentiments patterned closely upon the Declaration of Independence. It read in part as follows:

> When in the course of human events it becomes necessary for one portion of the family of man to assume among the people of the earth a position different from that which they have hitherto occupied, . . . a decent respect to the opinions of mankind requires that they should declare the causes that impel them to such a course.
>
> We hold these truths to be self-evident: that all men and women are created equal; that they are endowed by their Creator with certain inalienable rights; that among these are life, liberty, and the pursuit of happiness. . . . Whenever any form of government becomes destructive of these ends, it is the right of those who suffer from it to refuse allegiance to it. . . .
>
> The history of mankind is a history of repeated injuries and usurpations on the part of man toward woman, having in direct object the establishment of an absolute tyranny over her. To prove this, let facts be submitted to a candid world.
>
> He has never permitted her to exercise her inalienable right to the elective franchise.
>
> He has compelled her to submit to laws, in the formation of which she had no voice. . . .
>
> He has made her, if married, in the eye of the law, civilly dead.

In the covenant of marriage, she is compelled to promise obedience to her husband, he becoming to all intents and purposes her master—the law giving him power to deprive her of her liberty, and to administer chastisement. . . .

He has monopolized nearly all the profitable employments. . . .

He has denied her the facilities for obtaining a thorough education, all colleges being closed against her. . . .

He has created a false public sentiment by giving to the world a different code of morals for men and women. . . .

He has usurped the prerogative of Jehovah himself, claiming it as his right to assign her a sphere of action, when that belongs to her conscience and to her God.

He has endeavored, in every way that he could, to destroy her confidence in her own powers, to lessen her self-respect, and to make her willing to lead a dependent and abject life.

Now, in view of this entire disfranchisement of one-half the people of this country, their social and religious degradation, . . . we insist that they have immediate admission to all the rights and privileges which belong to them as citizens of the United States. . . .

The success of this first experimental meeting caused woman's rights conventions to be of almost yearly occurrence until the outbreak of the Civil War, when the leaders merged all lesser interests in the national cause. Contemporary opinion of these "Tomfoolery Conventions" is picturesquely expressed in the following editorial from the Syracuse *Daily Star:* "The poor creatures who take part in the silly rant of 'brawling women' and Aunt Nancy men, are most of them 'ismizers' of the rankest stamp, Abolitionists of the most frantic and contemptible kind, and Christian (?) sympathizers with such heretics as Wm. Lloyd Garrison, Parker Pillsbury, C. C. Burleigh, and S. S. Foster. These men are all Woman's Righters, and preachers of such damnable doctrines and accursed heresies, as would make demons of the pit shudder to hear."

The ridicule and vituperation of the press and pulpit seemed merely to spur the leaders to greater endeavors

although it undoubtedly prevented thousands of less confident members of the sex from declaring their allegiance to
the movement. Many prominent men lent their support.
The great anti-slavery agitators, Garrison and Wendell
Phillips, spoke at their meetings; Ralph Waldo Emerson,
John Greenleaf Whittier and Horace Greeley wrote and
lectured in their behalf. Far in the West Abraham Lincoln
approved the principle of sharing the government with those
who bore its burdens, "by no means excluding the women."

The three decades of feminine self-assertion closing in
1850 had not been without effect in bettering the condition
of women as a sex. However reluctantly the new gospel
was received, gradual but certain improvements in the legal
and social position of women began to appear in various
parts of the country. In 1839 Mississippi granted to married
women the control of their own property; and in the next
decade similar laws were passed in Texas, Indiana, Pennsylvania, New York, California and Wisconsin. In 1836 the
first woman's seminary of college rank, Mt. Holyoke, was
opened at South Hadley by Mary Lyon. The project of co-
education was an even more daring venture, but in 1833
Oberlin College was founded and from the outset admitted
men and women on equal terms. Twenty years later the
second co-educational college, Antioch, was opened by
Horace Mann at Yellowsprings, near Xenia, Ohio. When
the State University of Iowa opened its doors in 1855, it
set a bold example for other state universities by admitting
women to its first classes; but three years later when several
young women applied for admission to the University of
Michigan, their request was refused.

III

In the exciting decade preceding the Civil War the influence of women continued to be felt in all forward-looking

movements. It was during these years that Dorothea Dix performed her great work in securing the reorganization and proper construction of asylums for the insane. Her services were epoch-making in the history of public philanthropy, especially in the West and the South, but she met with one tragic disappointment when in 1854 President Pierce vetoed a bill she had finally induced Congress to pass, granting ten million acres of public land for the purpose of aiding the states to care for the insane. In New York state the women formed secret societies called the Daughters of Temperance, and some zealous individuals took the law into their own hands, visiting saloons, breaking windows and emptying whiskey barrels into the street.

Women were now emboldened to make their initial appearance in the professions. The first woman to receive a diploma in medicine after completing the regular college course was Elizabeth Blackwell, who attained that distinction in Geneva, New York, in 1848. Six years later she founded the New York Infirmary, the first adequate woman's medical institution. The ministry was not entirely a new calling for women, for certain sects such as the Quakers and the Shakers had always permitted women preachers; but the first regularly ordained woman in the United States was Mrs. Antoinette Brown Blackwell of the Congregational Church, who began her life work in 1852. Women were as yet unknown in the legal profession; but in the literary field they were more at home. Catherine Sedgwick, the novelist, Alice and Phœbe Cary, the poets, and Margaret Fuller, brilliant journalist and founder of the *Dial* magazine, were all familiar household names in the middle of the century.

The slavery question inevitably overshadowed all other interests of the time, and to this cause public-spirited women gave their chief attention. In 1852 Harriet Beecher Stowe published her great propagandist novel, *Uncle Tom's Cabin,* which in the next few years stirred the North to its depths. Women speakers in the North took an active part in enkindling public indignation over the Kansas-Nebraska Act in 1854; and when the Republican party was born out of the intense feeling of the time, women stimulated the men to active participation in the new party. Then occurred the Civil War and the energies of the women were for four terrible years turned to other purposes.

The story of the Civil War without an account of the part borne by the women in the struggle is a story but partly told and but poorly comprehended. Women became a part of the war machine quite as fully as the men, contributing services almost as indispensable to national success as the troops in the field. Organized relief work, attempted by the women of Philadelphia on a small scale during the Revolutionary War, was now developed to a high degree of perfection, a harbinger of what the women of America were to accomplish through even abler organization in the World War. A few days after the surrender of Fort Sumter the leading women of New York City met at Cooper Union and under the inspiration of Dr. Elizabeth Blackwell formed the Woman's Central Relief Association of New York. At the solicitation of this body the United States government was shortly thereafter induced to authorize the establishment of the so-called United States Sanitary Commission, charged with the duty of sustaining the morale and protecting the health of men in the camps, and of aiding in the care of the sick and wounded.

The work of this organization, the counterpart of our modern American Red Cross (established in 1882), was made possible largely through the exertions of the women. In nearly every community of the North, Soldiers' Aid Societies were formed, in which the women met together, scraped lint and rolled bandages, made clothing for the soldiers, and collected supplies and food for transmission to the nearest depot of the Sanitary Commission. The Chicago branch of the Sanitary Commission had one thousand aid societies constantly sending in money and supplies; five hundred societies united in supporting the Cleveland and Cincinnati branches. A suggestive description of the activities of such organizations is presented by the final report of the Wisconsin Soldiers' Aid Society: Six thousand packages were dispatched; gifts amounting to $200,000 collected. Bureaus were organized for getting state pay for the families of soldiers, for securing pensions and arrears, for obtaining employment for the wives and mothers of volunteers, for securing work for men partially disabled in the war, and for supplying the wants of those who had been permanently crippled in the service.

Perhaps no feature of the war was more remarkable than the series of Sanitary Fairs held in the large cities of the North in the final years of the war. Probably more than seven million dollars had been laboriously raised by the Sanitary Commission by a variety of means prior to Gettysburg. Shortly thereafter the first Sanitary Fair was launched in Chicago under the directing genius of Mrs. Jane Hoge and Mrs. Mary A. Livermore with the idea of raising $25,000. To the amazement of many who regarded the project as quixotic, more than $80,000 was realized. Other cities imitated and improved upon the example of Chicago, and not less than ten million dollars was contributed to the support of the Sanitary Commission by means of the fairs.

To supplement the labors of the Sanitary Commission, the Christian Commission was established in November, 1861, primarily as an enterprise for carrying on evangelical work among the soldiers. This organization was also largely sustained by the women, its most unique service being the establishment of a system of diet kitchens for injured soldiers which extended to every corps of the army. In the third year of the war a special Ladies' Christian Commission was organized, which by 1865 possessed two hundred and sixty-five branches in all parts of the North, mostly connected with evangelical churches. During the latter part of the war Soldiers' Homes and Soldiers' Rests were established by the women at all important railroad junctions, where the wants of traveling and wounded soldiers might be cared for. Thousands of women, distinguished by such heroines as Clara Barton, went to the front as nurses, enduring the hardships and horrors of camp life and battlefield with the men. Many women assumed masculine garb and served in the army. Of a different character though not less important were the services of the women on the western prairies, who when the men obeyed the nation's call took up the work of farming and helped to maintain agricultural production at a high degree of efficiency.

Speaking of the work of the women during the war, Lincoln said: "I have never studied the art of paying compliments to women; but I must say, that if all that has been said by orators and poets since the creation of the world were applied to the women of America, it would not do them justice for their conduct during this war."

In the South the burdens borne by the women were even heavier. A larger proportion of the white men were in the army and the responsibility of the women was correspondingly greater. The women brought into use old spinning-wheels and looms in order to make clothing for the soldiers; they denied themselves meat and drink that it might be sent to the army; they nursed wounded soldiers and worked in munition plants. The suggestion publicly made by one of them late in the war that all southern women cut off their hair and sell it to Europe, where it was believed it might bring $40,000,000, failed of execution only because it was impossible to run the federal blockade. Living in an invaded country, they experienced the horrors of war all about them —homes destroyed, fields devastated, hostile soldiers on every hand. Yet they faltered not; and when their cause was crushed on the battlefield, they welcomed their soldiers home and, under conditions of bitter deprivation and deep humiliation, helped their husbands and sons to build a new South.

The interest of leading women of the North in the cause of emancipation suffered no cessation in the midst of their war duties. Although the government made official announcement at the outset that the war was being waged for preservation of the Union, these women insisted that it should be turned into a war for freedom. Several months after Lincoln's election Susan B. Anthony and Mrs. Stanton in company with some of the old time abolitionists sought to hold a series of conventions in the leading cities of the North to arouse public opinion to the pitch of demanding immediate emancipation; but the meetings were broken up at every point. The fact was that the majority of northerners were not at this time enamoured of the idea of prosecuting a "nigger war"; and the Lincoln administration was deeply convinced of the necessity of avoiding the issue in order to retain the allegiance of the four border slave states that had chosen to remain in the Union. The Emancipation Proclamation when it appeared was greeted by these women with only partial approval, inasmuch as it declared the freedom merely of such slaves as were yet to be found in unconquered southern territory. A nationwide call was sent out for a convention of women to meet in New York for the purpose of taking appropriate action. Delegates from many states attended. The Woman's National Loyal League was formed; and resolutions were adopted urging the president to emancipate *all* the slaves in the nation and declaring that: "There never can be a true peace in this Republic until the civil and political rights of all citizens of African descent and all women are practically established." The next eighteen months were spent in rolling up a mammoth petition, signed by 265,000 men and women, urging that Congress take effective action for universal emancipation of the negroes. Charles Sumner, Horace Greeley and other public men believed that the activities of the Loyal League were a mighty educational factor in hastening the adoption of the thirteenth amendment.

During the war all active campaigning for woman's rights had been suspended despite the protests of Susan B. Anthony. The suffrage leaders in the women's war work believed that when with the return of peace justice was bestowed upon the enslaved negro the grateful government would also reward the women with a gift of equal rights. They were amazed and incensed therefore when they discovered that the reconstruction statesmen were determined to ignore their claims. The fourteenth amendment, proposed in Congress in 1866, provided in its second section for a reduction of the representation of such states as withheld the ballot from male citizens of voting age. Thereby the word "male" was to be placed in the federal Constitution for the first time; the intent of the amendment was to extend federal protection to male suffrage, leaving woman suffrage as heretofore to the mercy of the states. The women openly and repeatedly expressed their amazement that Congress should be willing to experiment with two million illiterate black men as voters while denying the ballot to women. They charged that the Republicans were not interested in establishing abstract justice as they professed but in building up a black Republican party in the South. In 1866 the American Equal Rights Society was formed through a merger of the former Woman Rights Society with a part of the old American Anti-Slavery Society; and through this agency Congress was flooded with petitions against the proposed amendment. Their protest was unavailing; and the cup of their humiliation was filled to the overflowing when an additional fifteenth amendment was passed by Congress prohibiting any abridgment of the right to vote "on account of race, color, or previous condition of servitude." With the addition of the word "sex" to the foregoing list, the suffrage leaders would have given their unqualified support to the amendment. The protagonists of woman rights now sought to turn defeat into victory by claiming that the fourteenth amendment, in declaring that all persons born or naturalized in the United States were citizens, had thereby really enfranchised all women. Acting upon this interpretation women actually attempted to vote in several states and in some cases succeeded; and it was not until a Supreme Court decision was rendered upon the point in 1875 that the women were convinced that the right of citizenship did not carry with it the right to vote.

But the woman suffragists did not confine their efforts to Congress in the reconstruction period. In 1867 they presented their case to a state constitutional convention for the first time in history, that of New York, and fought a vigorous campaign to amend the constitution of Kansas. Their only success came two years later when in the far-off West the territory of Wyoming was organized on the basis of equal political rights for men and women. The same year the women began to re-form their ranks in preparation for the long struggle that lay ahead of them. The American Woman Suffrage Association was organized by suffragists who believed in centering their efforts upon the state legislatures; and the next year the National Woman Suffrage Association succeeded the Equal Rights Society, pledged to the policy of concentrating suffrage efforts upon the national government. These two organizations, divided as to tactics but agreeing fundamentally in purpose, remained apart for more than twenty years and involved a useless division of forces. Thus the period of reconstruction, which had seemed so full of hope for the woman's cause, closed with no substantial advances for the sex. The most promising opportunity which had yet come to them passed quickly into history and was soon forgotten by the nation in the thronging of other interests.

IV

The half-century from 1870 to 1920 was destined to witness the triumph of the principle of sex equality. New elements, materialistic and spiritual, entered into the situation which made inevitable at the end of the period what was scarcely thinkable at its beginning. Chief among these new factors was the great physical revolution in the woman's world which drove an unprecedented number of women into industry and trade; but, as we shall see, there were also other influences at work which were making for their intellectual and social advance and for their enlarged influence in government and society.

The Civil War was followed by an era of rapid industrial development without equal in American history. The phenomenal demand for wage labor could be satisfied only by drawing into the factories great armies of women and children where they worked under precisely the same conditions as did the men. Already by 1870 one-seventh of the women over sixteen years of age were engaged in gainful pursuits; and three decades later the proportion had increased to more than one-fifth. For hundreds of thousands of women, married and single, it thus happened that outside interests relegated the home to a secondary place, not because the women were discontented and insurgent but because modern conditions of industry had forced them out of their traditional sphere. Wage-earning women were compelled in self-protection to take an interest in far-reaching questions of governmental and industrial policy affecting their welfare. In the seventies and eighties they began to enter the trade union movement; others became zealous workers in the growing Socialist movement. The existence of this great class of wage-earning women gave fresh point to all the arguments for sex equality; and out of their ranks came many hearty workers for the elimination of sex barriers.

With the widening of the industrial sphere new opportunities of higher education began to open up to women, and educated women began to find new outlets for their energies and creative power. In 1865 the first women's college possessing ample funds was founded at Poughkeepsie, New York, by Matthew Vassar, whose ideal it was to maintain educational standards as exacting as those prevailing in the best men's colleges. The establishment of Vassar College cast a glamour of respectability about all subsequent enterprises for the higher instruction of women. The western state universities began to fall in with the movement. Under a law of 1867 Wisconsin admitted women to the normal department of the university; and three years later Michigan reversed the practice of almost thirty years by opening all the regular courses to women. The movement, so diffidently begun, gathered momentum until in 1920 more than one hundred institutions of higher learning devoted their entire time to women students, and about three hundred and fifty colleges and universities were classed as co-educational.

On the whole it proved easier for women to establish their rights to a liberal education than to gain admission to the professional and technical courses. Notwithstanding the hopeful beginnings made in the period before the Civil War, women were for many years excluded from the best schools of medicine, law and theology. One of the leading medical schools, Johns Hopkins, opened its doors to them in 1893; but when the medical schools of Columbia and Yale took similar action in 1916, there still remained twenty-eight medical colleges closed to women, among them the medical departments of seven state universities. Law schools, other than those connected with the state universities, have been even slower to admit women. But in spite of all discriminations and discouragements, women forged ahead in the professions. Although the first woman lawyer was admitted to the bar as late as 1869, there were more than one thousand women lawyers in the United States in 1910. At the same time there were more than seven thousand women doctors, three thousand five hundred women preachers, two thousand women journalists, besides great numbers in teaching, commerce, the civil service, and other pursuits. To women of this class the arguments for the equalization of sex opportunities seemed axiomatic and they instinctively aligned themselves with Susan B. Anthony and Elizabeth Cady Stanton in the woman movement. Many individuals among them possessed organizing ability of a high order and the gift of eloquence; and to them, as we shall see, fell the responsibility as well as the credit of leading the suffrage cause to its final triumph.

Another factor working in the interests of feminine emancipation was the rise and development of women's clubs throughout the United States. The pioneers of the movement were the New England Woman's Club at Boston and the Sorosis at New York, both founded in 1868. The latter grew out of the discourteous treatment accorded to the women by the Press Club of New York on the occasion of the Dickens dinner. At first such clubs were few in number and purely literary or social in purpose, but the number of clubs increased as domestic conveniences became more common and the housewife gained more time from domestic duties. By 1890 the clubs were so numerous and so wide-spread that they became federated in a great national system; and the units began to communicate with each other and receive new ideas and inspiration. As time went on, the women paid less attention to art and literature and more to civic and social problems, for they had come to realize that under modern conditions the "home" is not bounded by four walls but is directly affected by all the good and evil influences of the community and of the state and nation. Thus they became interested in such problems as child welfare, education, food adulteration and inevitably in the suffrage question. The General Federation of Women's Clubs represented a total membership of nearly one million women in 1910. The typical woman's club never became a center for strenuous suffrage agitation; but it was a means of educating many housewives to the significance of the demand and the lessons in organization that were learned served them in good stead in the battle for the ballot.

The great enterprises of moral reform in the period since the Civil War were led and supported, in very large part, by women. The close connection between women and the temperance cause was recognized in a unique way when the Prohibition party at its initial national convention in 1872 declared for equal suffrage, thus anticipating the major parties by forty-four years. In December of the following year began the remarkable Women's Temperance Crusade of 1873-1874, inspired by a temperance address delivered by Dr. Dio Lewis of Boston at Hillsboro, Ohio. The women of the town gathered in the streets to pray and entered saloons, two by two, and exhorted the bartenders and drinkers to cease their evil ways. The movement spread in every direction. In fifty days it swept the liquor traffic out of two hundred and fifty towns. But this exorcism was not lasting of effect; the saloon was found to be the outcropping of the liquor system entrenched in law and possessing ramifications in government and business. The women therefore saw need for revising their tactics, and in November, 1874, the Woman's Christian Temperance Union was founded. Under the guidance of Frances Willard this organization waxed strong, establishing branches in every state and territory and attaining the distinction of being the largest society composed exclusively of women and conducted entirely by them. The educational and political activities of the W. C. T. U. were a potent influence in preparing the public mind for the adoption of the federal prohibition amendment in 1919.

To women also must be given much of the credit for the rise and spread of the social welfare movement along scientific lines. One of the earliest and most successful settlement houses in America was Hull House, founded in Chicago by Jane Addams and Ellen G. Starr in 1889. The College Settlement Association of New York originated in 1887 among the students of Smith College. The playground movement and the development of agencies for scientific philanthropy also owe much to the initiative and continued support of women. The names of women workers in social service have been legion; the value of their labors beyond computation.

The entrance of great numbers of women into all fields of human activity made the ancient legal fetters of the sex an intolerable anachronism. Their enhanced influence in the world of affairs led inevitably to the removal of the worst discriminations. By the beginning of the twentieth century legislative enactments had gone far toward introducing the principle of sex equality into American law. Married women might own and control their separate property in three-fourths of the states; in every state a wife might dispose by will of her separate property. In about two-thirds of the states she was entitled to her own earnings; and in the large majority she might make contracts and bring suit. In many states the law provided that if the wife earned money outside the home the fruits of her labors were her own, but all her earnings within the household still belonged to the husband. Fathers and mothers possessed equal guardianship of children only in nine states and in the District of Columbia. Many inequalities in civil status remained; but the *right* of sex equality was no longer seriously questioned, and time alone was required to assure to woman her full position in the eyes of the law.

The expansion of woman's sphere in so many directions was accompanied by steady advances toward the cherished goal of equal political rights. The suffrage movement of the forties and fifties had possessed able heads but had lacked body; but with the exodus of great numbers of women from the home in the years following 1870, the movement continued to develop leaders and slowly gained a mass of followers among both men and women which spelt eventual success. It is true that the time never came when all women were convinced of the righteousness of the suffrage cause. Many of them had continued to live sheltered lives and knew little of the dynamic changes that had transformed the life of their sex; others felt that the problems of democracy were already sufficiently baffling without increasing the numbers of the electorate. In 1873 a committee of women protested to Congress against the proposal to grant equal suffrage; and some years later a National Association Opposed to the Extension of Woman Suffrage, composed of women, was formed.

The progress toward full equal suffrage was gradual but certain. In the early years following the Civil War some of the western states ventured to adopt the principle of woman suffrage in a local and limited sense. Kansas granted the vote to women in school elections in 1861; Michigan and Minnesota followed in 1875, and thereafter numerous other states emulated their example. In some states women were permitted to vote in local elections involving bond issues or taxation questions. Complete equality in voting was not granted by any state until the territory of Wyoming was admitted into the Union in 1890. Three other far western states followed by 1896; and then there came a lull of fourteen years during which no further advances were made toward complete equal suffrage.

While suffrage campaigns were being fought in the various states, renewed effort was being made to secure affirmative action from the federal government. One wing of the suffrage leaders was convinced that the swiftest road to success lay in an amendment to the federal Constitution. Beginning with 1870 they argued each year before Congressional committees for an equal suffrage amendment. Petitions by the thousands were poured into Congress. Finally in 1878, Senator A. A. Sargent of California introduced the amendment for action by Congress. The phraseology of Sargent's amendment is historic, for the language was framed by Susan B. Anthony and forty-two years later was embodied as the nineteenth amendment in the United States Constitution. The zeal of the women had other results as well. Between 1878 and 1896 committees of the Senate reported five times in favor of a suffrage amendment and House committees twice; but action went no further. Thereafter Susan B. Anthony ceased spending her winters in Washington and Congress ceased to concern itself with the matter until the suffrage movement entered a new era about 1910.

The situation of affairs at Washington clearly demonstrated that Congress was not disposed to give serious consideration to the demands of the women until a larger number of individual Congressmen owed their seats to the favor of women voters. The efforts of the years following 1896 were thrown very largely into state campaigns though uniformly without success. Finally in 1910 a new spirit of progressivism began to make itself felt throughout the land, creating schism within the Republican party and exciting wide public interest in legislation for social justice. Taking advantage of the new spirit of the times, suffrage leaders redoubled their efforts. The National American Woman Suffrage Association, led by Mrs. Carrie Chapman Catt, set to work with renewed determination. At the national capital a group of women under the leadership of Alice Paul formed the Congressional Union in 1913, resolved to bring the federal government to terms through the use of sensational and militant methods. Results began to appear. Again it was the trans-Mississippi West that pointed the way; and before New York acted in 1917, twelve states of that section had accepted women on equal political terms with men. A number of state legislatures finding constitutional barriers in the way of full enfranchisement followed the example of Illinois (1913) by granting the vote to women in presidential elections only.

As the number of equal suffrage states increased, the coercive effect of the vast body of new voters upon Congress became apparent. In the Senate of 1913 eighteen members had woman constituents. Irrespective of the merits of the question, party leaders could now foresee the outcome and they resolved to reap such partisan advantages as they might from their advocacy of the federal franchise for women. Hardly a year passed after 1913 without a vote being taken on the submission of a constitutional amendment, either in one or both houses of Congress. Finally in 1919, under the spur of a special message from President Wilson, the necessary two-thirds majority was obtained; and the states ratified the new amendment in time for the women to take part in the approaching presidential election.

V

The entrance of the United States into the World War in 1917 undoubtedly hastened the adoption of federal suffrage for women because of the indispensable part which the women of America played in making the war a success for the Allies. A few days after the declaration of war the National Woman's Committee was created by the Council of National Defense, with Dr. Anna Howard Shaw as President, and charged with the duty of coördinating the patriotic activities of the women of the nation. Branches of the national body were organized in every state and the state committees undertook to set up Woman's Committees in every county and city.

Under the supervision of these central committees the war work of the women attained a degree of efficiency unrivalled in the history of the world. No city or hamlet was without its circle of devoted women gathering daily or weekly under the auspices of the American Red Cross to roll bandages, make clothing, or prepare special foods for the soldiers. One department of the Red Cross was concerned exclusively with looking after the interests of families and relatives left dependent by the enlistment of the breadwinners in the army or navy. Women flocked into the civil service in order to enable the government to carry on its greatly expanded functions; they assisted actively in the flotation of the various Liberty Loans; they worked in munition factories and other essential industries, thus releasing men for active field service. They undertook protective work for girls in the neighborhood of the great army encampments and raised money for building dormitories and "community houses" where civilian friends and relatives of the soldiers might be accommodated. Thousands of women went abroad with the Expeditionary Forces, serving in a great variety of capacities from Red Cross nurses and Salvation Army workers to office clerks and Y. M. C. A. entertainers. In the maintenance of the morale of the troops perhaps no single factor was of more importance than the unswerving patriotism of the women.

Without any disparagement of the high importance of such services, it is probably true that the greatest contribution of the women to victory was made in an altogether different field, that of food conservation. From the outset the government recognized the supreme need of carrying food to the armies and exhausted populations of the Allied countries. The housewives of the nation rallied promptly to the call of the Food Administrator to conserve food and increase the local food supplies. Few homes were without "pledge-cards" in the windows; and few were the homes in which "wheatless days" and "meatless meals" were not as conscientiously observed as if prescribed by law. Women were also active in planting "war gardens," and the Woman's Land Army of America played no inconsiderable part in supplying woman farm labor.

No more fitting tribute has been accorded the war work of our women than that paid by Sir George Paish in a public address in London in April, 1920: "When I hear people say that America won the war, I assent. I go farther. I say that the war was won by the women of America. In the years of food shortage it was the American women who made it possible for us to have enough food to go round. American women ate maize that we might eat wheat."

Women are today standing upon the threshold of a new era in the history of their sex; and whatever affects the status of woman in America will affect the entire people of which they are so intimately a part. Women in the United States are now, in most respects, a part of human society literally and directly, not merely as represented by men to whom they "belong" in some relation. They are directly responsible for their choices and decisions and are placed in a position to increase immeasurably their contributions to American development. In speculating as to the use that women will make of the vote, it is not to be overlooked that the women are better prepared for their new responsibilities than any previous class admitted to the franchise. The beneficiaries of white manhood suffrage in Jackson's day were undisciplined and uneducated; and the black men, enfranchised a generation later, were on an infinitely lower plane of public morality and individual fitness. The value of the ballot to the women themselves as an educative force cannot be doubted; and any knowledge of the past services of women to American history is an assurance that the women will use their new power for the good of the nation and of humanity.

BIBLIOGRAPHICAL NOTE

Historians have generally ignored woman as a positive influence in American history and have usually omitted even any mention of her struggle for sex equality. This task has thus fallen to other hands. Belle Squire in her little volume entitled *The Woman Movement in America* (Chicago, 1911) was the first writer to attempt to set forth the part that women as a class have played in all periods of American history. The volume was originally written as a series of articles for newspaper use and was based very largely upon *The History of Woman Suffrage* by Elizabeth Cady Stanton and others, mentioned hereinafter. In the next year H. Addington Bruce published his book *Woman in the Making of America* (Boston, 1912), which attempted to accomplish the same purpose but with less success. Since the appearance of these books, little has been done toward making further applications of the point of view; and the only history school book which has availed itself of this approach to the subject is Charles A. Beard and William C. Bagley's *The History of the American People* (New York, 1918). It is unthinkable that this neglect should continue in the new era of historical writing ushered in by the adoption of the nineteenth amendment.

For a long period of years appreciative studies have been made by writers interested in the influence of women in special periods of American history. Some of the more important of these special studies are the following: Alice Morse Earle's *Colonial Dames and*

Housewives (Boston, 1895) ; Sydney George Fisher's *Men, Women and Manners in Colonial Times* (2 v.; Philadelphia, 1898) ; Harry Clinton Green and Mary Wolcott Green's *The Pioneer Mothers of America* (3 v.; New York, 1912) ; Elizabeth F. Ellet's *The Women of the American Revolution* (4th ed., New York, 1849) ; Gaillard Hunt's *Life in America One Hundred Years Ago* (New York, 1914), chap. x; Elizabeth F. Ellet's *The Pioneer Women of the West* (New York, 1852); L. P. Brockett and M. C. Vaughan's *Woman's Work in the Civil War* (Philadelphia, 1867) ; Frank Moore's *Women of the War* (Hartford, 1866) ; Mary Forrest's *Women of the South* (New York, 1865) ; John L. Underwood's *The Women of the Confederacy* (New York, 1906).

The great arsenal of facts pertaining to the woman rights movement in America prior to 1902 is the monumental work entitled *The History of Woman Suffrage* (4 v.; 2d ed., Rochester, 1889-1902) by Elizabeth Cady Stanton, Susan B. Anthony, Matilda Joslyn Gage and others. All subsequent writers have made generous use of the materials brought together in these volumes. Since 1902 many valuable studies have been made of special aspects of woman's life and activities in the United States, among which may be mentioned Edith Abbott's *Women in Industry* (New York, 1910) ; Arthur W. Calhoun's *Social History of the American Family from Colonial Times to the Present* (3 v.; Cleveland, 1917-1919) ; E. A. Hecker's *Short History of Women's Rights* (New York, 1911) ; Bertha A. Rembaugh's *The Political Status of Women in the United States* (New York, 1911) ; J. M. Taylor's *Before Vassar Opened* (Boston, 1914) ; Jennie Lansley Wilson's *The Legal and Political Status of Women in the United States* (Cedar Rapids, 1912) ; Mary I. Wood's *The History of the General Federation of Women's Clubs* (New York, 1912). Of considerable value also is Mrs. J. C. Croly's *The History of the Woman's Club Movement in America* (New York, 1898).

In dealing with women in American history the biographical approach has been most popular. As examples of this type of literature the following books may be cited: Elmer C. Adams and Warren D. Foster's *Heroines of Modern Progress* (New York, 1913); Gamaliel Bradford's *Portraits of American Women* (Boston, 1919) ; Grace Humphreys's *Women in American History* (Indianapolis, 1919) ; Mary R. Parkman's *Heroines of Service* (New York, 1917) ; Virginia Tatnall Peacock's *Famous American Belles of the Nineteenth Century* (Philadelphia, 1901) ; Kate D. Sweetser's *Ten American Girls from History* (New York, 1917) ; Lillian Whiting's *Women Who Have Ennobled Life* (Philadelphia, 1915). Excellent biographies have also appeared of individual women, such as Susan B. Anthony, Margaret Fuller, Clara Barton, Harriet Beecher Stowe and Mary A. Livermore.

CHAPTER VII

THE AMERICAN REVOLUTION

When the representatives of George V rendered homage a few years ago at the tomb of the great disloyalist and rebel of a former century, George Washington, the minds of many Americans reverted, with a sense of bewilderment, to the times when another King George was guiding the destinies of the British nation. The fact is that the average American still accepts without qualification or question the partisan justifications of the struggle for independence which have come down from the actual participants in the affair on the American side. These accounts, colored by the emotions and misunderstandings of the times and designed to arouse the colonists to a warlike pitch against the British government, have formed the basis of the treatments in our school textbooks and have served to perpetuate judgments of the American Revolution which no fair-minded historian can accept today. Indeed, many Americans of the present generation who readily admit that there is much to be said for the southern side in the Civil War condemn as unpatriotic any effort to consider the origins of the War for Independence from a standpoint of scientific historical detachment. Fortunately our conception of patriotism is undergoing revision, for Germany has taught us the danger of teaching propaganda in the guise of history; and the teacher and writer of history today is charged with the responsibility of being as scrupulously fair to other nations as to the United States in dealing with the subject matter of American history.

In yet another way the popular understanding of the revolutionary movement is strangely at fault. We are inclined to think of the Revolution as a spontaneous uprising of the whole colonial population without faction or disagreement among them. Nothing could be farther from the truth according to the testimony of the patriots themselves. Thomas Hutchinson, the royal governor of Massachusetts, declared to a committee of Parliament in 1779 that at the outbreak of the war not one-fifth of the people "had independence in view"; and John Adams, who would scarcely be inclined to understate the number of the patriots, gave his opinion that about one-third of the people were opposed to the measures of the Revolution in all its stages. The great problem of the patriot leaders, Adams admitted in after years, was to keep the spirit of protest and revolt burning with equal intensity in the thirteen colonies or, as he said more crisply, to get the thirteen clocks to strike at the same time.

Nor was the American Revolution the sedate and gentlemanly affair that the popular historians have pictured it. Sydney George Fisher is amply justified in charging that since the people who write histories usually belong to the class who take the side of government in a revolution, they "have accordingly tried to describe a revolution in which all scholarly, refined, and conservative persons might have unhesitatingly taken part." The fact is that the American Revolution, as we now know it to have been, is infinitely more interesting and human, and provocative of patriotism, than the make-believe revolution handed down by tradition.

I

The very term "American Revolution" is not without difficulties and its use has led to misconception and confusion. In letter after letter John Adams tried to teach a headstrong generation some degree of accuracy in the use of an expression of whose meaning they had knowledge only by hearsay. "A history of the first war of the United States is a very different thing from a history of the American Revolution," he wrote in 1815. ". . . The revolution was in the minds of the people, and in the union of the colonies, both of which were accomplished before hostilities commenced. This revolution and union were gradually forming from the years 1760 to 1776." And to another correspondent he wrote: "But what do we mean by the American Revolution? Do we mean the American war? The Revolution was effected before the war commenced. The Revolution was in the minds and hearts of the people."

This distinction is not only valid in point of fact but it offers a helpful avenue of approach for a consideration of the circumstances of the nation's birth. If the period from 1760 to 1776 is not viewed merely as the prelude to the American Revolution, the military struggle may frankly be regarded for what it actually was, namely a war to dismember the British empire, an armed attempt to impose the views of the revolutionists upon the British government and a large section of the colonial population at whatever cost to freedom of opinion or the sanctity of life and property. The major emphasis is thus placed upon the clashing of economic interests and the interplay of mutual prejudices, opposing ideals and personal antagonisms—whether in England or America—which made inevitable in 1776 what was unthinkable in 1760.

Without considering here the remote and latent causes of the revolt, a discussion of the American Revolution may profitably begin with the effort of the British government to reorganize the British empire after the Peace of Paris of 1763. Of this empire the thirteen colonies along the Atlantic seaboard had, by virtue of the recent peace, become but a

small part. British statesmen felt the imperative need of
correcting the slothful and unsystematic methods of colonial
management by which some of the older colonies had been
granted more liberal government than that enjoyed by
organized territories of the United States today, and under
which all the continental American colonies had become
neglectful or defiant of ordinary imperial obligations. There
was a need that all the outlying British possessions should
be more closely integrated for purposes of administration
and that the far-flung empire should be defended against the
ambitions of England's traditional enemies, France and
Spain, as well as against the restlessness of the alien subject
populations. The problem which confronted the British
government was much more difficult than the questions of
colonial organization with which the American government
has wrestled since 1898; but the American adventure in
imperialism, involving, as it did, the question of whether the
Constitution followed the flag, should enable Americans of
the present generation to view with sympathy the British
experiment of the eighteenth century.

The king's ministers glimpsed too narrowly the task before
them. What they regarded as an exercise in the mechanics
of legislation was really an innovation in imperial relations
that touched the dynamic currents of colonial opinion and
colonial economic interest at many vital points. Moreover,
their attempt was being made at a time when the colonies
were, for the first time in their history, relieved of their
most urgent need of British protection by the removal of
the French menace from their frontiers. Under the earlier
imperial policy of "salutary neglect" the colonies had grown
in wealth and political experience, so that by the middle of
the eighteenth century they had become accustomed to conduct themselves toward England as substantially equal
commonwealths in a federation united by a common mon-

arch. For the colonists the new imperial policy involved unaccustomed tax burdens, the loss of trading profits, and limitations of self-government—advantages that were none the less precious because derived from an unwritten and unsanctioned constitution. Fundamentally, the great problem of the decade following the peace of 1763 was the problem of the reconciliation of centralized imperial control with colonial home rule. This, unfortunately, was never clearly perceived by the dominant element on either side, the issue being obscured by a blind officialism on the one hand and by an unillumined particularism on the other.

Perhaps the problem was incapable of solution; but we can see now that the best opportunity for a satisfactory outcome lay in the application to the situation of an enlightened statecraft on the part of Great Britain. To this the posture of political affairs in that country was not well adapted. George III, who had ascended the throne in 1760, was already devoting every political and financial resource in his power to the task of converting the British government from an aristocracy of great Whig families into a personal autocracy. His Parliament and ministers did not seek to reflect the aspirations of the British public and therefore lacked a potent incentive for the formulation of a conciliatory program of colonial subordination. The minority in Parliament represented by Pitt and Burke readily identified the struggle of the colonists to preserve home rule with their own struggle in England against autocratic rule. Pitt was thinking primarily of Englishmen at home when he exclaimed on the occasion of the Stamp Act commotions: "I rejoice that America has resisted." If his counsel had been followed, it is possible that the colonial revolt might have been forestalled by some plan of imperial federation.

II

With this brief glance at affairs in Great Britain it is now possible to consider the situation in America. Conditions there were both simpler and more complex than the traditional accounts represent. In place of thirteen units of population thinking alike on most public questions, there were in fact three major bodies of population, differentiated by physiographical conditions, economic interest and political ideals. The communities on the coastal plain from New Hampshire to Pennsylvania constituted one of these divisions; the settlements of the tidewater region from Maryland to Georgia formed another; and the third, less clearly defined geographically, consisted of the frontier districts of many of the provinces. These three divisions represented modes of living and mental attitudes much more fundamental than those signified by the artificial groupings of population within provincial boundaries.

The first area consisted of the commercial colonies; the dominant economic interest of the people was the carrying trade and shipbuilding. In the port towns of New England and the Middle Colonies great mercantile families had grown up, who had gained their wealth through smuggling with the West Indies or else through legitimate trading enterprises that embraced the entire world. The merchants were keenly alive to the golden benefits which membership in the British empire had always yielded; and like the business interests of any generation or clime, they might be expected to combat any effort to tamper with the source of their profits. For the merchants the unfolding of the new imperial program involved a very serious interference with their customary trading operations; and during the decade from 1764 to 1774 their constant aim was to effect a restoration of the commercial conditions of 1763. As a class they entertained neither earlier nor later the idea of independence, for withdrawal from the British empire meant for them the loss of vital business advantages without corresponding benefits in a world organized on a basis of imperial trading systems. They strove to obtain the most favorable terms possible within the empire but not to leave it. Indeed, they viewed with no small concern the growth of republican feeling and leveling sentiment which the controversy occasioned.

The great ports of the north—Boston, New York, Philadelphia, Newport—bore eloquent testimony to the prosperity of the mercantile class; and on the continuance of this prosperity depended the livelihood of the mechanics and petty shopkeepers of the towns and, to a lesser degree, the wellbeing of the farmers whose cereals and meats were exported to the West Indies. This proletarian element was not inclined by temperament to that self-restraint in movements of popular protest which was ever the *arrière pensée* of the merchant class; and being for the most part unenfranchised, they expressed their sentiments most naturally through boisterous mass meetings and mob demonstrations.

In the second of the three areas, the tidewater region of the South, colonial capital was invested almost exclusively in plantation production; and commerce was carried on chiefly by British mercantile houses and their American agents, the factors. The only town in the plantation provinces that could compare with the teeming ports of the North was Charleston, for the prevailing form of life was rural in character. All political activity sprang from the periodical meetings of the great landed proprietors in the assemblies. Under the wasteful system of marketing, which the apparent plenty of plantation life made possible, the planters found themselves treading a morass of indebtedness to British merchants from which it seemed that nothing less than virtual repudiation could extricate them. As Jefferson testified, "these debts had become hereditary from father to son, for many generations, so that the planters were a species of property annexed to certain mercantile houses in London." In the last quarter of a century prior to independence the provincial assemblies passed a succession of lax bankruptcy acts and other legislation detrimental to non-resident creditors; but these laws nearly always ran afoul the royal veto. This fact, together with the sturdy sense of self-determination which the peculiar social system fostered, made the plantation provinces ready to resent any fresh exercise of parliamentary authority over the colonies, such as the new imperial policy involved.   Georgia, the infant colony of the thirteen, still dependent upon the mother government for subsidies and for protection against a serious Indian menace, was less affected by these considerations, and indeed lagged behind her southern sisters throughout the revolutionary period.

On the western fringe of the two coastal areas lay an irregular belt of back-country settlements whose economy and psychological outlook were almost as distinctive as those of the two tidewater regions.   Certainly the western sections of many of the provinces had grievances in common and resembled each other more than they did the older sections with which they were associated by provincial boundaries. These pioneer settlements extended north and south, up and down the valleys between the fall line of the rivers and mountains, from New England to Georgia.   Outside of New England the majority of the settlers were dissenters of non-English strains, mostly German and Scotch Irish; but throughout the long frontier the people cultivated small isolated farms and entertained democratic ideas in harmony with the equalitarian conditions in which they lived.   As has already been pointed out elsewere in this volume, the back-country inhabitants in many of the provinces had long been discriminated against by the older settlements in the matter of representation in the assemblies, the administration of justice and the incidence of taxation; and they were thus familiar, of their own experience, with all the arguments which the Revolution was to make popular against non-representative government and unjust taxation. Being self-sustaining communities economically, their zeal for popular rights was in no wise alloyed by the embarrassment of their pocketbooks. Although out of harmony with the popular leaders of the seaboard in both the commercial and plantation provinces on many matters of domestic politics, they could join forces with them in protest against the new imperial policy; and they brought to the controversy a moral conviction and bold philosophy which gave great impetus to the agitation for independence.[1]

The history of the American Revolution is, in very large part, the story of the reaction of these three sections to the successive acts of the British government and of their interaction upon each other. The merchants of the commercial colonies were the most seriously affected by the new imperial policy and at the outset assumed the leadership of the colonial movement of protest. They were closely seconded by the planters of the south as soon as enough time had elapsed to make clear to the latter the implications of the issue of home rule for which the merchants stood. The democratic farmers of the interior, more or less out of contact with the political currents of the seaboard, were slower to take part; and it is largely true that their measure of participation varied inversely to the degree of their isolation. Patrick Henry and his fellow burgesses from the western counties

[1] In Georgia, however, the frontier settlers were pro-British in their sympathies because of their dependence on the home government for protection against the ever-present menace of the Creeks. Twenty-five years ago Professor J. S. Bassett, in a discriminating study, showed why the people of the interior counties of North Carolina became loyalists when the issue of independence was raised. Had the friction between the interior democracies and the coastal minorities developed to the point of armed rebellion in other provinces prior to 1776, the back-country folk might everywhere have thrown their weight on the side of the British government and thus have defeated the Revolution.

of Virginia began to undermine the conservatism of the tide-water statesmen as early as 1765, but the Germans and Scotch-Irish of Pennsylvania did not make their influence fully felt until the critical days of 1774-1775.

A complicating factor in the revolutionary movement was supplied by the religious conditions existing in the colonies, of which only brief mention can be made here. Religious antagonisms were of chief importance in accentuating differences between the colonies and the mother country that already existed because of economic and geographic reasons. This is not gainsaying that sectarian feeling, which had been an important motive in colonization, played a larger part in shaping the political conduct of people in colonial times than it has at any later period of American history. The great majority of the colonists belonged to the dissenting sects; and for historic reasons it was natural that there should be more or less distrust and jealousy felt by them toward adherents of the Church of England, among whom the royal officials and their hangers-on were prominently to be found. Indeed, the two hundred and fifty Episcopal clergymen officiating in the colonies on the eve of the Revolutionary War had all received ordination in England, and most of those in the northern provinces were pensioners of an English missionary society. The antagonism to England on this score was undoubtedly increased during the revolutionary period in many parts of America by the persistent rumor that the English government was planning to send bishops to the colonies. It was John Adams's belief, expressed in after years, that the widespread dread of an Anglican episcopate and an established church contributed "as much as any other cause" to sharpening the keen edge of popular antipathy against the mother country. As the radical party grew stronger, Anglican clergymen had to decide whether they would observe the patriotic fast days proclaimed as a protest against England and, finally, whether they would omit in their services the prayers for the king. Those who persisted were in many cases roughly handled.

The Congregational ministers of New England were active agents in keeping alive colonial discontent. It was a royal office-holder who noted that the women of the flocks aided American manufactures by spinning flax six days of the week and "on the seventh, the Parsons took their turns and spun out their prayers and sermons to a long thread of Politics." The only organic and official action taken by a religious denomination in behalf of the American cause was that of the Presbyterians, who delegated the only minister in the Congress of 1776 to give their vote for independence. Some insight into contemporary opinion of the relation of religion to politics is afforded, for instance, by the customary usage of the terms Presbyterians and Episcopalians by Judge Thomas Jones, the New York loyalist, as almost synonymous with the terms rebels and loyalists. Joseph Galloway, another loyalist, who had attained high office in Pennsylvania by the suffrages of his fellow-colonists, ascribed the colonial revolt largely to the machinations of the Presbyterians and the New England Congregationalists and believed that the alliance formed by the two sects in 1764 was a factor of prime importance in the promotion of the spirit for independence. Such generalizations may be pushed too far, however, for numerous exceptions may be noted. Thus the Episcopalians of the southern tidewater region, where the ministers were supported locally, were as strongly opposed to the importation of English prelates as were the Congregationalists of New England, and many of the clergy and laity took active part in the Revolutionary War.

III

The new British policy of imperial control assumed its first form under George Grenville (1764-1765). The numerous regulations of trade, which need not be analyzed here, injured fair traders and smuggling merchants alike and threatened bankruptcy to the great mercantile houses of Boston, New York and Philadelphia. The prohibition of colonial legal tender added to their woes and indeed made the hard-pressed planters of the South sharers in the general distress. The Stamp Act, with its far-reaching taxes burdensome alike to merchant and farmer, sealed the union of commercial and plantation provinces at the same time that it afforded an opportunity for placing the colonial argument on constitutional grounds; and because of the character of the taxation, it rallied to the colonial position the powerful support of the lawyers and newspaper proprietors. The plan of the British to garrison their new acquisitions in America and to station a few detachments of troops in the older colonies was, in the feverish state of the public mind, envisaged as a brazen attempt to intimidate the colonies into submission. The merchants of some of the ports, intent on restoring the conditions of their former prosperity, adopted resolutions of non-importation; and little recking the future, they aroused the populace to a sense of British injustice, even to the extent of countenancing and instigating mob excesses and the destruction of property.

In the end Parliament resolved upon the passage of certain remedial laws (1766), an outcome which, from the standpoint of the more radical colonists, can be regarded as little more than a compromise. The Stamp Act was indeed repealed and important alterations were made in the trade regulations; but the Currency Act, the regulations against smuggling and the provisions for a standing army remained unchanged. In addition the Declaratory Act was passed; and the new molasses duty was an unvarnished application of the principle of "taxation without representation" announced in the Declaratory Act. The rejoicing of the colonists can be explained only on the ground that the merchants of the North dominated colonial opinion; and like practical men of affairs, they were contemptuous, if not fearful, of disputes turning upon questions of abstract right.

The passage of the Townshend Acts in 1767 was the second attempt of Parliament to reconstruct the empire in the spirit of the Grenville experiment. Again the merchants of the commercial colonies perceived themselves as the class whose interests were chiefly imperiled; but sobered by the mob outrages of Stamp Act days, they resolved to guide the course of American opposition in orderly and peaceful channels. They, therefore, began an active agitation for corrective legislation through merchants' petitions and legislative memorials to Parliament; and after much questioning of each other's good faith they succeeded in developing an elaborate system of commercial boycott, which united the commercial colonies in an effort to secure the repeal of the objectionable laws. After a year or so this movement in a much modified form spread to the plantation provinces, where, under the leadship of Washington and other planters, it was employed as a means of preventing the landed aristocracy from falling more deeply into the toils of their British creditors.

Meantime the merchants began to see that in organizing their communities for peaceful resistance to Great Britain they were unavoidably releasing disruptive forces which, like Frankenstein's monster, they were finding it impossible to control. The failure of non-importation to effect swift redress compelled the merchant bodies, as the months passed, to depend more and more upon the tumultuous methods of the proletariat in order to keep wavering merchants true to the cause. Increasing friction between smuggling merchants and customs officers also produced outbreaks of mob violence in many provinces, and led by a broad, smooth road to such distressing affairs as the Boston "Massacre" on the one hand

and to the destruction of the revenue cutter *Gaspee* on the other. As the political agitators and turbulent elements gained the upper hand, the contest began to assume more clearly the form of a crusade for constitutional and natural rights; and when word arrived in May, 1770, that Parliament had repealed all the Townshend duties except the trifling tax on tea, the merchants found it difficult to reassert their earlier control and to stop a movement that had lost all significance for hard-headed men of business. The merchants of New York, under the leadership of their newly formed Chamber of Commerce, were the first who were able to wrench loose from their enforced alliance with the radicals; and the cancellation of their boycott resolutions was soon followed by similar action in the ports of Philadelphia and Boston. The plantation provinces were coolly left in the lurch notwithstanding that Parliament had not receded from its position of arbitrary taxation, and the movement there soon died of inanition.

The two or three years that followed the partial repeal of the Townshend duties were, for the most part, years of material prosperity and political calm. The merchants had grown to look askance at a doctrine of home rule which left it uncertain who was to rule at home. As a class they eagerly agreed with the merchant-politician Thomas Cushing that "high points about the supreme authority of Parliament" should best "fall asleep." And so—John Hancock as well as Isaac Low—they deserted politics for business, even to the extent of importing dutied tea which people imbibed everywhere except at Philadelphia and New York, where local conditions made it possible for merchants to offer the cheaper Dutch tea to consumers. The sun of the radicals had suffered an eclipse; and quietly biding their time, they began to apply to their own following the lessons of organization that they had learned from the "mercantile dons." In the commercial colonies Sam Adams—"that Matchiavel of

Chaos" as Thomas Hutchinson loved to call him—sought, through the establishment of town committees of correspondence, to unite the workingmen of the port towns and the farmers of the rural districts in political action; and the burgesses of Virginia launched their plan of a provincial committee of correspondence that might give uncensored expression to the political grievances of the southern planters. Under the spur of fresh irritations both plans were to spread to the other provinces where, by supplementing each other, they came in time to form the basis of the radical party organization throughout British America.

In May, 1773, a new tea act was passed by Parliament, which stampeded the merchants into joining forces once more with the political radicals and irresponsible elements. This new law, if put into operation, would have enabled the great East India Company to monopolize the colonial tea market to the exclusion of both American smugglers and law-abiding tea traders. Alarmed at this prospect and fearful lest further monopolistic privileges in trade might follow from the success of the present experiment, the colonial merchant class joined in an active popular agitation for the purpose of preventing the landing of any of the tea importations of the East India Company. Though their efforts for a vigorous but restrained opposition met with substantial success elsewhere, they were overreached at Boston by the superior management of Sam Adams and the unintelligence of Governor Hutchinson, whose sons were tea consignees; and the British trading company became the involuntary host at a tea party costing £15,000.

IV

The Boston Tea Party marked a turning point in the course of events both in America and Britain. In both countries it was regarded by the merchants and moderates as a lawless destruction of private property and an act of wanton defiance which no self-respecting government could wisely ignore. Plainly the issue between the colonies and the mother country had ceased to be one of mere trading advantage. Outside of New England, colonial opinion, so far as it expressed itself, greeted the event with a general disapproval and apprehension. In the mother country Parliament proceeded to the passage of the severe disciplinary measures of 1774.

The effect of this punitive legislation cannot be overestimated, for it convinced many colonists who had disapproved of the Boston vandalism that the greater guilt now lay on the side of Parliament. "They look upon the chastisement of Boston to be purposely rigorous, and held up by way of intimidation to all America . . ." wrote Governor Penn from Philadelphia. "Their delinquency in destroying the East India Company's tea is lost in the attention given to what is here called the too severe punishment of shutting up the port, altering the Constitution, and making an Act, as they term it, screening the officers and soldiers shedding American blood." From this time on there occurred in the several provinces a contest for the control of public policy between the moderates on the one hand and the radicals or extremists on the other, the former receiving aid and comfort from the royal officials and their circle of friends. This line of cleavage is unmistakable in the case of practically every province.

The moderates as a group wanted to pay for the tea destroyed and to propose to Parliament an act of union which should automatically dispose of all controversial questions for the future. The radicals were opposed to compromise and as a class desired a comprehensive and drastic boycott of Great Britain with which to exact from Parliament recognition of the colonial claim to complete home rule. Both parties were willing to make a trial of strength in an intercolonial congress; and after bitter contests in each province to control the *personnel* of the irregularly elected delegations, the First Continental Congress assembled in Philadelphia in September, 1774. In this notable gathering the moderates discovered to their dismay that they were outnumbered; and, in the disconsolate phrase of a Maryland merchant, "Adams, with his crew, and the haughty Sultans of the South juggled the whole conclave of the Delegates." Indeed, this extra-legal body, by adopting the Association for the establishment of non-importation, non-consumption and non-exportation, decreed that the merchants of America should sacrifice their trade for the benefit of a cause from which they had become alienated; and the radicals in Congress provided for spreading a network of committees over the continent to insure obedience to their decree.

In the popular conventions called prior to the First Continental Congress and in the provincial meetings that were held to ratify its doings, the people from the back-country counties of many provinces were, for the first time, admitted to that full measure of representation which had long been denied them by the unequal system of apportionment in the colonial assemblies. Deeply stirred by the political slogans of the tidewater radicals, they ranged themselves by their side and lent momentum to an agitation that was hastening toward independence. In closely divided provinces like Pennsylvania and South Carolina their voice was undoubtedly the decisive factor.

The proceedings of the First Continental Congress were received with mixed feelings by the colonists. The moderates who had lingered in the popular movement in order to control it began to withdraw, although it required the outbreak of hostilities at Lexington or even the Declaration

of Independence to convince some that their efforts could be
of no avail. The merchants perforce acquiesced in the regulations of the Association, which, in the early months, were
not without profit to them. The popular committees of the
coast towns, formerly controlled by the merchants, began to
fall into the hands of the democratic mechanic class. In
New York, Boston and Philadelphia alike, "nobodies" and
"unimportant persons" succeeded to power; and even in
Savannah, Governor Wright declared that "the Parochial
Committee are a Parcel of the Lowest People, Chiefly Carpenters, Shoemakers, Blacksmiths, &c. . . ." Flushed with
success, the radical leaders busied themselves with consolidating their following in town and country through the
creation of committees of observation and provincial committees and conventions. Little wonder was it that, in this
changed aspect of public affairs, a worthy minister of
Charleston, S. C., should be dismissed by his congregation
"for his audacity in . . . saying that *mechanics* and country
clowns had no right to dispute about politics, or what kings,
lords and commons had done," or that the *Newport Mercury*
of September 26, 1774, in reporting the affair should add:
"All *such* divines should be taught to know that mechanics
and country clowns (infamously so called) are the real and
absolute masters of king, lords, commons and priests. . . ."
    Events had reached a stage where the extremists in both
countries were in control. What Chatham and Joseph Galloway might have adjusted to their mutual satisfaction could
not be rationally discussed by North and Sam Adams.
Under the circumstances it was inevitable that the policy of
commercial coercion, adopted by the First Continental Congress, should soon be superseded by armed warfare as the
weapon of the radicals, and that open rebellion should in
turn give way to a struggle for independence. The thronging events of these later months are familiar enough in out-

line and need not be recounted here. The key to these times is to be found in the fact that the radical elements were a minority of the colonial population and that only through their effective organization and aggressive tactics could they hope to whip into line the great body of timid and indifferent people who lacked either organization or a definite program.

The successive steps leading to independence were not taken without great mental travail, without suspicion of each other's motives, without sordid consultation of economic advantage, or without doubt as to the rectitude of the course or fear of the consequences. Thousands of men of recognized social and business connections, who had been active in the earlier agitation for colonial home rule, opposed separation and left their native land rather than be witnesses to its undoing. One of these earnestly warned his countrymen in April, 1776, that "a set of men whom nobody knows . . . are attempting to hurry you into a scene of anarchy; their scheme of Independence is visionary; they know not themselves what they mean by it." On the other hand, John Adams found food for sober reflection in the rejoicing of a horse-jockey neighbor of his: "Oh! Mr. Adams, what great things have you and your colleagues done for us! . . . There are no courts of justice now in this Province and I hope there never will be another." Many a man of property, like the patriot Henry Laurens, wept when he listened to the reading of the Declaration of Independence, or else, like John Ross of Philadelphia, "loved ease and Madeira much better than liberty and strife," and decided to be neutral in the struggle.

The real significance of the American Revolution, however, is not to be measured in terms of the conflicting emotions and purposes of those who, wittingly or unwittingly, helped to bring it about. What great issue in history has

not been scarred by sordid motives, personal antagonisms
and unintelligent decisions? Fundamentally the American
Revolution represented the refusal of a self-reliant people to
permit their natural and normal energies to be confined
against their will, whether by an irresponsible imperial government or by the ruling minorities in their midst.

V

The popular view of the Revolution as a great forensic
controversy over abstract governmental rights will not bear
close scrutiny. How could a people, who for ten years
were not in agreement among themselves as to their aims
and aspirations, be said to possess a common political philosophy? Before assuming that Otis or Dickinson or Thomson
Mason spoke the voice of the colonists, the historian must
first ascertain what class or section of the population each
represented and how widespread its influence was. At best,
an exposition of the political theories of the anti-parlia-
mentary party is an account of their retreat from one strategic position to another. Abandoning a view that based
their liberties on charter grants, they appealed to their constitutional rights as Englishmen; and when that position
became untenable, they invoked the doctrine of the rights of
man. Likewise, their sincere devotion to the kingship was
not open to question through ten years of controversy, when
suddenly, a few months before the end, the English immigrant Tom Paine in the pamphlet *Common Sense* jerked the
bandages from their eyes and revealed the goal of republicanism and independence at which they had already arrived
in fact. Without discounting in any way the propagandist
value attaching to popular shibboleths as such, it may as well
be admitted that the colonists would have lost their case if
the decision had turned upon an impartial consideration of
the legal principles involved.

Some of the difficulties in arriving at the truth concerning the Tories may also be apparent. Prior to 1774, it would be a distortion of the facts to picture the country as divided into two major parties, one representing blind attachment to the doctrine of parliamentary supremacy and the other a blind partisanship of the doctrine of colonial home rule. Rather, the American colonists, united in desiring a large degree of colonial autonomy, differed in opinion as to what limitations of home rule were admissable and as to what methods of opposition were best adapted to secure the relief they desired. In this period every true American was a loyalist in the sense that he favored the permanent integrity of the British empire. Indeed, to regard "Tory" and "loyalist" as equivalent terms would place the historian in the predicament of classing practically the entire colonial population as Tories until 1776.

Excepting always the royal official class and its social connections, the terms "Tory" and "patriot" became intelligible for the first time when the First Continental Congress set forth the radical program in the Continental Association and stigmatized those who opposed the program as "enemies of American liberty." As the radical program advanced from commercial coercion to armed rebellion, the local committees applied a new test of patriotism, that of allegiance to the rebellion. It should be remembered, however, that the original object of this armed uprising was not independence but, as often in English history, a change in ministerial policy. With the Declaration of Independence patriotism became for the first time synonymous with disloyalty to England. Many men, like Daniel Dulany and Joseph Galloway, who may rightly be considered broad-minded patriotic Americans in the earlier years of the revolutionary contest, became Tories by the new definitions; and John Dickinson is the example of a man who narrowly escaped the infamy of not making up his mind in favor of independence as quickly as the majority of the Second Continental Congress. The disorders of the Confederation period were a justification of the decision made by the Tories; but the reconstructive forces in American society which built a nationalistic republic under the Constitution have eloquently vindicated the choice made by the revolutionists.

BIBLIOGRAPHICAL NOTE

A history of the histories of the American Revolution should go far toward revealing the ideals and purposes which have governed historical writing in this country in the various periods of the past and should explain why the Revolution has had to be re-discovered and re-constructed from the source materials by the present generation of historians. Sydney George Fisher has undertaken such a survey in his essay "The Legendary and Myth-Making Process in Histories of the American Revolution," originally published in the *Proceedings* of the American Philosophical Society, vol. 51 (1912), pp. 53-76, and reprinted in the *History Teacher's Magazine*, vol. iv (1913), pp. 63-71, and elsewhere. Pertinent information on the same subject may be found in the "Critical Essay on Authorities" in George Elliott Howard's *Preliminaries of the Revolution, 1763-1775* (in *The American Nation: a History*, vol. 8; New York, 1905).

Charles Altschul's study, *The American Revolution in Our School Text-Books* (New York, 1917), is excellent, so far as it goes, in showing the one-sided and misleading treatment of the American Revolution contained in the school histories of a generation ago.

Reappraisement of the conflict by historians using scientific methods began in the nineties and the most valuable work along this line has been done since 1900. The pioneer labors of Charles McLean Andrews and Herbert Levi Osgood in showing that the history of the colonies must be studied as an integral part of British imperial history were of basic importance to this reappraisement. Their point of view, arrived at as the result of independent studies, was first presented in the form of papers before the American Historical Association in 1898. See "American Colonial History, 1690-1750" by Professor Andrews and "The Study of American Colonial History" by Professor Osgood in the *Annual Report* of the American Historical Association for 1898, pp. 46-60, 63-73. The actual, as contrasted with the fancied, effects of the British acts of trade and navigation on the colonies were first set forth by George Louis Beer in his monograph *The Commercial Policy of England toward the American Colonies* (New York, 1893), developed by the English economist, W. J. Ashley, in his *Surveys*

Historic and Economic (New York, 1900), pp. 309-360, and further amplified by George Louis Beer in a series of volumes entitled *British Colonial Policy, 1754-1765* (New York, 1907), *The Origins of the British Colonial System, 1578-1660* (New York, 1908), and *The Old Colonial System, 1660-1754* (New York, 1912). The sectional and economic basis of colonial discontent, ignored or misunderstood by the earlier historians, has been the subject of careful study in such works as Mellen Chamberlain's "The Revolution Impending" in Justin Winsor's *Narrative and Critical History of America* (8 v.; Boston, 1884-1889), vol. vi, pp. 1-112; William Wirt Henry's *Patrick Henry; Life, Correspondence and Speeches* (3 v.; New York, 1891); John Spencer Bassett's "The Regulators of North Carolina (1756-1771)" in the *Annual Report* of the American Historical Association for 1894, pp. 141-212; C. H. Lincoln's *The Revolutionary Movement in Pennsylvania, 1760-1776* (Philadelphia, 1901); Carl L. Becker's *The History of Political Parties in the Province of New York, 1760-1776* (Madison, 1909); H. J. Eckenrode's *The Revolution in Virginia* (Boston, 1916); Charles McLean Andrews's "The Boston Merchants and the Non-Importation Movement" in *Publications* of the Colonial Society of Massachusetts, vol. xix (1917), pp. 159-259; Arthur Meier Schlesinger's *The Colonial Merchants and the American Revolution, 1763-1776* (New York, 1918); and Edith Anna Bailey's *Influences toward Radicalism in Connecticut, 1754-1775* (Northampton, 1920). Some light has been thrown upon the organization and methods of the popular party by Henry B. Dawson's *The Sons of Liberty in New York* (New York, 1859); Richard Frothingham's *The Rise of the Republic of the United States* (Boston, 1881); and E. D. Collins's "Committees of Correspondence of the American Revolution" in the *Annual Report* of the American Historical Association for 1901, vol. i, pp. 243-271. The activities and views of the loyalist element of the population received partisan justification in such early works as Lorenzo Sabine's *Biographical Sketches of Loyalists of the American Revolution* (2 v.; Boston, 1864) and Egerton Ryerson's *Loyalists of America and Their Times* (2 v.; Toronto, 1880), and have since been studied from a disinterested viewpoint by George E. Ellis in "The Loyalists" in Winsor's *Narrative and Critical History* (cited above), vol. vii, pp. 185-214, by Moses Coit Tyler in *The Literary History of the American Revolution, 1763-1783* (2 v.; New York, 1897), by Alexander C. Flick in *Loyalism in New York in the American Revolution* (New York, 1901), and by Claude Halstead Van Tyne in *Loyalists in the American Revolution* (New York, 1902). Religious and sectarian influences in the revolutionary movement have received attention in W. P. Breed's *Presbyterians and the Revolution* (Philadelphia, 1876); Mellen Chamberlain's *John Adams, the Statesman of the American Revolution, with Other Essays* (Boston, 1884); George E. Ellis's "The Sentiment of Independence, Its Growth and Consummation" in Winsor's *Narrative and Critical History* (cited above), vol. vi, pp. 231-255; Arthur Lyon Cross's

The Anglican Episcopate and the American Colonies (Cambridge, 1902); Martin I. J. Griffin's *Catholics and the American Revolution* (3 v.; Ridley Park, Pa., 1907); and Claude Halstead Van Tyne's "Influence of the Clergy, and of Religious and Sectarian Forces, on the American Revolution" in the *American Historical Review,* vol. xix (1913), pp. 44-64.

The best general summaries of the American Revolution today are Sydney George Fisher's *The Struggle for American Independence* (2 v.; Philadelphia, 1908); Edward Channing's *A History of the United States,* vol. iii (New York, 1912); Carl Lotus Becker's *Beginnings of the American People* (Boston, 1912), chaps. v-vi. A forthcoming book by Clarence W. Alvord under the projected title of *Imperial Muddlers and the American Revolution: an Essay about Propaganda and Politics* promises to be of great importance in this connection. Of the English accounts the best continues to be W. E. H. Lecky's *History of England in the Eighteenth Century* (8 v.; London, 1878-1890), vol. iii, chap. xii, edited in a separate volume by J. A. Woodburn under the title *The American Revolution, 1763-1783* (New York, 1898).

An important conference devoted to a discussion of our present knowledge of the American Revolution was held in conjunction with the recent meeting of the American Historical Association at St. Louis (December, 1921). The principal papers were presented by Professor Van Tyne and Professor Alvord.

CHAPTER VIII

ECONOMIC ASPECTS OF THE MOVEMENT FOR THE CONSTITUTION

I

In the year 1781 the Articles of Confederation were ratified by the last of the thirteen states and went into effect as the first written constitution of the federal union. In the same year occurred the battle of Yorktown, which from a military point of view assured independence to the struggling colonies. The war was practically at an end. Emerging from six years of armed conflict, the young republic had to solve even more difficult problems in the six years of peace that followed.

The population was deeply affected by *post bellum* unrest, and public life gave evidence of that lowering of moral tone that seems an inevitable aftermath of a great war. The frame of government under which the new nation made its start had been drawn up by men laboring under a desperate fear of centralized power as embodied in the British government and who were determined that the new federal government, notwithstanding its different source of authority, should exercise as little power as possible. Under the circumstances the Articles of Confederation could hardly be more than a feeble instrument. All essential powers remained with the individual states; and it was only by virtue of an extraordinary majority vote that the general government might perform certain carefully stipulated functions in behalf of all the states. Obviously, such a government was unfitted to cope with the social and political disturbances that were to mark the period.

The instability of the times were far-reaching in its effects and pervaded not only the operations of the state and federal governments but also the life of the people in their social and business relations. The ill-paid revolutionary army, seething with unrest, was a prolific source of uneasiness. The main body of the troops were encamped at Newburg on the Hudson, and they faced a return to their home and families, after their arduous campaigns, "without a settlement of their accounts, or a farthing of money in their pockets." Only the personal intervention of Washington at a critical juncture prevented the consummation of a plot to effect a forcible presentation of their claims to Congress. A band of mutinous Pennsylvania troops stationed at Lancaster did indeed march on Philadelphia and frightened Congress into changing the seat of government to Princeton.

On the trans-Alleghany frontier the spirit of lawlessness also stalked abroad. For three years backwoodsmen living in what is now eastern Tennessee defied their parent state of North Carolina and, on their own cognizance, demanded admission into the union as the State of Franklin. The integrity of Virginia was likewise menaced by a movement for independent statehood among the settlers of Kentucky. Congress sought to promote further settlement of the western country under national supervision by the Ordinances of 1784 and 1785; but none but the most daring were willing to brave the perils of frontier life without military protection against the savages.

The public finances were in unbelievably bad shape. Continental paper money had depreciated to a point where an enterprising barber found it a matter of economy to paper his shop with scrip; and the general disgust resulted in the coining of a phrase that has survived to our own time—"not worth a continental." Lacking taxing power, the Confederation government was unable to pay the interest on the national debt, and the common selling price of national securities in good markets varied from one-tenth to one-sixth of their face value, sometimes falling as low as one to twenty. State securities were depreciated almost as badly.

Commerce and business were in a languishing condition. The lack of a stable circulating medium was a contributing factor but other conditions were equally unfavorable to the conduct of business. It proved impossible for the feeble Confederation government to re-establish the old commercial relations with Great Britain and the British Empire, whence had sprung the abundant prosperity of the colonial merchants and shipbuilders. Spain, the mistress of Louisiana and the Floridas, spurned all efforts to find an outlet for our inland trade through opening up the mouth of the Mississippi. The infant manufactures which had sprung up during the war were being destroyed by the price-cutting competition of British manufacturers; and the Confederation lacked power to stimulate domestic industries by a protective tariff. Strangest of all to Americans of today, commercial intercourse among the states of the union was embarrassed and impeded by restrictions and tariffs imposed by the various states upon each other; and again Congress was impotent to take any measures to improve the situation.

The men who suffered the direct and immediate effects of the derangement of business and commerce were the common people throughout the states, who had no surplus upon which to fall back in times of financial stringency. In the early years of the Confederation period some parts of the country had enjoyed a degree of prosperity; but each succeeding year brought an increasing measure of hard times. By the years 1785 and 1786 the country was in a condition of pronounced depression. Money was scarce, crops were rotting in the ground, and poor people were reduced to the expedient of barter. The debtor classes everywhere turned to their state governments for relief from the scarcity of specie. If the cause of their difficulties was the lack of money, then, they reasoned, let the government manufacture more money and put an end to the hardships of the poor. However naïve this solution may seem to us today, we should remember that it was the natural reaction of a people who found themselves in desperate economic straits without any other proposals for their relief. Along with these paper money demands went others which, in the language of Luther Martin of Maryland, were designed "to prevent the wealthy creditor and the moneyed man from totally destroying the poor, though even industrious, debtor." Of this class were measures to suspend the collection of debts ("stay laws") and acts declaring cattle and produce the equivalent of money when offered in payment of debts.

In all the states political contests began to take the form of struggles between the debtor and creditor classes—that is, between the small farmers and mechanic classes on the one hand and the merchant and capitalist group on the other. The paper money men carried the legislatures of seven states in elections of 1786, being unsuccessful only in Virginia, Delaware, Maryland, Connecticut, New Hampshire and Massachusetts. In New Hampshire several hundred men, armed with muskets, swords and staves, entered Exeter where the legislature was sitting and demanded a release from taxes and an issue of paper money. The lower house wavered but, the Senate standing firm, the rebels were routed the next day. The most alarming uprising took place in Massachusetts, a revolt that took six months to suppress. The adjournment of the state legislature in July, 1786, without authorizing any measures of relief for debtors led to mob demonstrations which prevented the courts from sitting in several of the larger districts. Encouraged by these successes, a motley army of insurgents formed under the leadership of Daniel Shays, a veteran of Bunker Hill, and they set forth to plunder the national arsenal at Springfield as preparatory to further measures. As the legislature was not in session and there were no funds to pay the state troops, a number of wealthy gentlemen loaned the necessary funds for this purpose; and prompt action on the part of General Lincoln prevented the breaking out of a civil war.

Echoes of the Shays uprising rang throughout the country. What had occurred in Massachusetts might easily be repeated, with more disastrous results, in other states. Moreover, the troubles in Massachusetts had been accompanied by the enunciation of doctrines in some quarters that far outran paper money vagaries. Mass meetings in various towns and counties had broached the doctrines that taxation ought to be eliminated as an unnecessary burden, and that all property should be held in common since all had made sacrifices to save it from England. The very foundations of society seemed threatened. Washington, who cannot be regarded as an alarmist, expressed the thought of many responsible and conservative people when he wrote: "There are combustibles in every State which a spark might set fire to. . . . I feel . . . infinitely more than I can express to you, for the disorders which have arisen in these States. Good God! Who, besides a Tory, could have foreseen, or a Briton, predicted them?"

II

The instability and tumult of the times drove home to the substantial classes of the population the imperative need for a stronger form of national government. Some of these men were animated by motives of disinterested patriotism, their love of country being outraged by the affronts offered

America by foreign nations, in particular by the fact that Great Britain and Spain continued to occupy western territory which had been ceded to the United States by the treaty of peace of 1783. Others were by temperament repelled by the radicalism and lawlessness that prevailed under the Articles and were inclined to favor any movement which promised a strong hand at the helm of state. Religious and racial sympathies were also an indirect and not negligible factor in consolidating the opposing groups in their attitude toward the Articles of Confederation. But of all the motives that caused men to strive for a more vigorous national government the most potent was undoubtedly the desire to re-establish conditions under which property rights and contracts might be secure, investments be safe, and commerce and business prosper.

It is with the economic aspects of the movement for the Constitution that the present discussion is concerned since this phase of the subject has, until recently, been largely neglected by the historians. No discriminating reader need feel that such a presentation carries with it the imputation of ignoble or unworthy motives to the Fathers of the Constitution; rather, it forms an illuminating commentary on the fact that intelligent self-interest, whether conscious or instinctive, is one of the motive forces of human progress. Individuals may indeed have joined in the movement with no other prompting than a desire for personal gain irrespective of the public welfare; but the group as a whole undoubtedly were moved by the conviction that the changes they advocated would benefit the nation at large as well as their own personal economic station.

Under the Articles of Confederation men of substance and position found their property holdings imperiled and the gates to economic advancement closed. Persons who had speculated in western lands and were holding them for a rise found that their holdings remained at an abnormally low price because of the weakness of the Confederation government, the lack of proper military protection on the frontier, and the uncertainty as to the legal title. Holders of the depreciated public securities could have no respect for a government which had not only failed to provide for the eventual redemption of its obligations but was unable even to make the current interest payments. Men with money to lend found the avenues to profitable investment blocked by the general derangement of business and the action of the state legislatures in annulling private contracts and issuing worthless paper currency. The merchants, manufacturers and shipbuilders were likewise affected by the inability of the government to enact protective tariffs and navigation laws or to secure favorable commercial treaties with foreign nations. This general contempt for the government was fully shared by the great slave owners of the South who believed that the government should possess adequate power to insure the return of runaway slaves and to quell servile insurrections. Indeed, the southern planters were as vitally concerned in maintaining order against the possibility of slave revolts as the creditors of Massachusetts were in preventing recurrences of Shays' rebellion.

The lodestone of a common material interest inevitably drew together the men of large economic interests irrespective of state boundaries or other artificial distinctions, and consolidated them into a compact group opposed to the poor and the debtor classes. Efforts had been made at various times to strengthen the Articles with amendments conferring commercial and taxation powers upon Congress, but these attempts had all been defeated by the requirement that any changes must be accepted by act of all the state legislatures. In 1782 the New York legislature had proposed a convention to revise the Articles, and the suggestion had been repeated by the legislature of Massachusetts three years later, but without effect.

The train of events which culminated in the meeting of the Constitutional Convention was inspired and set in motion by men aroused to action by the commercial chaos that reigned in the country. In 1785 commissioners of Virginia and Maryland came together for the purpose of adjusting questions involving jurisdiction over the navigation of the Potomac River and Chesapeake Bay. It quickly developed that the question of trading regulations was one that affected the neighboring states as well; and Maryland proposed that Pennsylvania and Delaware should be invited to participate in a subsequent meeting. Virginia, however, enlarged the scope of the proposed conference by formally calling upon all the states to send delegates to Annapolis in 1786 to "consider how far a uniform system in their commercial relations may be necessary to their common interest and their permanent harmony."

The response of the states to this invitation was disappointing, for only five states were represented at the Annapolis convention. No definite action affecting commercial relations could be taken under the circumstances; but the meeting went on record in favor of another convention, to be held in Philadelphia the following year, to "devise such further Provisions as shall appear to them necessary to render the Constitution of the Federal Government adequate to the exigencies of the Union." The interesting phraseology of this resolution was the work of Alexander Hamilton. The resolution further provided that any changes recommended by the proposed convention should be adopted in the manner provided by the Articles of Confederation, namely, ratification by the legislatures of all the states. The Confederation Congress ignored the resolution of this extralegal body for a time; but when it became clear that the states were planning to act upon it anyway, Congress hastened to lend its sanction to the gathering.

To what extent the large economic interests directed and controlled the selection of delegates to the Constitutional Convention is necessarily a matter of conjecture except as indirect evidence may shed light on the matter. In every state the delegates were elected by the legislature and it is difficult, if not impossible, to ascertain what arguments and pressures were brought to bear to influence the members in their action. According to John Adams, "The Federal Convention was the work of the commercial people in the seaport towns, of the slave-holding states, of the officers of the revolutionary army, and the property holders everywhere"; and this judgment of a distinguished contemporary is largely borne out by the recent researches of Dr. Charles A. Beard.

Of the fifty-five members who attended the convention at one time or other not one represented in his own personal economic interests the small farming or mechanic classes On the contrary the great majority, at least five-sixths of the membership, were directly and personally interested in the outcome of their labors through their ownership of property, real or personal, and were, to a greater or less extent, economic beneficiaries of the adoption of the Constitution. While detailed figures must necessarily be inexact, it is worth noting that speculative investments in land were represented by at least fourteen members. Public security interests were extensively represented among the members in sums varying from negligible amounts up to more than $100,000. The precise number of public creditors in the convention will probably never be known, but the names of no less than forty appeared upon the records of the United States Treasury Department when Hamilton's funding scheme was carried into operation shortly after the adoption of the Constitution. Personalty in the form of money loaned at interest was represented by at least twenty-four members. The mercantile, manufacturing and shipping interests had spokesmen in at least eleven members. Fifteen or more members were slaveholders. Thus the membership of the convention consisted not of political visionaries or closet philosophers but of men of the world determined, above all things else, to erect a government that would be effective and workable from a practical man's point of view.

III

The Constitutional Convention held its sessions in secret; and not until the publication of the official journal by act of Congress in 1819 was the bare record of its proceedings divulged. Many more years passed before James Madison's notes on the debates were made public. From these accounts and other fragmentary versions of the convention's activities the historians have been able to reconstruct a picture of the stormy controversies and grudging concessions that marked the various stages of the framing of the Constitution. To quote Professor Max Farrand, the completed Constitution was "neither a work of divine origin, nor 'the greatest work that was ever struck off at a given time by the brain and purpose of man,' but a practical, workable document . . . planned to meet certain immediate needs and modified to suit the exigencies of the situation."

The document contained every protection which the interests of the conservative classes had demanded for the safeguarding of their property rights. The structure of the new government with its intricate system of checks and balances was designed to prevent the populace from giving free rein to its whims and passions. Of the three principal departments of the government the qualified voters in the states were permitted to vote directly for only one house of Congress; and ample provision was made by which the will of the popular house might be defeated. More specifically, provisions were inserted for conferring full revenue powers upon Congress and for making the debts of the Confederation government an obligation upon the new government. Congress was further given plenary power to raise and support military and naval forces, for the protection of the country against both foreign and domestic foes. Over foreign and interstate commerce Congress was given substantially complete control, which made it possible for the new government to enact protective tariffs and to prevent the erection of tariff barriers between the states. The new government also received unrestricted powers of treaty-making with ample authority to enforce treaties when made. Not less significant were the clauses which forbade the states to issue paper currency, or to make anything but gold and silver legal tender, or to make laws impairing the obligation of contracts. By such provisions conditions were assured under which holders of public securities might be paid in full, social disturbances quelled, the western frontier protected, advantages secured in dealing with foreign nations, manufactures fostered, and the financial follies of the states prevented.

But it was one thing for the Philadelphia Convention to agree upon such a document in secret session, and another to secure the acceptance of these sweeping provisions by the country after public consideration. Technically, the instrument framed by the Convention was only a revision of the Articles of Confederation, and hence must go through the regular process prescribed for alterations and amendments of the Confederation government. But the members of the Convention early recognized the impossibility of securing approval by the *legislatures* of *all* the states; and so they decided to disregard the existing legal machinery, and they put forth a document which provided for its own method of ratification. The proposed Constitution declared that the states should signify their approval through *special conventions* chosen upon the express issue, and when *nine* state conventions had ratified the instrument, it should go into effect among the states so acting. The whole procedure was a departure from the provisions of the fundamental law under which the Convention had been called; and this action of the Convention, from a legal point of view, cannot be regarded otherwise than unlawful and revolutionary. As one distinguished jurist has remarked, if such an act had been committed by Julius or Napoleon, it would have been pronounced a *coup d'état*.

The future of the Constitution now hung upon the decision of the state ratifying conventions. From November, 1787, to the following July a campaign of continental proportions was carried on. Since the Constitution was not submitted to direct popular ratification, as are state constitutions today, the best indication that we have of popular sentiment is found in the selection of delegates to the state conventions. But here allowances must be made for the fact that perhaps one-third of the adult white male population were excluded from the franchise by the property qualifications that prevailed in every state. In New York alone a temporary exception was made, and all· adult men were allowed to vote. A considerable proportion of the qualified voters in every state abstained from voting through indifference or ignorance; and in general it seems highly probable that not more than one-fifth or one-fourth of the adult white males participated in the election of delegates to the state conventions.

The arguments urged for and against ratification were much the same in the several states; but each state campaign had its local peculiarities due to the special social, economic and geographic conditions. In Massachusetts the eastern counties with their dominant commercial and financial interests favored ratification, while the farmers of the interior, who had recruited the ranks of Shays' army, fought it. In Rhode Island wealth and commerce supported the Constitution but were outweighed by the agricultural class who were advocates of "cheap money." The forces opposed to ratification in Connecticut were very feeble but drew their strength from those parts of the state that contained the debtor class and from the men who had sympathized with Shays' rebellion. The rural counties of New York were in opposition while the business section of the state in and about New York City were ardent ratificationists. New Jersey was favorable to the new instrument because of the trading restrictions that had been imposed upon her by New York and Pennsylvania but a note of dissent was heard from the debtor and paper money regions. In Pennsylvania the merchant and propertied classes united in supporting the Constitution in face of the opposition of the Scotch-Irish and German radicals of the backcountry, who had dominated state politics since revolutionary times. In Virginia the long-standing social and economic antagonism between east and west, between the great planters and merchants of the tidewater and the small farmers of the interior, reappeared. Eighty per cent of tidewater Virginia, containing the monied and commercial interests, supported the Constitution whereas seventy-four per cent of the back-country voted against it. Much the same alignment was found in the Carolinas, with the agrarian element in an actual majority in North Carolina. Georgia gave a speedy endorsement to the Constitution because, as the southern frontier state, the people felt the imperative need of a strong general government to assist in warding off Indian attacks. West of the Alleghanies the people were a unit in opposing ratification.

John Marshall, an active supporter of ratification and

later Chief Justice of the United States Supreme Court, wrote in his *Life of Washington* some years later: "So balanced were the parties in some of them [the states] that even after the subject had been discussed for a considerable time, the fate of the constitution could scarcely be conjectured; and so small in many instances, was the majority in its favor, as to afford strong ground for the opinion that, had the influence of character been removed, the intrinsic merits of the instrument would not have secured its adoption. Indeed it is scarcely to be doubted that in some of the adopting states a majority of the people were in the opposition. In all of them, the numerous amendments which were proposed demonstrate the reluctance with which the new government was accepted; and that a dread of dismemberment, not an approbation of the particular system under discussion, had induced an acquiescence in it."

In the words of Woodrow Wilson, the friends of the Constitution had on their side the tremendous advantage of "a strong and intelligent class, possessed of unity and informed by a conscious solidarity of material interest." But "economic determinism" was not all to be found on this side of the contest. Although the foes of adoption had strong theoretical grounds for fearing a highly centralized federal government, they also had definite pecuniary reasons for condemning the many restrictions imposed upon popular government in general and upon the authority of the state governments in particular. It was Alexander Hamilton's cynical comment that the new frame of government encountered the "opposition of all men much in debt, who will not wish to see a government established, one object of which is to restrain the means of cheating creditors." It is a mistaken notion that all of the distinguished men of the country were to be found in the ranks of the ratificationists, for among the active opponents were such men as Patrick

Henry, Richard Henry Lee and Edmund Randolph of Virginia, Elbridge Gerry of Massachusetts, and George Clinton of New York. The last two later occupied the office of vice-president of the United States.

Although the enemies of ratification were poorly organized, it appears that in the case of four states—New Hampshire, Massachusetts, New York and Virginia—the conventions were, at the time of their election, either opposed to the Constitution or else so closely divided that their action was in doubt. A change of ten votes in Massachusetts, six in New Hampshire, six in Virginia and two in New York would have prevented ratification by the conventions of those states. In North Carolina the Constitution was rejected by vote of the convention; and the authorities in Rhode Island refused to summon a convention to consider it. Both states failed to take part in the first presidential election.

On the basis of the new fundamental law the new national government was in due form established. The bitter animosities which had characterized the struggle over ratification subsided and were soon forgotten. All elements united in support of the Constitution and for the moment the political waters seemed tranquil. But the underlying economic and social conflict could not be so easily stilled. Forced to assume new forms by the changed circumstances, the commercial and monied interests on the one hand and the agrarian and debtor interests on the other prepared to wage battle for the control of the new government. Here we find the fundamental explanation of the rise of political parties during Washington's presidency.

BIBLIOGRAPHICAL NOTE

The chief authority on the economic phases of the movement for the Constitution is Charles A. Beard, who presented the results of his researches in his work: *An Economic Interpretation of the Constitution of the United States* (New York, 1913).

Most of the early historians dealing with the movement for the Constitution had largely overlooked the economic conflict involved, one conspicuous exception being John Marshall who in discussing the matter in his *Life of George Washington* (5 v.; Philadelphia, 1804-1807) showed a keen appreciation of the economic motivation of events. John Bach McMaster in his *History of the People of the United States* (8 v.; New York, 1883-1913), vol. i, and Andrew Cunningham McLaughlin in his *The Confederation and the Constitution* (in *The American Nation: a History*, vol. 10; New York, 1905) deal with social and economic conditions in this period, but their treatments are largely surveys of outward events.

Progress toward an economic and social explanation of events began to be made with the appearance of a notable series of monographic studies which had been worked out independently of each other: James C. Welling's "The States'-Rights Conflict over the Public Lands" in the *Papers* of the American Historical Association (New York, 1889), vol. iii, pp. 167-188; Orin Grant Libby's *The Geographical Distribution of the Vote of the Thirteen States on the Federal Constitution, 1787-1788* (Madison, 1894); Samuel B. Harding's *The Contest over the Ratification of the Federal Constitution in the State of Massachusetts* (Cambridge, 1896); F. G. Bates's *Rhode Island and the Formation of the Union* (New York, 1898); William A. Schaper's "Sectionalism and Representation in South Carolina" in the *Annual Report* of the American Historical Association for 1900, vol. i, pp. 237-463; and Charles Henry Ambler's *Sectionalism in Virginia from 1776 to 1861* (Chicago, 1910).

The appearance of Dr. Beard's volume in 1913, at a time when popular criticism of the courts was rife, caused it to be greeted with a storm of criticism and protest. As a matter of fact, his chief contribution to the subject beyond what had already been done lay in his painstaking analysis of the economic interests of the members of the Constitutional Convention and his emphasis upon the public security holdings of members of the Federal and state ratifying conventions. Perhaps the most incisive scholarly criticism of Dr. Beard's book was made by E. S. Corwin in the *History Teacher's Magazine* for February, 1914. Dr. Beard's answer to his critics may be found in his *Economic Origins of Jeffersonian Democracy* (New York, 1915), pp. 1-9.

The point of view set forth by Dr. Beard has been generally accepted by scholars who have written on the Confederation period since 1913; for example, Allen Johnson's *Union and Democracy* (Boston, 1915), chap. ii; Homer C. Hockett's *Western Influences on Political Parties to 1825* (Columbus, 1917), pp. 27-40; and Frank Tracy Carlton's *Organized Labor in American History* (New York, 1920), pp. 45-52.

CHAPTER IX

THE SIGNIFICANCE OF JACKSONIAN DEMOCRACY

The habit of the earlier historians of thinking of American history as a chronicle of political and constitutional development has given currency to a very misleading conception of "Jacksonian Democracy." To the ordinary reader of history the phrase refers to a violent change in American government and politics effected during the years from 1829 to 1837 by an irresponsible and erratic military chieftain at the head of the newly enfranchised and untutored masses. Notwithstanding the changing emphasis of historical writing in late years this notion has tended to persist, perhaps through a natural desire of the human kind to seek a simple explanation of events rather than a complex one, and perhaps also because of our tendency to picture a superman or a malign genius—as the case may be—as the moving force in historic changes.

The researches that have been conducted into the life of the people of the United States in the twenties and the thirties have thrown an entirely different light upon the democratic upheaval of that period. The great changes that occurred are to be regarded as a transformation of American society that made itself manifest not only in the sphere of government but in almost every other phase of human thought and endeavor. Jackson himself was a product, rather than the creator, of the new democratic spirit, for he rode into power on a tide of forces that had been gathering strength for more than a decade and which he had done little or nothing to bring into being. It will appear that the new democracy was "Jacksonian" only to the extent that Jackson stamped the political phase of the movement with the imprint of his personality, lending it certain picturesque characteristics and dramatic qualities.

In the present discussion the origins and development of this new spirit in American life will be traced in the period of a decade or so before Jackson's elevation to the presidency, as well as during his term of office; and its liberating and liberalizing effects will be followed in the rise of a new society west of the Alleghanies, in the development of a dynamic labor movement in the East, in the literary, social and religious aspirations of the people, and in the profound changes in political organization and governmental practice.

I

The growth of the West affords one vital approach to an understanding of the new democratic outlook of America. Reference has been made elsewhere in this volume to the fact that in the first quarter of the century the whole physical basis of American life was changed by the expansion of the American population across the Alleghanies. In 1800 only one-twentieth of the people lived west of the mountains; but when Jackson was inaugurated president, one-third of them were to be found in that region. Meantime the population of the nation had increased from five and one-third millions to thirty millions; so that the West in 1829 contained almost twice as many people as the entire United States at the beginning of the century. In the train of western migration there sprang up mighty frontier commonwealths, increasing the original number of states from thirteen to twenty-two. By the time Jackson entered the presidency the entire domain east of the Mississippi river had been carved into states save only Michigan, Wisconsin and Florida, and be-

yond the great river Louisiana and Missouri had won acceptance as members of the Union.

All the conditions of life in the West made for the promotion of equalitarian ideas. The democracy of the frontier
was not derived from the reading of philosophical disquisi-
tions but grew out of the hardy experiences of the pioneers
in wresting the land from savage foe and the primitive
resistance of Nature. A man was deemed a man if he could
survive the struggle for existence, irrespective of his social
antecedents; and land was so abundant that every man
might attain a position of economic independence. Political
equality was thus based upon a real equality. It was a
democracy as yet without organization, one that depended
upon personal leadership. The man most successful as an
Indian fighter was expected to make the best judge or the
best Congressman. It was a democracy opposed to an
office-holding class and moved by a deep conviction that any
upstanding man was competent to hold any office. Yet on
clearcut political issues the people were independent and
intelligent. Their political code had as its main tenets:
political democracy, equality of economic opportunity, and
opposition to monopoly and special privilege.

Distinction between north and south did not as yet exist
in the trans-Alleghany region. The difficulties of the pioneer of the Old Northwest in hewing a clearing out of the
hard woods of his region were matched by the trials of the
Mississippi pioneer in wrestling with the pine forests of the
south.

The West with all its crudenesses and virtues came to
play a large part in American life in the twenties and the
thirties, deepening the channels of democracy and driving
through them a roaring tide that threatened to inundate the
banks. Henry Clay of Kentucky, Thomas H. Benton of
Missouri and Andrew Jackson of Tennessee were all products

of western conditions, though with curious variations, and by their tremendous energy and personal gifts they helped to impress the ideals and prejudices of the frontier upon the national government.

The life of the westerner was crowded with the exigencies of daily living and secondarily with the political problems which the necessity for self-government thrust constantly upon his attention. He had as yet no contribution to make to creative literature or to the fine art of living. The life of the frontier democracy bore the promise of original contributions but its expression had to await the oncoming of the children and grandchildren of the first pioneers.

II

While democracy was working out its destiny in the forests of the Mississippi valley, the men left behind in the eastern cities were engaging in a struggle to establish conditions of equality and social well-being adapted to their special circumstances. To understand the difficulties and oppressive conditions against which this movement of protest was directed, it is necessary to consider the changed circumstances of the life of the common man in the new industrial centers of the East since the opening years of the nineteenth century. Since the days of Jefferson's embargo, New England and the Middle Atlantic states had been undergoing a transformation from a section of predominant agricultural and shipping interests to a section increasingly devoted to manufacturing. This growth of manufacturing marked the advent of the factory system in American history; and while manufacturing was conducted only in scattered districts and upon a comparatively small scale as measured by modern standards, it profoundly influenced the lives of the working class immediately concerned.

Prior to the introduction of the factory system, such

manufacturing as was known in America had been carried on under the "domestic system." Each employer or "master" worked side by side with his journeymen and apprentices, sharing their hard conditions and long hours; and every workingman expected in time to become an employer. There was no sharp division between capital and labor, and no distinct and permanent laboring class. With the application of machinery to work that had hitherto been performed by hand, the situation of the workingman changed radically. Under the new conditions the mass of hired labor shifted from the farm and the village to the trades and the manufactures in the towns in the first quarter of the century. The customary workday on the farm from "sun to sun" or "dark to dark" was carried over into the factory and the trades notwithstanding the greatly altered conditions of labor, and women and children were employed at the same ruinously long hours as the men.

An estimate of the average workday in the manufacturing districts was made in 1839 by James Montgomery, superintendent of the York Factories at Saco, Maine, who calculated that the day's work at Lowell averaged a little more than twelve hours the year around for six days a week, and that in many of the Middle Atlantic and southern states the ordinary working hours approached thirteen a day. There is abundant evidence to show that these figures may be regarded as a conservative statement of the conditions prevailing in the earlier years of the century. The Lowell factories were said to employ 3,800 women and 1,200 men in 1833; at about the same time it was estimated that two-fifths of all the factory workers in New England were children under sixteen years of age. Wages had risen nominally, but since they had lagged behind the rise of prices, the workingmen could buy less with their earnings than earlier.

Factory manufacture tended to concentrate in cities; and the period was marked by the rapid growth of urban population. In 1800 there were only six cities in the nation with a population of eight thousand or over; three decades later the number had increased to twenty-six, including three whose population ranged from seventy-five thousand to a quarter of a million. The wage-earners, forced to live near their source of employment, became congested into squalid and unwholesome tenements, where they lived under conditions of destitution, disease, vice and crime. The city of Lowell, Massachusetts, which in 1820 did not even exist, had a population of over twenty thousand in 1840, collected there largely to work in the mills.

The pressure of industry not only tended to degrade the wage-earners morally and physically but left no place for the education of the children. In 1825 a committee of the Massachusetts legislature engaged in investigating the opportunities of children for schooling was able to discover only two towns where the children between the ages of six and seventeen worked as few as eleven hours of steady labor a day; elsewhere the usual working hours were twelve and thirteen. Even when the time could be found, the children of the poor were everywhere excluded from attendance at the better schools. Although the principle of free, tax-supported schools had long been established in Massachusetts and most of New England, public schools were generally much less efficient than private schools, and Rhode Island had no public educational system whatever. In such states as New York and Pennsylvania, private schools were conducted for the children of the well-to-do, and such free schools as were maintained were regarded as dispensers of charity to paupers with all the odium attached thereto. In 1833 it was estimated that in the entire country one million children of the ages from six to fifteen were not in any school, and eighty thousand of these were in the state of New York.

Other conditions of their daily life convinced the laboring

class that the law and the courts bore unequally upon the poor and the rich. The eastern states were slower than the western in bestowing the franchise upon the unpropertied class. Even when this concession was reluctantly granted, much injustice remained in the operation of the laws. The compulsory militia system permitted the rich to escape by paying a small fine whereas the poor man must serve or go to prison. The debtors' prisons still swallowed thousands of worthy but unfortunate men. Labor combinations to raise wages were prosecuted under the old English common law as illegal conspiracies. The banking system of the times afforded the workingmen none of the advantages of credit and frequently caused them to be paid in bank notes of doubtful value.

The revolt of labor against these hard conditions of life formed an integral part of the democratic upheaval of Jackson's time. Theoretically the workers might have escaped most of these hardships by joining their venturesome brethren who had taken up public land on the frontier; and in fact many individuals of self-reliance and a little cash surplus did so. But to the average mill-hand, burdened with a family, the public domain west of the Alleghanies seemed inaccessible from distance and expense; he felt obliged to work out his salvation in the community where he resided and with such means as lay readily at his hand.

The first awakening of American wage-earners occurred in the late twenties. Before that time a sullen discontent had shown itself occasionally in strikes and in the sporadic formation of labor unions; but the working class as a whole remained unorganized, and unaware that their greatest hope for relief lay in combined and aggressive action. About 1825, however, this fact dawned upon their consciousness and they began to make use of their collective strength for the betterment of social conditions. Their efforts fell in the two more or less related spheres of industrial and political action.

From 1825 dates a rapid multiplication of labor unions, or "trade associations" as they were then called. In every large city the different trades succeeded in organizing. At the outset the various trade associations in a city were unconnected with each other; but in 1827 a movement began in Philadelphia to join together the several trade associations into an effective central organization of the wage-earners of the entire city. The new organization was called the "Mechanics' Union of Trade Associations," and its constitution declared that its object was "to avert, if possible, the desolating effects which must inevitably arise from a depreciation of the intrinsic value of human labor" and "to promote equally the happiness, prosperity and welfare of the whole community."

The idea of central federations spread to other cities; so that within a few years all the large cities had similar organizations. In 1834 occurred the next logical step when the city federations came together in a national federation. At about the same time some of the stronger crafts began to organize upon a national basis, namely the cordwainers, the printers, the comb makers, the carpenters and the handloom weavers. By 1836 it was estimated that union membership in the seaboard cities of the North amounted to three hundred thousand.

These labor organizations sought not only to improve conditions of employment through strikes and other forms of industrial action but they also directed their efforts to effecting reforms of a broader social import through political action. The transition to active political participation was natural and easy. At first the city federations pledged the candidates of the old parties "to support the interests and claims of the Working Classes" in the city council and the state legislature; but when these halfway expedients failed to obtain results, the wage-earners proceeded to organize their own parties in state after state. The first Working Men's party appeared in Philadelphia in 1828; New York followed in the next year; and within a short time Working Men's parties of varying strength were to be found in all the seaboard states north of Maryland. These parties enjoyed local successes, occasionally sent members to the state legislatures and to Congress, and forced the old parties in some instances to name candidates favorable to labor.

The aims of the organized labor elements harmonized with the new democratic aspirations of the age and did much toward vitalizing those aspirations. The strikes carried on by the trade associations sought to increase wages, to secure what we now call the "closed shop," and to shorten the workday to ten hours. The demands of the labor parties were broader in scope, touching on most of the conditions that made life arduous for the less fortunate classes and seeking to create broader opportunities for the common man. As summed up by the *Mechanics' Free Press* of Philadelphia in its issue of April 16, 1831, the program of labor comprised these leading demands: "Universal education, abolition of chartered monopolies [including the United States Bank], equal taxation, revision or abolition of the militia system, a less expensive law system, all officers to be elected directly by the people, a lien law for laborers, no legislation on religion." The abolition of imprisonment for debt might properly have been included in this list.

The paramount emphasis placed by labor organizations everywhere upon education grew out of the conviction, often expressed, that since "our government is republican, our education should be equally so." In the words of the Philadelphia Trades Union, nothing less was demanded than that "an open school, and competent teachers, for every child in the State, from the lowest branch of an infant school to the lecture rooms of practical science, should be established, and those to superintend them to be chosen by the people." Fortunate it was for the republic that at a time when the untutored masses were receiving the boon of political equality the battering away of the organized workingmen was making possible the establishment of popular education. In general the working people not only fought against their own immediate ills but as individuals were in sympathy with all the reform movements of the period, from temperance and the outlawing of lotteries to the abolition of capital punishment.

The labor movement reached its floodtide while Andrew Jackson was in office. Indeed, he could not have been elected president if the votes of the laboring men of the Northeast had not been added to those of his followers in the Southeast and the West. Jackson capitalized this support when he waged battle against the great financial monopoly, the United States Bank, and gave express recognition to its demands when he established the ten-hour workday in the federal shipyards in 1836.

The industrial depression following the panic of 1837 destroyed most of the labor unions and federations; and the strength of the labor parties was sapped by internal dissensions and by the action of the Democratic party in taking over many of the workingmen's chief demands. But this pioneer labor movement had already made a lasting impression on American democratic ideals and practice. Jackson's successor, Martin Van Buren, applied the principle of the ten-hour day to all government works in 1840; and indeed by that date the shorter workday was established in most mechanical branches. By that time, also, imprisonment for debt had been abolished in most of the states; and the foundations of popular education had been laid. Further than this, Miss Helen Sumner has well said: "though the Working Men's party had little success in electing its candidates to office and though its immediate tangible results were small, it succeeded in forcing its measures into the foreground of public attention, and eventually all the specific evils of which it complained were abolished and all its constructive measures were passed."

III

The democratic ferment of the twenties and the thirties was also active in the intellectual and spiritual life of the people. Hidden forces seemed to be set free which emboldened writers and thinkers to loftier flights than had been their wont and gave them a robust faith in the perfectibility of mankind. The new spirit flowered luxuriantly in the literature of the period, which for the first time cast off its servile dependence on England in literary manners. In 1819 appeared Washington Irving's *Sketch Book,* which immortalized the Hudson river in world literature. In 1821 James Fenimore Cooper published *The Spy,* a purely American novel, to be followed two years later by *The Pioneers,* the first of the *Leatherstocking Tales.*

The Spy has been termed by discerning critics "our literary Declaration of Independence," and it marked the opening of an era of a truly indigenous American literature. The writers of the next quarter-century became definitely "American" in their outlook, originality and subject matter. It was in this period that John Greenleaf Whittier, Oliver Wendell Holmes, James Russell Lowell, Ralph Waldo Emerson and Henry Wadsworth Longfellow began their literary careers—all of them men who, without losing their kinship with the literature of the world, derived much of their inspiration from their American environment and displayed strong humanitarian sympathy with the moral unrest of the times. Out of this period, too, came Edgar Allan Poe, a tragic and solitary genius, the Ishmael of letters, who shows no reflection of place or time in his work but through whom America made her most significant contribution to general literature—the short story.

The trend of the times inspired men of scholarship to rewrite the history of the republic with a new dignity and with a purpose to glorify democratic institutions and deify the founders of the nation. George Bancroft began his monumental history of the United States in the thirties, thoroughly imbued with the belief, as Professor Dunning has aptly remarked, that the American republic represented "the culmination of God's wonder-working in the life of mankind." Late in the twenties Jared Sparks took up his vast labors of collecting and editing historical documents, taking care to alter and embellish such writings as he selected for publication on the theory that his fellow countrymen should not be disillusioned by observing the patriot fathers in their unguarded moments. Or as one of his admirers put it in defense of Sparks's method, he was resolved to defeat the "prurient curiosity" of the public "to see a great man in dishabille."

The awakened interest in literary self-expression was further evidenced by the establishment of the first substantial literary periodicals in America and the founding of great publishing houses. In 1815 the *North American Review* made its appearance; and before Jackson left the presidency, the *New England Magazine* (1831), the *Knickerbocker Magazine* (1832) and the *Southern Literary Messenger* (1834) were added to the list. D. Appleton started his career as a book publisher in 1831; and by the close of the decade the foundations had been laid of the well known houses of Harper & Brothers, J. B. Lippincott & Company, Little, Brown & Company, and G. P. Putnam & Sons.

The liberation of the American mind from time-honored

traditions and rigid conventions appeared markedly in the ecclesiastical revolts and religious revivals of the age. In Lowell's epigram, "Protestantism had made its fortune and no longer protested"; a new religious spirit better suited to the times was needed. The stern Calvinistic theology, which had so long held sway in New England, felt the first impact of the democratic tide. Under the leadership of Channing, Unitarianism was organized in 1815 by dissenting members of the Congregational Church, on a creed opposing the sombre doctrines of total depravity and predestination and affirming the infinite possibilities of human development. The new system exerted an influence altogether out of proportion to the number of its adherents, and attained its loftiest expression in the philosophic movement known as "Transcendentalism," of which Ralph Waldo Emerson was the foremost exponent. Transcendentalism was a combination of the spiritual earnestness of Puritanism and an untrammeled individualism, which strove to emphasize the dignity and freedom of the human spirit.

The spread of Unitarianism throughout New England was checked only by the work of men like Horace Bushnell, who sought to harmonize the Calvinistic theology of the old Congregational system with the new precepts of democracy. Other sects were experiencing similar difficulties in the attempt to keep pace with the changing ideals of the age. The Quakers were rent in twain by the teachings of Elias Hicks. The Campbells, father and son, led a departure from the established Presbyterian order. Universalism took its rise at this time; and in the West there occurred a rapid growth of the Methodists, Baptists and other denominations which were able to satisfy the religious cravings of a people impatient of theological hair-splitting. The religious zeal of the frontiersmen found characteristic expression in the democratic camp-meeting, where the revivalist might use his knowledge of crowd psychology to arouse his audience to ecstasies of religious excitement.

The new interest in the well-being of the masses found expression in countless projects for social betterment. In 1824 began the first organized movement against strong drink. The use of intoxicants in the United States was well-nigh universal. Even at the chief colleges liquor was openly sold from booths on public days; and municipal officials provided free punch for those who marched on a training-day. On the dinner tables of the inns were to be found decanters of brandy free to the guests. The movement began in Boston with the formation of societies pledged to abstinence. Within five years more than one thousand of these societies had been formed in all parts of the country. By that time more than fifty distilleries had gone out of business, and the importation of foreign spirits was greatly reduced. The movement now took the form of the "Washington societies," and in the forties blossomed forth into a demand for state statutes forbidding the liquor traffic altogether

Other reform movements found inspiration in the temper of the times. In the twenties the woman rights movement had its inception. At first directed to the improvement of female education and enlarged rights for married women, it speedily broadened its scope and, in the forties, extended to a demand for woman suffrage. The anti-slavery movement underwent a significant change. Surcharged with the new democratic spirit, it lost its former philanthropic and hortatory character; and in the hands of William Lloyd Garrison it became a militant crusade for equal racial rights regardless of existing legal and constitutional barriers. The American Anti-Slavery Society was founded; and by 1840, two thousand centers of abolition propaganda existed in all parts of the North.

But the new humanitarian spirit also had immediate practical effects. Massachusetts now founded the first public hospital for the insane. Stephen Girard of Philadelphia, who died in 1831, left the bulk of his fortune for the establishment of the orphan school that still bears his name. Special schools for the deaf and the blind were instituted in many states; and state provision for the separation of juvenile delinquents from adult criminals was begun. The growing demand for higher education was met and strengthened by the establishment of Colby, Amherst, Oberlin, Kenyon, Mt. Holyoke, Randolph-Macon, Haverford, Knox, Muskingum and Marietta colleges, of Denison, Tulane, Wesleyan, Western Reserve and New York universities, and of Hartford, Lane and Union theological seminaries.

Characteristic of the illimitable faith in humanity were the optimistic attempts to establish communistic colonies in various parts of the country between 1820 and 1840. Robert Owen, who had already attempted to found a model industrial town in Scotland, came to America and established a community at New Harmony, Indiana, where labor and property were to be in common. A little later the New England Transcendentalists founded a coöperative society at Brook Farm, near Boston, an enterprise which Hawthorne, one of the participants, subsequently satirized in *The Blithedale Romance*. More than thirty other communities and "phalansteries" were established, some of which are still in existence. Emerson remarked: "Not a man you meet but has a draft of a new community in his pocket!" Although most of these experiments turned out to be failures, the fine idealism underlying them proved to be a fount of inspiration for later generations of social reformers in American history.

As the foregoing account suggests, the restlessness of the times had its fantastic offshoots as well as its elements of permanent value. James Russell Lowell in his essay on Thoreau (1865) gives us his humorous recollections of these years: "Every possible form of intellectual and physical dyspepsia brought forth its gospel. Bran had its prophets. . . . Plainness of speech was carried to a pitch that would have taken away the breath of George Fox. . . . Everybody had a mission (with a capital M) to attend to everybody-else's business. No brain but had its private maggot, which must have found pitiably short commons sometimes. Not a few impecunious zealots abjured the use of money (unless earned by other people), professing to live on the internal revenues of the spirit. Some had an assurance of instant millennium so soon as hooks and eyes should be substituted for buttons. Communities were established where everything was to be common but common-sense. . . . Many foreign revolutionists out of work added to the general misunderstanding their contribution of broken English in every most ingenious form of fracture. All stood ready at a moment's notice to reform everything but themselves."

But Lowell was not willing to dismiss this ebullience with a jest. "There was a very solid and serious kernel, full of the most deadly explosiveness," he added; and then he put his finger upon the fundamental significance of the unrest: "It was simply a struggle for fresh air, in which, if the windows could not be opened, there was danger that panes would be broken, though painted with images of saints and martyrs. . . . There is only one thing better than tradition, and that is the original and eternal life out of which all tradition takes its rise. It was this life which the reformers demanded, with more or less clearness of consciousness and expression, life in politics, life in literature, life in religion." It required the broad sympathy and keen insight of a Lowell to recognize that Andrew Jackson, James Fenimore Cooper, Ralph Waldo Emerson and William Lloyd Garrison, however differing in external qualities and interests, were essentially products of the same era.

IV

The irrepressible desire of the common man for political self-expression, to which Lowell alluded, led to many radical changes in political precept and practice. A natural concomitant was the liberalization of the suffrage. The new western commonwealths came into the union as self-confessed democracies. With the exception of one or two states, all adult white males were given the right to vote; and everywhere, too, the principle was accepted that representation should be based upon population and not upon property. The action of the western states proved to be a vast makeweight in favor of greater democracy in the older states, reinforced, as the demand was, by the agitation of the laboring elements of the seaboard towns. New York, Massachusetts, Virginia and other states proceeded to modify their suffrage provisions so as to admit great numbers of the unenfranchised classes.

The presidential campaign of 1832 revealed to what extent the new political forces had gained mastery of the situation. The old method of nominating presidential candidates by means of a congressional clique, a practice that had already broken down eight years before, was now replaced by national party conventions, in which the rank and file of the party had representation. All parties in the campaign employed the new device. At the same time was begun the practice, essentially democratic in its purpose, of informing the public by means of a party platform of the policies which the party intended to adopt if successful in the election. Even the organization of the Anti-Masonic party in this campaign may be regarded as a product of the fierce democratic spirit of the times; it represented a determination, however misguided, to rid America of what was thought to be a secret and dangerous influence in American life.

Changes of like character were being introduced into state government and politics. Property qualifications for officeholding were removed. The governor was made elective by the people instead of by the legislature as heretofore in many states. The principle of popular election was even applied to the judges of the state courts. In Connecticut and Massachusetts the church establishments were overthrown.

The choice of Andrew Jackson or of a man like him was almost inevitable under the circumstances. The popular demand was for a president who should symbolize the apotheosis of the common man. No mistake was made in this respect in the case of Jackson. He had been born in the backwoods country of North Carolina, where he had passed his boyhood in bare poverty. Picking up some necessary scraps of knowledge he removed to the newer frontier of Tennessee to practise law. His public career began almost at once, for he was a natural leader and maintained his mastery of men by pistol or blow, by vehement assertion or rude intellectual force, as the amenities of the occasion demanded. As president of the United States, he displayed most of the virtues and many of the defects of the masses from which he sprang. The scrambling, punch-drinking mob which invaded Washington at the inauguration, crowding and pushing into the White House and tipping over tubs of punch, did so in the spirit of copartners who at last had gotten an opportunity to take account of the assets of the firm. Though this scene was not countenanced by Jackson, he placed his seal of approval upon the aspirations of the rank and file when he introduced the "spoils system" of appointments. What could seem more equitable to the primitive democracy of his day than the principle of "rotation in office," and what more undemocratic than the older conception of a permanent officeholding gentry?

His democratic instincts again received full play in his great battle against the United States Bank, an institution controlled by wealthy investors in England and the United States and one which he envisaged as a money monopoly dangerous to free institutions. Once again he interpreted the inarticulate will of the people when he issued his flaming manifesto against South Carolina nullification. Had Congress heeded the advice given in each one of his eight annual messages, the Constitution would have been amended to provide for the election of president and vice-president by direct popular vote. His great contribution to American history was the establishment of the principle that the government should be responsive to the will of the masses.

Yet Andrew Jackson without his background of social revolt and humanitarian idealism could not be understood or explained. He was possible because the times had prepared the way for his coming and had ripened the popular mind for his message. Like Rostand's *Chantecler,* his crowing did not summon the sun of a new dawn, but his voice rang out in clarion tones when the morning light was breaking.

BIBLIOGRAPHICAL NOTE

The facts which are brought together in the foregoing treatment may be found scattered through many secondary works; but the vital relationship of these facts to each other and to the democratic upheaval of the twenties and the thirties was first made clear by Willis Mason West in his *American History and Government* (Boston, 1913), chap. xiii.

The western elements in the democratic movement have been best set forth by Frederick Jackson Turner in his essay, "Contributions of the West to American Democracy" (1903) in his *The Frontier in American History* (New York, 1920), chap. ix; and in his volume *Rise of the New West, 1819-1829* (in *The American Nation: a History,* vol. 14; New York, 1906), chaps. v-viii.

The facts concerning the pioneer labor movement in America were first set forth in documentary form in the monumental work edited by John R. Commons and four associates entitled *Documentary History of American Industrial Society* (10 v.; Cleveland, 1910-1911), of which vols. v and vi are devoted to "Labor Movements from

1820 to 1840." This material was put into the form of an historical narrative by John R. Commons and six other scholars in the work entitled *History of Labour in the United States* (2 v.; New York, 1918). Vol. i, parts ii and iii, deal with the period from 1820 to 1840.

The literary awakening has been treated with relation to its historical background by William B. Cairns in his monograph *On the Development of American Literature from 1815 to 1833 with Especial Reference to Periodicals* (Madison, 1898), and more adequately by William J. Long in his *American Literature* (Boston, 1913), chaps. iii-iv. The new tendencies in historical scholarship are the theme of John Spencer Bassett's volume *The Middle Group of American Historians* (New York, 1917).

The new religious trend may be studied in the histories of the various denominations. The facts concerning the Garrisonian abolition movement may be found in many places but nowhere more clearly than in Albert Bushnell Hart's *Slavery and Abolition, 1831-1841* (in *The American Nation: a History*, vol. 16; New York, 1906), chaps. xi-xviii, xxi. For the woman's movement in this period, see the Bibliographical Note at the close of chap. vi of the present volume. The educational awakening has been most appreciatively set forth with reference to the social and political background of the times by Ellwood P. Cubberley in his *Public Education in the United States* (Boston, 1919), chaps. iv-ix.

A synthetic treatment of the communistic experiments may be found in John Humphrey Noyes's *History of American Socialisms* (Philadelphia, 1870), and more briefly in Morris Hillquit's *History of Socialism in the United States* (New York, 1903), part i. The widespread interest in social reform is treated from the standpoint of transcendentalist philosophy by Ralph Waldo Emerson in his lecture entitled "New England Reformers," delivered in 1844 and reprinted in his *Complete Works* (12 v.; New York, n. d.), vol. iii, pp. 237-270. The political aspects of the democratic movement have been treated in an enlightening manner in M. Ostrogorski's *Democracy and the Organization of Political Parties* (2 v.; New York, 1902), vol. ii, chap. ii; Charles Edward Merriam's *A History of American Political Theories* (New York, 1903), chap. v; and William MacDonald's *Jacksonian Democracy, 1829-1837* (in *The American Nation: a History*, vol. 15; New York, 1906), chaps. iv, xiv, xv.

Of the many biographies of Andrew Jackson the most recent and best is that by John Spencer Bassett (2 v.; Garden City, 1911).

CHAPTER X

THE STATE RIGHTS FETISH

I

The doctrine of state rights is one that is intimately associated with American history, especially with certain movements and controversies that fell in the period before the Civil War. Writers and teachers of American history are accustomed to use the phrase as if it furnished a fundamental explanation of the motivation of events. That this is far from true any detailed examination of American history should make apparent; and indeed the expression itself has borne different meanings at different epochs or as understood by different leaders in the same epoch. At one period of our history the foremost exponents of the state rights theory were believers in nullification. At another time the doctrine was epitomized in the claim of the right of secession. In either of these forms the doctrine might more properly be called "state sovereignty." Yet again, those who promulgated state rights views had nothing more in contemplation than a peaceful political purpose to induce the federal government to allow freer play for the authority of the state governments.

These contrasting schools of state rights opinion did not essentially differ with each other as to fundamental purpose but, as we shall see, they held different views as to a practical program of achieving results. The kernel of all forms of the state rights doctrine was the desire of the state governments to enhance their power or, at least, to resist encroachments of the federal authority. Since the respective spheres of power of state and nation are defined in the federal Constitution, advocates of state rights, however they may have differed among themselves, all joined in professing a belief in a "strict construction" of that instrument. They held that the powers granted to the federal government in the Constitution should be understood in the most literal sense and, in the language of the tenth amendment, that the powers "not delegated to the United States by the Constitution, nor prohibited by it to the States," were "reserved to the States respectively, or to the people." [1]

The origin of the great controversy is to be found in the Federal Constitutional Convention. In a less direct sense, the state rights question is not to be regarded as an American problem at all, but rather as the inevitable fruit of any attempt to reconcile centralized federative control with local self-government. In this sense, the Revolutionary War may be regarded as a victory for state rights, or colonial self-government, carried to the point of secession; and the Articles of Confederation were a codification of that victory in the guise of a formal constitution under which the separate states became freer of their own central government than they as colonies had desired to be of the British home government. The chief task that confronted the leaders of the Federal Constitutional Convention was, in its essence, the same that the British government had failed to solve a dozen years before: the problem of harmonizing central unified control with state sovereignty.

The solution was worked out in the Constitutional Convention by men of practical vision who were resolved to

[1] It is interesting to note that the state-rights strict constructionists were always one-sided in the application of their doctrine, and were never willing to apply strict construction as a criterion when defining the rights reserved to the states. From this point of view those who are known in history as the broad constructionists, the men who desired to preserve or enlarge the powers of the federal government, may be regarded as strict constructionists in respect to state authority.

make the national government a going concern at whatever cost to preconceived theories of state sovereignty. The constitution they produced magnificently justified their method; but from the standpoint of pure theory the document necessarily contained compromises, concealments and inconsistencies which were eagerly seized upon by later disputants to justify their peculiar views of the nature of the federal system that had been created. Leaders of both the nationalist and state rights schools could find aid and comfort in the wording of the Constitution; but neither group could make out an impregnable case for its manner of thinking without ignoring or explaining away phrases and implications which supported the contrary position.

Readers of the older American histories are likely to get the impression that the state rights theory, like cotton and slavery, was a peculiar product of the South, and that in the political field it has dominated the beliefs and policies of the Democratic party. On the basis of these assumptions the history of the United States prior to the Civil War, and to some extent since, is pictured as a great struggle between two schools of governmental theory, the Democrats, and the South generally, being wedded by temperament and intellect to the one view, and the rival party supported by a majority of the northerners having a psychological affinity for the other. There is, of course, a measure of truth in all this; but the picture as a whole is in wrong perspective and blurs the essential facts.

It is the purpose of the present discussion to show, as Alexander Johnston has so well said, that "almost every state in the Union in turn declared its own 'sovereignty,' and denounced as almost treasonable similar declarations in other cases by other states," and, secondly, that political parties have been almost as variable in this respect as the states. Throughout the discussion it will appear that economic interest or some other local advantage has usually determined the attitude of states and parties toward questions of constitutional construction.

II

The first notable attempt by any state legislatures to formulate the state rights doctrine appeared in the well-known Virginia and Kentucky resolutions of 1798 and 1799. We know now that these resolutions had a political animus behind them. Drafted respectively by Madison and Jefferson, they were adopted by the legislatures of Virginia and Kentucky as a spectacular protest against the action of the Federalists in Congress in passing the Alien and Sedition Acts and other laws which seemed to contravene a plain reading of the Constitution. Far from being carefully reasoned documents, these resolutions resorted to extravagant language in much the same manner as modern political platforms and for exactly the same purpose: the arousing of popular indignation against the party in power.

By both states the Union was pronounced a compact formed by sovereign states which retained the right to decide when the federal government was acting beyond its constitutional powers. The Virginia resolutions asserted, somewhat vaguely, that when, as in the present case, the federal government was guilty of exceeding its authority, the states had the right "to interpose for arresting the progress of the evil"; and the Kentucky legislature, while bravely resolving that nullification was "the rightful remedy," ended up rather lamely by declaring that against the acts objected to "this Commonwealth does now enter . . . its solemn protest." In view of the next turning in the history of the state rights theory, it is interesting to note that the New England legislatures, controlled by Federalist opinion, were a unit in decrying the dangerous tendency of the Virginia and Kentucky resolutions and in asserting that the power of passing upon the constitutionality of acts of Congress was vested by the Constitution exclusively in the federal courts.

The second important development of the state rights doctrine grew out of very different circumstances. In December, 1807, the Republican party in Congress under the leadership of President Jefferson passed the embargo as an act of retaliation against British and French interferences with American trade during the Napoleonic wars. New England was the center of the shipbuilding industry and the chief carrier of world commerce at this time, and the people there bitterly resented a regulation which meant the total destruction of their chief source of wealth. They therefore embarked upon a career of obstruction and opposition to the federal government, that was to last far into the war that the United States waged with Great Britain from 1812 to 1815.

Forced to resort to minority tactics, the New England leaders found their most effective weapon in the adoption of the state rights doctrine which Jefferson and Madison had sponsored a few years earlier. In February, 1809, the Massachusetts legislature resolved that the embargo measures were, "in many respects, unjust, oppressive and unconstitutional, and not legally binding on the citizens of this state," though the citizens were counselled "to abstain from forcible resistance, and to apply for their remedy in a peaceable manner to the laws of the commonwealth." The Connecticut legislature resolved in a similar spirit that it would not "assist or concur in giving effect to the . . . unconstitutional act, passed to enforce the Embargo."

With the outbreak of the war with Great Britain, the New England leaders found new grounds for disaffection. One cause for complaint was the insistence of the United States government that the state militia should be called into service under federal officers. The Connecticut legislature solemnly resolved that "the state of Connecticut is a FREE SOVEREIGN and INDEPENDENT state; that the United States are a *confederacy* of states; that we are a confederated and not a consolidated republic," and that the demand of the War Department was in plain violation of the Constitution. When a conscription bill was proposed in Congress, the Connecticut legislature denounced it in October, 1814, as subversive of the "freedom, sovereignty and independence" of the state and "inconsistent with the principles of the constitution of the United States." The "free, sovereign and independent State of Massachusetts" gave vent to its disapproval in a succession of resolutions centering about the thought: "Whenever the national compact is violated, . . . this legislature is bound to interpose its power, and wrest from the oppressor his victim"; and it recalled that "This is the spirit of our Union" as "explained by the very man [President Madison], who now sets at defiance all the principles of his early political life."

The festering discontent reached its climax in the Hartford Convention of December, 1814, made up of official delegates from Massachusetts, Connecticut and Rhode Island, and of representatives from local conventions in New Hampshire and Vermont. We do not know to this day what occurred behind the closed doors of the convention hall although there is no doubt that talk of secession ran rife. Soberer counsels won the day, however. Resolutions were adopted repeating the gist of the Virginia resolutions of 1798 and demanding seven amendments to the federal Constitution which, if adopted, would remove all of the New England grievances. "If the Union be destined to dissolution," the convention announced to the world, " . . . it should, if possible, be the work of peaceable times, and deliberate consent."

The geographical center of the state rights agitation shifted once more with the renewal of the controversy over the United States Bank. When a bill for re-charter of the First Bank was pending in Congress, the Pennsylvania legislature in January, 1811, announced its conviction that the proposed measure was unwarranted by the Constitution, and asserted that the Constitution, "being to all intents and purposes a treaty between sovereign states, the general government by this treaty was not constituted the exclusive or final judge of the powers it was to exercise." The legislature of Virginia agreed that the passage of the bill "would be not only unconstitutional, but a dangerous encroachment on the sovereignty of the states."

When the Second United States Bank was finally established in 1816, hostility to the bank reappeared, being aggravated by the hard times attending the crisis of 1819 and by the opposition of the state banks. In several states the legislatures levied heavy taxes on the branches of the United States Bank within their boundaries; but the Supreme Court in the McCulloch v. Maryland decision in 1819 sustained the constitutionality of the bank and its exemption from state taxation. Nothing dismayed by this turn of events, the General Assembly of Ohio reaffirmed its right to tax the branch banks, endorsed the Virginia and Kentucky resolutions of 1798 and 1800, and denounced the dogma that the powers of "sovereign States" may be determined and settled by the United States Supreme Court.

The federal government found an outspoken friend in South Carolina and a somewhat unexpected defender in Massachusetts. In resolutions of 1821 and 1822 both states asserted the full right of Congress to enact laws establishing a national bank with branches in the several states, and Massachusetts, with an odor of self-righteousness, explicitly championed the right of the United States Supreme Court to settle all questions involving the constitutionality of legislation. Even Pennsylvania, which had pronounced the bank unconstitutional twenty years before, rallied to its support in 1831, and requested Congress to renew its charter!

Georgia was the next state to lift the standard of state rights. Her interest in the matter was the outgrowth of a long controversy with certain Indian tribes within her boundaries, in which the United States government was acting the part of protector of the Indians. In December, 1827, the legislature officially recorded its approval of a statement made by Governor Troup to the Secretary of War, that he felt it "to be his duty to resist to the utmost any military attack which the Government of the United States shall think proper to make on the territory, the People or the sovereignty of Georgia." When the United States Supreme Court handed down a decision favorable to the Indians, the legislature passed resolutions enjoining the officers of the state to ignore "every mandate and process" issued by the court, and requiring the governor to defend the rights of the state "with all the force and means placed at his command by the Constitution and laws of this state."

The action of Georgia aroused the attention of other states whose Indian problems had long since been settled. The legislatures of Massachusetts and Pennsylvania passed resolutions in support of the supremacy and integrity of the federal judiciary; and Connecticut, erstwhile defender of the compact theory, resolved in 1831 that "we regard the judicial department . . . as sacred in its origin, and invaluable in its purposes and objects." It must have been out of the fullness of her experience that she asserted that the legislatures "of the several states partake too readily of local jealousies and excitements to be entrusted with the final determination of questions involving the validity of the federal laws."

While the Georgia Indian controversy was being aired,

a new movement for state rights was gathering strength in a different quarter of the Union. The sentiment of South Carolina statesmen had hitherto been distinctly nationalistic; and when the legislature was urged in 1820 to denounce the protective system as unconstitutional, resolutions were adopted by the House of Representatives reprobating "the practice, unfortunately become too common, of arraying upon questions of national policy, the states as *distinct and independent sovereignties* . . . with a view to exercise a control *over* the general government."

It was the tariff question, however, that was soon to cause the planters of South Carolina the same bitterness of spirit that the merchants of New England had felt toward the embargo. A high tariff to foster manufacturing could be of no possible assistance to the South, and indeed damaged that section by greatly raising the prices of the manufactures they must buy. So by December, 1825, the South Carolina legislature made the expedient discovery that a protective tariff was "an unconstitutional exercise of power." In a like category, it placed federal aid to internal improvements, a measure which was chiefly beneficial to northern merchants seeking to broaden their domestic markets. In the next few years South Carolina was joined in her new convictions by the nearby states of Virginia, Georgia, Alabama and Mississippi.

But South Carolina soon began to press forward to positions and views in advance of those of her sister states of the South. Having arrived at the opinion in 1827 that the Constitution was a compact of the states "as separate, independent sovereignties," the South Carolina legislature in the next year adopted the famous "Exposition," written by John C. Calhoun, which explicitly announced the right of a state to nullify federal laws that were regarded by the state as unconstitutional. A few years later, in November, 1832,

South Carolina put her threat into execution through the passage of an "Ordinance of Nullification" by a state convention expressly assembled for that purpose. In her opposition to the protective tariff South Carolina had carried her state rights views to lengths that had never been more than hinted at by any of her predecessors. When Congress granted her a measure of relief through the passage of the compromise tariff of 1833, the South Carolina convention solemnly repealed the Ordinance of Nullification and adopted a new ordinance nullifying the so-called Force Bill of Congress.

The leaders of South Carolina in this crisis had at their tongues' end the earlier history of the state rights doctrine in America, but they sought in vain for friends and defenders where they had every right to expect them. In the first stages of the controversy, Ohio and Pennsylvania, both former expounders of the state rights position, expressed their belief that the tariff was entirely constitutional. Even those states of the South which had earlier declared a belief in the unconstitutionality of the tariff system were not willing to follow the logic of South Carolina into nullification. The Virginia legislature officially resolved that the Virginia resolutions of 1798 did not sustain the nullification proceedings in South Carolina. The Georgia legislature, which only recently had defied the Supreme Court and the federal government in her dispute over the Indian lands, could now declare with good conscience: "we abhor the doctrine of Nullification as neither a ·peaceful, nor a constitutional remedy, but, on the contrary, as tending to civil commotion and disunion." The resolutions of Alabama and North Carolina were no less emphatic, Mississippi adding, with myopic vision into the future, "we stand firmly resolved, . . . in all events and at every hazard, to sustain" the president in "preserving the integrity of the Union—that

Union, whose value we will never stop to calculate—holding it, as our fathers held it, precious above all price." Perhaps the most unkindest cut of all was administered by the Kentucky legislature, which in 1799 had first announced the right of nullification. The Kentucky resolutions proclaimed the unqualified right of the majority to govern through laws of Congress, and denied that either South Carolina or any other state had the constitutional right to defeat the will of the majority.

From the close of the nullification episode of 1832-1833 to the outbreak of the Civil War, the agitation of state rights was intimately connected with a new issue of growing importance, the slavery question, and the principal form assumed by the doctrine was that of the right of secession. The pro-slavery forces sought refuge in the state rights position as a shield against federal interference with pro-slavery projects; and, as we shall see, many southern states which had hitherto been hostile or apathetic to the doctrine as a philosophical abstraction became its foremost advocates. As a natural consequence, anti-slavery legislatures in the North were led to lay great stress on the national character of the Union and the broad powers of the general government in dealing with slavery. Nevertheless, it is significant to note that when it served anti-slavery purposes better to lapse into state rights dialectic, northern legislatures did not hesitate to be inconsistent.

Thus the legislature of Massachusetts resolved in 1844 that "the project of the annexation of Texas," if carried through to success by the pro-slavery forces, "may tend to drive these states into a dissolution of the union"; and when, notwithstanding, annexation was accomplished in the following year, the legislature resolved that "Massachusetts hereby refuses to acknowledge the act . . . authorizing the admission of Texas, as a legal act, in any way binding her from using her utmost exertions in coöperation with other States, by every lawful and constitutional measure, to annul its conditions, and defeat its accomplishment." Vermont, Ohio and Connecticut likewise protested that the federal government had exceeded its constitutional powers in annexing Texas as a state. With the outbreak of the Mexican War, the Massachusetts legislature denounced it as a pro-slavery war of conquest, and in 1847 resolved that the struggle was "unjust and unconstitutional in its origin and character" and that all good citizens should unite to stop it.

The New Jersey legislature found occasion as late as 1852 to declare, in solemn resolutions, that the Constitution was "a compact between the several States" and that the general government had been granted by the sovereign states only limited powers. The passage of the Fugitive Slave Act of 1850 called forth fresh evidences of latent state rights feeling in the North. Many of the legislatures of that section passed so-called Personal Liberty Laws, designed to obstruct the recovery of fugitive slaves under the federal act. "They were dangerously near the nullification of a United States law," James Ford Rhodes tells us. In 1855 and 1856, resolutions were passed by the legislatures of Massachusetts and Ohio pronouncing the Fugitive Slave Act unwarranted by the Constitution. In Wisconsin the state Supreme Court held the law to be "unconstitutional and void"; and when the federal Supreme Court reversed the decision, the state legislature resolved in 1859, on the verge of the war to preserve the Union, that the several states which had formed the federal compact, being "sovereign and independent," had "the unquestionable right to judge of its infractions" and to resort to "positive defiance" of all unauthorized acts of the general government.

The authority of the federal judiciary was also assailed from many quarters when the Supreme Court handed down the Dred Scott decision opening the federal territories to slavery. Ohio and other northern states lost no time in declaring the decision to be "repugnant to the plain provisions of the Constitution"; and the Maine legislature joined Ohio in calling for a reorganization of the court.

Notwithstanding these occasional instances of reversion to type on the part of northern states, the state rights theory received its most important development in this period at the hands of the southern legislatures. In the struggle over the tariff, South Carolina had developed the theory and technique of nullification to a high point of perfection, only to find, on trying out the method, that it was certain to be ineffective in practice unless accompanied with the tacit concurrence of the federal government. The incident had shown conclusively that, in a test of force, a resolute federal government would always be able to enforce United States law in a nullifying state. The implications of the compact theory readily suggested a logical substitute for nullification in secession; and this measure henceforth became the great shibboleth of the southern state rights school.

Already in 1831 the South Carolina legislature had announced that "This is a confederacy of sovereign States, and each may withdraw from the confederacy when it chooses"; and in the Ordinance of Nullification, the South Carolina convention of 1832 had warned the United States government that, if any act of coercion were directed against that state, the people would "hold themselves absolved from all further . . . political connexion" with the Union. In reply to these assertions, Maryland, Delaware and Kentucky, all of them slave states, declared expressly against the constitutional right of secession. But as the fundamental character of the conflict between slavery and freedom became apparent in the subsequent years, one southern state after another began, rather reluctantly, to array itself at the side of South Carolina in her advanced constitutional position.

By 1850 the controversy over slavery reached an acute
stage; and the actual secession of several southern states
was prevented only by the enactment of Clay's famous compromise measures. These measures, in the nature of the
case, were only partially satisfactory to the South; and
special conventions were called in a number of southern
states to consider the advisability of secession. The conventions of Georgia and South Carolina agreed that, although
the occasion was provocative, they would await further
aggressions of the federal government before seceding; but
Mississippi and Tennessee, with no premonition of the events
of 1861, roundly denounced secession as unsanctioned by
the Constitution.

The irritations produced by another decade of sectional
strife gave to the South the united front that had hitherto
been lacking; and with the election of Lincoln and the firing
on Fort Sumter, eleven southern states enacted ordinances of
secession through special state conventions, and one other
state, Kentucky, standing athwart the military highway
between the sections, announced its sovereign decision
in favor of neutrality. In an eloquent indictment of northern policy, the Mississippi convention presented the
case of the South in its most favorable light: "We must
either submit to degradation and to the loss of property
[in slaves] worth four billions of money, or we must secede
from the Union framed by our fathers, to secure this as
well as every other species of property. For far less cause
than this our fathers separated from the Crown of England."

The victory of the federal government in the Civil War
forever settled the theory of state rights so far as nullification and secession were concerned. Express disavowal of
doctrines so utterly discredited on the battlefield was hardly
required; but the southern state conventions of 1865, held
to reorganize the state governments under President Johnson's supervision, solemnly proclaimed the invalidity of their

ordinances of secession. The conventions of South Carolina and Georgia, with a fine, if futile, consistency, preferred to repeal rather than to repudiate their ordinances.

Since the Civil War the federal government has progressed with unprecedented rapidity toward a consolidation of authority. Steam and electricity, and the dwindling importance of state boundaries in matters of commerce, have made many matters fit subjects for national control which seemed better off in the hands of the states one hundred years ago. Edward A. Freeman, the English historian, observed while traveling in the United States in 1883 that "where the word 'federal' used to be used up to the time of the civil war or later, the word 'national' is now used all but invariably. It used to be 'federal capital,' 'federal army,' 'federal revenue,' and so forth. Now the word 'national' is almost always used instead."

Protests against this centralizing tendency have been expressed again and again; but in these latter years the remonstrances have not usually been uttered by the states in their organic capacities, nor have the protests been designed to accomplish anything more than a revulsion of public sentiment from the current drift of events. In this sense, stripped of its disunionist tendencies, the state rights doctrine will doubtless always be with us. Senator Joseph E. Ramsdell, speaking before the constitutional convention of Louisiana in 1921, represented the views of many present-day believers in state rights when he said: "The Nation is rapidly growing in power and importance as compared with the States. Amendments to the Constitution increasing Federal power have been frequent, but whoever heard of one in the interest of the States? I have never believed in the extreme doctrine of State rights taught by many Democrats of the old school. My leaning has been toward a relatively strong central government, without giving up wha*

I deem essential to the States, but the pace of Federal encroachment which we have been traveling for 20 years has been too fast for me. I wish to see it slowed up, and a movement backward rather than forward. . . ."

III

The same pervasive influences which played upon states and geographical sections and helped to mold their constitutional views have affected the attitude of political parties on questions of constitutional interpretation. But, in addition, another element must be taken into account, arising from the psychology of politics: the party in power always feels that the Constitution, however broadly construed, is perfectly safe in its keeping, while the minority party is convinced that the welfare of the people demands that the majority should be restrained to a very narrow exercise of governmental authority. Hence the "Ins" have always tended to be strong nationalists, and the "Outs" strict constructionists and advocates of state rights.

American history is rich in illustrations of the instability of the constitutional beliefs of parties. The Jeffersonian Republican party originated in Washington's first administration as a party of strict construction and state rights. Jefferson's argument against the constitutionality of the United States Bank remained for many years the classic exposition of strict construction doctrine; and the Virginia and Kentucky resolutions, drawn up by Madison and Jefferson, proved a veritable Pandora's box of future state rights philosophy. It seemed to the Republicans that the Federalists, dominated by the broad construction views of Hamilton, were intent on converting the federal government into an engine of centralization and virtual monarchy, and that the nation could be saved from this fate only by a rigid insistence that the government should abide by the phraseology of the Constitution literally construed.

But when Jefferson and his party came into power, the need for applying brakes to the federal government became insensibly less important to them. The opportunity to acquire the vast territory of Louisiana from France in 1803 showed Jefferson, greatly to his own surprise, how far he had drifted from his earlier convictions. In an amazingly frank letter written at the time, he confessed: "The constitution has made no provision for our holding foreign territory. . . . The executive, in seizing the fugitive occurrence which so much advances the good of our country, have done an act beyond the constitution. The Legislature, in casting behind them metaphysical subtleties, and risking themselves like faithful servants, must ratify and pay for it, and throw themselves on the country for doing for them what we know they would have done for themselves had they been in a situation to do it." In other words, it was all right to violate the Constitution if Congress and the president thought that the mass of the voters approved.

The change of front of the Republicans was only equalled by a similar reversal on the part of the Federalists. High priests of nationalism and broad construction while in power, Federalist leaders began to view with alarm the centralizing tendencies of their successful opponents. In Congress they resisted the Louisiana cession as unconstitutional because the treaty provided for future membership in the Union. The Federalists were pledged to the development of commerce and shipping; and the creation of new states out of the Louisiana wilderness meant new recruits for the agricultural policies of the Republicans. Acceptance of the Louisiana treaty would have been for them a form of political suicide. When the treaty was ratified in spite of their protests, some of the Federalist leaders plotted, in their extremity, to bring about the secession of New England and New York from the Union. The adhesion of New York seemed to depend upon the election of Aaron Burr to the governorship in 1804; and when Burr proved unsuccessful, the conspirators were forced to defer their plans to a more propitious time. The nationalistic trend of the Republicans gave the Federalists many further causes for complaint in the next ten years and, as we have already seen, led finally to the assembling of the Hartford Convention in 1814, under the inspiration of disgruntled Federalist politicians, to consult upon measures to restore New England to its ancient position in the Union.

By 1816 the Republicans had become thoroughly nationalized, their remaining scruples being dispelled by the patriotic impulses born of the War of 1812. The legislation passed by Congress in 1816 and 1817 shows how complete the conversion was. Although the Republicans had refused to re-charter the First United States Bank in 1811, the party now proceeded to create a Second United States Bank more than three times as large as the one Hamilton had founded. A protective tariff was also enacted; and had President Madison withheld his veto, a permanent fund would have been set aside for internal improvements at national expense.

The attitude of two young members of this Congress deserves especial mention in this connection. Daniel Webster, a Federalist hailing from Massachusetts and not yet conscious of the relation of manufacturing to the future prosperity of his section, opposed all this nationalistic program. On the contrary, John C. Calhoun, of South Carolina, equally heedless of the rôle that cotton was soon to play in the prosperity of the South, was an eloquent advocate of broad construction. In words that he was never after permitted to forget, he denounced all tendencies toward sectionalism and disunion, and declared that the Constitution "was not intended as a thesis for the logician to exercise his ingenuity on" but should be construed in a generous spirit and with plain good sense. By 1830 the two men had exchanged positions. With a truer appreciation of the sources of the economic prosperity of their respective sections, Webster became the greatest advocate of nationalism that the country possessed prior to the Civil War, and Calhoun became the inspired leader of the state rights extremists.

There is no time to dwell upon the shades of difference between the Jackson Democrats and the Calhoun Democrats as to state rights doctrine. Suffice it to say that after Jackson retired from office the southern Democrats gained control of the party organization and, in very large part, stamped their peculiar views upon the party creed. Democratic platforms adopted in 1840 and thereafter demanded a strict construction of the Constitution ("it is inexpedient and dangerous to exercise doubtful constitutional powers"), and specifically denounced the protective tariff, the United States Bank and national internal improvements. Yet, notwithstanding these earnest avowals, some of the most striking events of the period down to the Civil War came as a result of the exercise of broad construction powers by these very Democrats!

Although, as Jefferson had admitted in 1803, the Constitution nowhere expressly authorized the acquisition of foreign territory, the Democrats of this period proved to be the most aggressive expansionists in our history. Texas. was annexed in 1845, followed three years later by the acquisition of a goodly portion of the neighboring republic of Mexico. Polk, Pierce and Buchanan, unsated, pressed forward schemes to annex Cuba and other Caribbean territories. Equally clear was the illegality of internal improvements by a strict reading of the Constitution; yet Jefferson Davis himself, as Secretary of War under Pierce, proposed the construction of a transcontinental railway along a southern route at a cost estimated at perhaps one hundred million dollars to the federal government. President Pierce endorsed the project and it would probably have been adopted by Congress had not Stephen A. Douglas inopportunely revived sectional bitterness by the introduction of the Kansas-Nebraska Act in 1854.

Not less instructive was the attitude of the Democratic party toward the Dred Scott decision of 1857. As long as the Supreme Court remained a transmitter of doctrines unfavorable to southern interests, that tribunal had been assailed by state rights advocates as a usurper of unconstitutional powers. No principle had been more firmly fixed in state rights thinking than that the federal judiciary could not pass judgment on the constitutionality of the acts of the federal government. Now southern leaders everywhere endorsed this pro-slavery decision of the Supreme Court and, in the language of Stephen A. Douglas, maintained that "whoever resists the final decision of the highest judicial tribunal aims a deadly blow to our whole republican system of government." These lapses from state rights orthodoxy were without doubt dictated by the self-interest of the South, but in no wise detracted from the earnestness with which pro-slavery Democrats on all other occasions asserted their constitutional right of nullification and secession.

In the first presidential campaign after Appomattox the Democrats hastened to clear their official creed of those elements of state rights doctrine that had been rendered obsolete by the Civil War. Their platform of 1868 recognized "the questions of slavery and secession as having been settled for all time to come by the war or the voluntary action of the Southern States in constitutional conventions assembled, . . . never to be renewed or reagitated." Hopelessly in the minority for many years thereafter and distrustful of the political capacity of the Republicans, the Democrats declared in their platforms again and again for a strict construction of the Constitution and denounced Republican "centralizationism." In 1892 and again in 1912 they even took the doctrinaire position that the protective tariff was a violation of the Constitution.

Their criticism of the Republicans was fully warranted so far as it related to the undoubted fact that the power of the government at Washington was being greatly enlarged beyond the dreams of a Hamilton or a Webster. But the explanation for this centripetal trend lay deeper than party. In the era of great economic expansion following the Civil War, business overleaped state boundaries and became nationwide. Labor and education were likewise nationalized. The silent march of events was making a nationalistic program the inevitable code of action of the general government irrespective of which party might be in control.

Extreme tariff protection, national supervision of state elections, lavish subsidies to railroads and other internal improvements—all these were Republican contributions to the new nationalism at the expense of a literal interpretation of the Constitution. But the advent of the Democrats to power in 1885 was marked by no attempt to reinvigorate the power of the states. A startling new assertion of national authority came in the passage of the Interstate Commerce Act, which President Cleveland signed; and in the case of the Pullman strike of 1893, he sent troops to Chicago in defiance of the traditional reading of the Constitution. In the latter instance Governor Altgeld of Illinois, who had refused to apply for federal assistance, felt called upon to remind the Democratic president that "The principle of local self-government is just as fundamental in our institutions as is that of federal supremacy."

In the opening years of the twentieth century the artificial nature of party gestures on constitutional questions has appeared clearer than ever before. Roosevelt in his administration of the government proved to be an aggressive nationalist, and aroused the bitter animosity of the Democrats because of the alleged unconstitutional character of many of his acts. The Democratic platform of 1904 denounced the "strained and unnatural constructions upon statutes," stigmatized Roosevelt's interference in the Panama Revolution as unconstitutional, and called for the election of a president "who will set his face sternly against executive usurpation of legislative and judicial functions, whether that usurpation be veiled under the guise of executive construction of existing laws, or whether it take refuge in the tyrant's plea of necessity or superior wisdom."

But the tables were turned with the accession of Wilson and his party to power in 1913. Eager to meet the imperative needs of the times, the Democrats used their power to pass law after law that could be justified only by a very elastic interpretation of the Constitution. A child labor law was placed upon the statute books in 1916, based upon the interstate commerce power of Congress; and when the act was pronounced unconstitutional by the Supreme Court, Congress proceeded to enact another law for the same purpose based upon the taxing power. The Federal Trade Commission Act, the Federal Reserve Act and the Federal Farm Loan Act represented other vast extensions of national authority by the Democrats. Of the Federal Reserve Act Senator Ramsdell, one of its southern supporters, said in an address before the Louisiana constitutional convention in 1921 that it "places colossal power in the Federal Government, a power which is intended for good . . . but . . . which in the hands of an ambitious autocrat or corrupt board can be used to work great evil." He further asserted that the Adamson Eight-Hour Law of 1916, establishing a standard eight-hour day for the railroads, "steps on the toes of the States pretty hard and in many ways."

When a country is engaged in war, one expects a great concentration of power in the hands of the government at Washington; but even in this respect the Democratic administration went to extremes. At President Wilson's behest, Congress passed the selective draft law; and this was soon followed by statutes vesting in the federal government far-reaching powers of control over railroads, telephones, fuel, food, prices, alcoholic beverages, and indeed over freedom of speech and of the press. However temporary some of these measures may have been in their importance, the Democratic Congress proposed two new amendments to the Constitution which invaded domains which had long been jealously guarded by the states, one providing for the abolition of intoxicating liquors and the other forbidding the states to deny the suffrage to women.

Many of these laws, particularly those adopted before the United States entered the World War, were hotly contested in Congress as unwarranted by the Constitution; and the Democratic president was bitterly denounced by his Republican opponents for his "unconstitutional and dictatorial course," just as Roosevelt had formerly been by the Democrats. In an almost perfect paraphrase of the Democratic platform of 1904, the Republican platform of 1920 said of President Wilson: "Under the despot's plea of necessity or superior wisdom, Executive usurpation of legislative and judicial functions . . . undermines our institutions." The chorus of opposition reached its climax when President Wilson returned from the Paris Peace Conference with the Covenant of the League of Nations. The Republican senators, unable to reconcile themselves to a pact which they claimed bound the United States contrary to stipulations of the national Constitution, managed to prevent ratification by the United States.

IV

The facts that have been presented in the foregoing discussion speak for themselves. There can be no doubt that state rights agitation has played a large part in American history; but it is equally clear that the controversy must always be studied in its relation to time and circumstances. The state rights doctrine has never had any real vitality independent of underlying conditions of vast social, economic or political significance. The group advocating state rights at any period have sought its shelter in much the same spirit that a western pioneer seeks his storm-cellar when a tornado is raging. The doctrine has served as a species of protective coloration against the threatening onslaughts of a powerful foe. As a well-known American historian has tersely said, "Scratch a Wisconsin farmer and you find a Georgia planter!"

BIBLIOGRAPHICAL NOTE

Beginning with the foundation of the federal government, innumerable treatises have been written and addresses made upon the nature of the Union. These discussions were usually controversial in purpose and designed to supply historical reasons to show why the general government should enjoy greater or less authority in its relation to the states and the people thereof. Some of the greatest minds in our history have grappled with this central problem of federated government, for example, James Madison, Alexander Hamilton, Thomas Jefferson, John Marshall, Joseph Story, Daniel Webster, John C. Calhoun and Abraham Lincoln; and more recently the legal aspects of the problem have been learnedly discussed from an academic point of view by John W. Burgess, J. Allen Smith, W. W. Willoughby and others. For an excellent historical summary of American political theory dealing with the nature of the Union, see C. Edward Merriam's *A History of American Political Theories* (New York, 1903), chap. vii, and his *American Political Ideas, 1865-1917* (New York, 1920), chap. viii.

The point of view, which forms the basis of the discussion in the present volume, was suggested by Alexander Johnston in John J. Lalor's *Cyclopedia of Political Science, Political Economy and of the Political History of the United States* (3 v.; New York, 1893), vol. iii, p. 794, so far as the relation of states to the federal government is concerned. Its detailed application in the case of particular states was worked out in David Franklin Houston's *A Critical Study of Nullification in South Carolina* (New York, 1896) ; William A. Schaper's "Sectionalism and Representation in South Carolina" in the *Annual Report* of the American Historical Association for 1900, vol. i, pp. 237-463; Ulrich Bonnell Phillips's "Georgia and State Rights" in the *Annual Report* of the American Historical Association for 1901, vol. ii; and later, in Charles Henry Ambler's *Sectionalism in Virginia from 1776 to 1861* (Chicago, 1910). In 1906 appeared Herman V. Ames's compilation of official documents entitled *State Documents on Federal Relations: The States and the United States* (Philadelphia), a collection which showed that what held true in the case of South Carolina and Georgia was likewise true of the other states in their attitude toward the general government. Every student of American history would do well to be acquainted with Dean Ames's volume.

Although the foregoing works are primarily concerned with the official attitude of the states on constitutional questions, the viewpoint readily furnishes a key to the constitutional doctrines of the great political parties. In the sketch in the present volume, some illustrations have been drawn from political history to show the changeable character of party views on the nature of the Constitution. In this connection a violently partisan book entitled *Logic of History. Five Hundred Political Texts: Being Concentrated Extracts of Abolitionism; Also, Results of Slavery Agitation and Emancipation* (Madison, 1864) is of interest. Annotated by S. D. Carpenter, a Copperhead editor, the work contains hundreds of excerpts from political speeches, party newspapers, and resolutions of local party conventions to show that expressions of strict construction and disunionism were by no means confined to the *ante bellum* Democratic party. It is perhaps worth noting that Alexander Johnston, who saw clearly the artificial character of the state rights theory as avowed by the several states, would probably not have agreed that the same conclusion held true of political parties. See passage in his *History of American Politics* (New York, 1882), p. 2.

CHAPTER XI

THE FOUNDATIONS OF THE MODERN ERA

I

It is the custom of students of European history to place the beginning of modern times several centuries ago, indeed at about the time that Christopher Columbus set sail for America; and when one reviews the long painful struggle of Europe, reaching back into the dim mists of antiquity, to attain its present stage of civilization, no serious question can be raised with this practice.[1] But the history of the white man in America is painted upon a smaller canvas; the total period of time embraced is comparatively short; and the physical environment has been such as to reproduce many of the primitive social and institutional conditions which the progress of European peoples had long since rendered obsolete in the Old World. Therefore it may be admissible to think of the modern era of America independently of the corresponding period in Europe; and without seeking to strain the analogy, there is an advantage in viewing the earlier history of America as divided into periods which are strongly suggestive of the ancient and medieval periods of European history.

Ancient American history was, from the standpoint of the white man, the age of discovery and European colonization, and was itself preceded by a "pre-historic" period of

---

[1] However, the suggestion of Harry Elmer Barnes, writing in the spirit of Wells's *Outline of History,* that modern times might more correctly be dated from neolithic man has large corrective value for the historical student. See "The Past and Future in History" in the *Historical Outlook,* vol. xii, p. 48 (February, 1921).

native Indian civilizations, the records of which have come to us in the form of monuments, ornaments, and picture-writing. The keynote of ancient American history was the transplantation of an advanced civilization to a primitive and undeveloped world. The transition to the medieval period came when the English colonies, and later the Spanish colonies, severed political connections with the Old World by means of revolutionary wars for independence. In the case of the United States the Middle Period was characterized by the dissensions and jealousies of baronies (or states) with the growing power of the overlord (or federal government), and the entire national life was strongly tinctured by the plantation system of the South with its feudal lords and black vassals.

Medieval American history was brought to a close by two epochal events. The first of these, the victory of the federal government in the Civil War, discredited forever the doctrine of state sovereignty and destroyed the anachronism of slavery. The other event was, in its lasting effects, more significant than the war itself, although, strangely enough, the historians of the period have little to say about it. This was the great economic revolution which swept through the nation at high tide from about 1860 to 1880 and willy nilly projected America into Modern Times.

Life in the United States before the Civil War had a peculiar static quality so far as the essentials of living were concerned. There were no great cities in our modern sense, and fewer than a half-dozen millionaires. People in general lived comfortably and wastefully. There was virtual equality of material possessions and always an opportunity for the man who could not make a livelihood in the crowded portions of the country to make a clean start on the frontier. An old letter recently discovered in the files of the United States Patent Office shows that in 1833 the head of that department wished to resign because he felt that the limit of human invention had been reached and there would be no further need of his services.

To be sure, mute forces were working beneath the surface of American society that were prophetic of future changes; but these were little heeded or understood at the time. There had occurred an industrial revolution in England in the latter part of the eighteenth century, the significance of which appeared in the introduction of the factory system into that country and the profoundly changed relations in industry and society that resulted. Under the influence of the embargo and the tariffs of 1816 and 1824, manufacturing had begun to develop in certain districts of the seaboard states of the North; but the country as a whole was untouched by the factory system, being predominantly agricultural in its interests and modes of living. Nearly four-fifths of the people continued to live on the farm.

In most respects the daily routine of life with which Webster and Lincoln were familiar was the same as that of George Washington and Benjamin Franklin; and there was in no sense the profound contrast that we have between the times of Lincoln and those we live in today. As Professor Cubberley has pointed out, if Lincoln were to return now and walk about Washington, he would be surprised and bewildered by the things he would see. Buildings more than three or four stories high would be new. The plate-glass show windows of the stores, the electric street-lighting, the moving-picture theatres, the electric elevators in the buildings and especially the big department stores would be things in his day unknown. The smooth-paved streets and cement sidewalks would be new to him. The fast-moving electric street-cars and motor vehicles would fill him with wonder. Even a boy on a bicycle would be a curiosity. Entering the White House, someone would have to explain to him such commonplaces of modern life as sanitary plumbing, steam heating, friction matches, telephones, electric lights, the Victrola, and even the fountain pen. In Lincoln's day, plumbing was in its beginnings, coal-oil lamps and gas-jets were just coming into use, and the steel pen had only recently superseded the quill pen. The steel rail, the steel bridge, high-powered locomotives, refrigerator cars, artificial ice, the cream separator, the twine binder, the caterpillar tractor, money orders, the parcels post, rural free delivery, the cable, the wireless, gasoline engines, repeating rifles, dynamite, submarines, airplanes—these and hundreds of other inventions now in common use were all alike unknown.

A number of things conspired to introduce a new economic and social order into American life in the sixties and the seventies. The high war tariffs caused men of capital to invest their money in manufacturing; and government contracts for war supplies gave impetus to this development. The state and national governments embarked on a policy of making vast grants of land and credit to railroad enterprises, thus laying the foundations for the modern era of railway development. The passage of the free homestead law of 1862 caused a rush of population toward the West, a movement that was vastly stimulated by the opening up of the less accessible regions by the railroads. These various factors reacted upon each other. Thus, the railroads called upon the factories for the manufacture of steel rails and locomotives, and by means of their iron highways supplied new markets for eastern manufacturers as well as for the western farmers. The unprecedented activity along all lines of economic endeavor imposed fresh demands upon American inventive genius to which it responded with countless new appliances and machines for farm and factory.

So rapid and comprehensive were the changes that occurred in the two decades following Lincoln's inauguration that no less a term than "economic revolution" is required to describe them. Referring particularly to American industrial development, the United States Industrial Commission declared in 1902 that "the changes and the progress since 1865 have been greater in many directions than during the whole history of the world before." In contrast to the industrial revolution in England, however, the economic revolution was not merely a revolution in manufacturing processes. In just as significant a sense it was an agricultural revolution and also a revolution in transportation. The United States was transformed in a generation from a nation employing primitive methods of agriculture and importing most of her manufactures from abroad, into an industrialized country with an export trade in farm and factory products that reached the outer fringes of the globe. It is to this new economic basis of American life that the historian must ascribe the characteristic events of recent history—the new issues, the changed character of political parties, the growing conflict between capital and labor, our complex social problems, indeed our very intellectual and cultural ideals and aspirations.

The full force of these new energies was not immediately apparent, because the attention of the public, after the great emotional experience of the Civil War, was for the time being riveted upon certain perplexing questions concerning the emancipated negroes and the political reconstruction of the South. But with the truer perspective made possible by the passage of years the historians are beginning to give less attention to southern reconstruction and more to northern reconstruction, since the financial and industrial reorganization of the North has proved to be of greater enduring importance.

Notwithstanding the transient importance of after-war issues, thoughtful people everywhere were conscious of an impending change in the fundamentals of American life or of a change perhaps already accomplished. In 1871, Henry Ward Beecher, speaking in a prophetic sense, declared: "We are today in more danger from overgrown pecuniary interests—from organized money—than we ever were from slavery, and the battle of the future is to be one of gold and silver." That amazing book published a few years ago, *The Education of Henry Adams,* has as its dominant recurring note the unwillingness or inability of a descendant of John and John Quincy Adams to accept the changed social order born of the economic revolution. In a revealing passage dealing with the great economic overturn, Henry Adams, following his habit of speaking of himself in the third person, confessed: "the result of this revolution on a survivor from the fifties resembled the action of the earthworm; he twisted about, in vain, to recover his starting-point; he could no longer see his own trail; he had become an estray; a flotsam or jetsam of wreckage. . . . His world was dead. Not a Polish Jew fresh from Warsaw or Cracow . . . but had a keener instinct, an intenser energy, and a freer hand than he—American of Americans, with Heaven knew how many Puritans and Patriots behind him, and an education that had cost a civil war. . . . One comfort he could enjoy to the full. Little as he might be fitted for the work that was before him, he had only to look at his father [Charles Francis Adams] and [John Lothrop] Motley to see figures less fitted for it than he. All were equally survivals from the forties—bric-à-brac from the time of Louis Philippe. . . ."

Political leadership naturally fell to men who were in harmony with the changed conditions of American life. The new school of statesmen were men of a practical stamp, not profound students of history like Madison nor keen theoreticians like Calhoun nor great orators like Webster. They have been men of affairs interested in directing the energies of the government in such a way as to permit the rapid development of the natural resources of the country and the building up of gigantic business enterprises. Such questions as "sound money," government aids to industry, the protective tariff and trust regulation became the dominant issues in politics. Some of these men were unscrupulous and corrupt; but most of them were sincere and patriotic, believing, rightly or wrongly, that the national prosperity depended upon the accumulation of wealth in a few hands. The newer statesmanship was represented by such men as Roscoe Conkling of New York, James G. Blaine of Maine, Samuel J. Randall of Pennsylvania, and, a little later, by Marcus Hanna of Ohio and Nelson W. Aldrich of Rhode Island. All these men made a strong impression upon their contemporaries, but few of their names will live in history. While their prototypes are still common in American politics, the group as a whole reached the zenith of their power before 1900 and have enjoyed less influence since.

The reform spirit was not without its exponents within the ranks of the dominant parties after the Civil War; but even the reformers, such men as Grover Cleveland, George W. Curtis and Carl Schurz, did not quarrel seriously with the political objects of the men who were usually in power. They warred, rather, against inefficiency and corruption in the conduct of government. Their efforts secured ballot reform, civil service reform and the entering wedge of tariff reform; but they never ceased to resent the charge that they were idealists or closet philosophers. It was Cleveland who expressed the thought of this earnest minority when he said in the course of fighting for one of his great reforms: "It is a condition that confronts us, not a theory." Indeed the idea of political reform for purely humanitarian objects has found a lodging place in the minds of effective party leaders only since about 1900, and the new conception represented a reaction against the materialistic bent of the political generation which had dominated public life down to that time.

II

The real significance of the economic revolution in the making of modern America is more readily seen upon a closer examination of the three great fields of transportation, agriculture and manufacturing, in which the chief changes occurred.

In 1860 there were thirty thousand miles of railroad in this country; this number had doubled by 1870 and trebled by 1880, being greatly increased by the building of the five transcontinental lines. By the close of the century it had reached the astounding total of almost two hundred thousand miles, equivalent to an eight-track railroad encircling the globe. The increase of mileage was attended by a growth of consolidation of management. Until about 1870, a railroad a few hundred miles in length constituted the maximum for efficient operation. A traveler from New York to the Mississippi might be required to make no less than a half dozen bodily transfers from one line to another. The Illinois Central, with seven hundred miles of track, was long considered one of the greatest railroads in the world. After 1870 began the development of "through lines," and the maximum length of a single railroad became five thousand miles. Since 1890, consolidation has progressed to new limits. Railroad systems have grown out of the amalgamation of through lines, some of them comprising twenty thousand miles of track under common control. The railway employees in 1900 represented an army of one million men, a number which has now swollen to two millions and which, including their families, means that today more than eight million persons are directly interested in the welfare of the railroad industry.

The rapid expansion of the railroads, with its attendant shrinkage of distances, was of incalculable value in helping to bring together again the South and the North in a new unity of purpose. But more obvious to people at the time was the service of the railroads in facilitating the settlement of the West. The world was astonished at the rapidity with which the virginal spaces of the West were occupied. By 1900 the Union had grown in forty years from thirty-three states to forty-five. Lands and natural resources which had seemed illimitable in 1860 thus passed, in very large part, into the possession of private owners. By 1890 the official frontier had vanished; and the lands left in the government's keeping were not such as to attract settlers.

As a result an important social force disappeared from American life. With this means of escape cut off, life has tended to become a bitter and sometimes hopeless struggle for men who cannot make their way against the fierce competition of the more populous sections of the country. Social conditions in the United States for the first time begin to approach the conditions of life in the Old World. In a somewhat tardy attempt to restore the earlier conditions of western settlement, the conservation movement, fathered by President Roosevelt, found one of its chief sources of inspiration. Since 1900 commendable progress has been made by the government in irrigating arid lands, draining swamp lands, protecting mineral resources owned by the government, and providing for the replanting of deforested tracts.

Another stream of influences flowed from the rapid growth of the railroads. The unscrupulous practices of the railroads in the early days of overcharging and discriminating against the western settlers led to a great farmers' movement of protest in the seventies, which has found a place in history as the "Granger movement." The outcome of this early attempt of American farmers at organized action was the enactment of the first state legislation to regulate railroads; and the acceptance of this novel principle by the states led in turn to its adoption by Congress in the Interstate Commerce Act of 1887. These laws were of epochal importance, for they represented the first systematic effort of the government to cope with the growing evils of corporate wealth.

While the agricultural revolution since the Civil War can not be considered apart from railroad expansion, it nevertheless left its own peculiar impress upon the modern American era. The farming industry grew at an unparalleled pace. Between 1870 and 1880 the farms of the nation were increased by an area equal to that of France; and between 1880 and the end of the century a domain was added equal to the European area of France, England, Wales and the German Empire of 1914. An important factor in this growth was the widely extended use of improved labor-saving machinery, including the substitution of horse power and steam power for manual labor, and the application of scientific methods to agriculture. The expansion of farming was too rapid for the needs of the country; "overproduction" followed, causing low prices for crops and a prolonged period of hard times for the rural population. The situation was aggravated by the fact that many of the farmers had borrowed heavily of eastern capitalists in order to finance their undertakings. According to the census of 1890, the mortgage indebtedness of agricultural lands had increased from $343,000,000 to $586,000,000 in a period of ten years. A very large percentage of the farm properties west of the Mississippi was under mortgage at the time of the census; and very bad conditions were also to be found in the states east of the river. Between 1890 and 1895 hundreds of settlers in the semiarid West were forced to give up their farms to the persons who held mortgages on them. In the South very similar conditions prevailed, where the lands devastated by the Civil War were in process of being brought under cultivation again and the old plantation system was being gradually replaced by small independent farms.

These were ideal conditions for the fertilization of unrest and discontent; and so it happened that for many years the agricultural population proved to be a hotbed of radical agitation. Untrained in the intricacies of economics, their minds turned naturally to certain simple and plausible remedies to relieve their distresses; and the precariousness of their means of livelihood lent a religious zeal to their convictions. Greenback inflation, free silver and Populism, all movements that bulk large in American history since the Civil War, recruited their chief strength in the farming states of the West and the South. It was not until about 1900 that the rural population came to take their place as the great conservative force in American politics. From 1894 down to 1900 a series of excellent crops of wheat and corn and an advance in the price of livestock occurred. Farm products also received preferential treatment in the Republican tariffs of 1890 and 1897; and after 1896 occurred an increase in the circulating medium of the country due to the discovery of new sources of gold supply. Thousands of mortgages on western farms were paid off with a consequent reduction of the rate of interest on farm loans. Farming thus became profitable again; and the farmer became interested in maintaining the *status quo*. With the outbreak of the World War unexpected difficulties faced the farmer; and the last few years have witnessed a return of aggressive farmer organizations seeking to achieve more favorable conditions for agriculture.

More significant than the revolution in transportation or even the agricultural revolution has been the transformation of our industrial system. The small beginnings in manufacturing made before the Civil War were completely eclipsed by the epochal developments since then. Indeed, according to the United States Industrial Commission reporting in 1902, these developments constituted "probably the most rapid change in the methods of industry observable at any time in history." It would be tedious, even if it were practicable, to sketch the marvelous advances in invention and mechanism upon which the industrial revolution was based. The records of the Patent Office throw some light on the matter. In the entire period before 1860, something less than 36,000 patents had been granted; in the remaining years of the century the number of patents issued reached the astonishing total of almost 640,000. The widespread use of improved mechanical appliances meant more efficient processes, labor saving, and a great cheapening in the cost of production.

Progress in invention was accompanied and fostered by improvements in the organization of industry. Manufacturing carried on in a small plant was discovered to be less efficient and less economical than production upon a large scale. Industrial organizations have tended to grow until, in many lines, they include vastly more than a single great factory but a unified system comprehending many factories and making by-products and accessory products as well as the major product. Within twenty years after the close of the Civil War the trust and other forms of large industrial combination had begun to occupy their dominant position in modern American life.

The industrial revolution was productive of colossal fortunes for those who were "captains of industry" or who speculated successfully in the stocks and bonds of industrial corporations. Inequality of wealth such as was unknown in the early days of the republic became the accepted state of society. The United States passed through the millionaire era into the multimillionaire era and by 1900 emerged into the age of billionaires.

While a comparative few were amassing enormous riches, vast numbers of men, women and children entered the factories as wage earners, and the foundations were laid for that most difficult of all modern problems, the labor problem. The location of plants at strategic commercial points was responsible for a tremendous movement of people from the country into the great industrial centers and the massing of the factory workers into poor quarters and slum districts. As industries were virtually unregulated by law until the nineties, the situation of the working class in respect to wages, hours and conditions of labor was utterly wretched. Since the government at this period was unwilling to take aggressive measures for mitigating these conditions, the workingmen were forced to rely upon their own resources. Imitating the great combinations of capital, they combined together in trade unions and soon sought to create a national alliance of all workingmen for common purposes. The Knights of Labor arose in the late sixties and ran their checkered career until the middle eighties. Out of the ruins of this organization arose the American Federation of Labor, which continues to be the greatest and most powerful body of organized labor in the United States. Efforts were made from time to time to organize the laboring class politically; but labor parties were always short-lived and never attained any marked political success. The country became torn periodically by tremendous conflicts between capital and labor, involving the loss of countless lives and millions of dollars' worth of property. Finally the government was forced to step in and, by legislation, remove some of the worst evils from which the working class suffered. Many injustices, real and fancied, remained, however, and the accentuation of class feeling constitutes today the most serious obstacle to the attainment of genuine national unity.

Notwithstanding the accumulated grievances of the working class the industrial revolution is not to be regarded as a calamity for the mass of the people. The final outcome has been an increase in the number of persons employed, a multiplication of the productive power of the community, an enormous reduction in the price of all the comforts of life, and an extension of the range of human enjoyments. The drudgery and wasteful toil of life have been greatly lessened. Wages have continued to advance though often not as rapidly as the cost of living; the advantages of education have been multiplied and extended; and health conditions in home and factory are better than ever before. As someone has pointed out, the average workingman can enjoy in his home lighting undreamed of in the days of tallow candles, warmth beyond the power of the old smoky soft-coal grate, kitchen conveniences that our New England ancestors would probably have thought sinful, and sanitary conditions and conveniences beyond the reach of the wealthiest man even half a century ago. If the owner of the poorest tenement house in our cities today were to install the kind of plumbing that George Washington possessed, he would promptly be locked up as a menace to the health of the community.

Large scale production with its great saving of labor has made it possible for labor unions to bring about a reduction in the hours of daily work. Hence people have leisure for personal enjoyment previously unknown. The trolley-car, the automobile, the amusement park and the "movies" have brought rest and recreation to millions of people who in earlier times knew only toil and whose pleasures consisted chiefly in church attendance, neighborhood gossip and alcoholic stimulants.

The intelligent workingman does not deny these palpable facts; but the crux of the problem, as he sees it, is his belief that the worker has not received a fair share of the enormous increase of wealth which has taken place in this country largely through his own grinding labor.

III

A marked characteristic of American history since the Civil War has been the development of new diplomatic interests. The changed direction of our foreign policy has been largely a consequence of the transformation of the United States from an importing nation requiring foreign capital for its economic development, to the greatest exporting nation of the world, operating in large degree independently of outside financial aid. On the one hand, the vast growth of farm and factory production has demanded ample foreign markets; and on the other, the accumulation of surplus capital has sought opportunity for overseas investment. The attention of our diplomats inevitably turned to the backward and undeveloped regions of the globe, particularly to those portions to which European enterprise had not yet penetrated. These materialistic motives found quick response in the traditional sympathy of the American people for less favored peoples and in the national faith in the uplifting influence of American ideals and institutions.

So it happened that American foreign policy in the modern period has been chiefly engaged in the annexation of islands in the Pacific Ocean, the promotion of trade and investments in the Far East, the construction of an interoceanic canal, and the fostering of commerce with Latin America. These new impulses reached their full momentum at the turning of the century, when, in a space of three years, Hawaii, Tutuila, the Philippines, Guam and Porto Rico were annexed; Cuba was converted into a protectorate; the United States proclaimed the policy of an "open door" for foreign trade in China; and the Hay-Pauncefote treaty cleared the way for the building of an isthmian canal under American control. By these events America was forced to issue from her chrysalis of isolation and take her place as a world power with a potential voice in the affairs of Europe, Asia and Africa.

It is not going too far to say that the Monroe Doctrine today has become largely an economic policy. Formerly the Monroe Doctrine was wholly political, aiming to prevent the further extension of European governmental systems to the soil of the New World. Purely economic operations and engagements were unknown to it. But, as Professor Ogg has pointed out, the United States was gradually forced to recognize that the investment of foreign capital in a backward Latin American country may easily lead to economic absorption and that economic absorption is likely to result in political control. Hence the Monroe Doctrine as we know it today is largely concerned with converting into American protectorates those countries whose financial laxness might tempt creditor nations to intervene in their affairs, and with discouraging foreign capitalists and corporations from acquiring lands and other concessions in Latin America on such a scale as to foreshadow political control.

In a very different sense the United States has contracted a series of difficult foreign relations through the invasion of our shores by great hordes of immigrants. The alluring prospects of employment and wealth opened up by the economic revolution in this country attracted European peasants in unprecedented numbers to our farms and factories, railroads and mines. Their presence has yielded its benefits as well as its evil results; but, however viewed, modern American life has been rendered infinitely more complex by reason of their coming. The problem of the assimilation of the alien ranks with the labor problem in its gravity for the future welfare of America.

IV

But the basic importance of the economic revolution to an understanding of modern America cannot be dismissed with a consideration of these concrete aspects of material and political development. What Mencken has termed, in sardonic vein, "the whole, gross, glittering, excessively dynamic, infinitely grotesque, incredibly stupendous drama of American life" has its sources in the new economic substructure of American society of the last sixty years. The high degree of specialization and the keen competition among individuals, exacted by the compulsions of modern existence, have lent a feverish intensity to living. Santayana has said of the contemporary American, with an element of truth, that "All his life he jumps into the train after it has started, and jumps out before it has stopped, and never once gets left behind or breaks a leg." There is a tendency for the American people to live on the latest sensations and exhaust themselves with superficial emotions. The "pursuit of happiness," proclaimed by the Declaration of Independence as an inalienable right, has ceased to be a leisurely and beguiling occupation and has become a frenzied and breathless chase. The ceaseless activity and the jaded mental condition characteristic of the average American outside of business hours have led him to value brevity and hurry above all other virtues. Symptoms of this state of mind are to be found on every hand—in "short orders" in the restaurants, vaudeville in the theaters, headline summaries in the newspapers, short stories in literature.

The prodigious strides made by science in the modern period and the demand for industrial efficiency have placed a premium upon the cultivation of the *practical* and the *actual* in all departments of human thought and endeavor. In the sphere of education the older ideals of a liberal education have been forced to yield to the demands for specialized and technical training. Due to the early importance of farming in our national economy, agricultural education was the first of the vocational subjects to be taken over by the schools and the colleges. In the eighties the high schools began to offer courses in manual training, business, and household economy; and gradually these subjects found places in the college curriculum. Today, we are told on high authority, our schools are no longer "mere disciplinary institutions where drill is given in the mastery of the rudiments of knowledge" but "institutions of democracy calculated to train for useful service in the office, the shop and the home, and intended to prepare young people for intelligent participation in the increasingly complex social and political life of our democratic society." The new direction and ideals of education have awakened a popular interest and support unknown to those simpler times when a man who had mastered the "three R's" could cope sufficiently well with the problems of life.

In literature the romantic school typified by Cooper, Irving and Hawthorne has succumbed to the realistic art of Howells and James, the dialect and local color writing of Harte and Mark Twain, and the sociological fiction of Frank Norris and Upton Sinclair. Our writers perceived the literary possibilities presented by the new America and sought to interpret and photograph the multifold aspects of the modern scene. An amazing new literature appeared, born of the people, for the people and by the people.

The same influences coursed through American music. Before the Civil War there was very little appreciation of music even by cultivated people. That great conflict was fought by soldiers singing songs, most of which had been composed in the Old World. Since then, music has been both vulgarized and popularized. The principal output of

American composers has been "popular music," seeking however crudely to express the new meanings and energies of American life. The period since Appomattox might be divided into the epoch of plantation melodies and "coon songs," the era of "ragtime," and the contemporary age of "jazz." But the apostles of the higher forms of music have had no reason for discouragement. Although the output of serious American music has been comparatively small and often imitative, some compositions of genuine beauty and individuality have been produced, notably the work of Edward MacDowell. Every large city today has its symphony orchestra and music courses; and American inventive genius has, by means of the phonograph, carried music of undying beauty into a million homes.

In the field of history the *social* point of view has become the characteristic mark of the present generation of historians; and the very concept of an "economic interpretation of history" is the product of an industrial age. Contemporary philosophy has become pragmatic in its treatment of ethics and naturalistic in dealing with the problems of metaphysics. Religion has turned from the contemplation of theological abstractions and is seeking to apply its precepts to the stubborn realities of modern life, or else to base its appeal upon the assurance of physical health as well as spiritual peace. Even the conservative spirit of the law has gradually undergone a process of socialization in an effort to adjust itself to living social, economic and political facts; and "mechanical jurisprudence" is reluctantly but inevitably yielding to the new school of "sociological jurisprudence."

Perhaps most significant of all is the new political philosophy which, with each passing decade, has gained fresh converts among the leaders of public opinion. The former ideal of *laissez faire*—the right of individuals to compete unrestrictedly with each other without governmental regulation—was well adapted to the conditions prevailing before the economic revolution, when land and natural resources were plentiful and cheap. But with the increasing complexities of modern life the feeling has grown that the liberty and opportunities of the individual can be properly safeguarded only by the protective oversight of the government. Conditions in the United States have not reached that degree of wretchedness which would give Socialism or Communism a strong popular appeal; and the dominant thought of America is agreed that intelligent social control furnishes the best preventive of ruthless individualism, on the one hand, and of government paternalism on the other.

BIBLIOGRAPHICAL NOTE

The great arsenal of information on the economic transformation of the United States since the Civil War is the *Report* of the United States Industrial Commission (19 v.; Washington, 1900-1902). The final volume is particularly useful. The student, however, should not overlook the detailed study made by David A. Wells in 1889 of the changes of the preceding quarter of a century, entitled *Recent Economic Changes and Their Effect on the Production and Distribution of Wealth and the Well-Being of Society* (New York). Although the revolutionary character of the changes is fully recognized in both of these works, the specific term, "economic revolution," seems to have been first used by Charles A. Beard in his *American Government and Politics* (New York, 1910) and again in his *Contemporary American History, 1877-1913* (New York, 1914). The term has not yet won general acceptance by the historians, the less accurate one of "industrial revolution" being ordinarily employed.

The facts of the economic revolution are excellently summarized in Katharine Coman's *The Industrial History of the United States* (New York, 1905), pp. 265-343; Ernest Ludlow Bogart's *The Economic History of the United States* (New York, 1907), part iv (especially good); Emory Richard Johnson and others' *History of Foreign and Domestic Commerce of the United States* (2 v.; Washington, 1915), vol. i, chap. xv; Arthur W. Calhoun's *A Social History of the American Family* (3 v.; Cleveland, 1917-1919), vol. iii, chap. iv; and Ellwood P. Cubberley's *Public Education in the United States* (Boston, 1919), chap. xi. The agricultural phases of the revolution have been studied separately by Louis Bernard Schmidt in his article "Some Significant Aspects of the Agrarian Revolution in the United States" in the *Iowa Journal of Politics and History*, vol. xviii (1920), pp. 371-395.

The present writer's view as to the vital relationship of the economic revolution to an understanding of all aspects of modern American life and society was presented in an article entitled "The Problem of Teaching Recent American History" in the *Historical Outlook*, vol. xi (1920), pp. 352-355. The first chapter of Charles Edward Merriam's *American Political Ideas, 1865-1917* (New York, 1920) is a brilliant exposition of the fundamental factors of the period. The same point of view has been worked out, with more or less conscious intent, in Charles A. Beard's *Contemporary American History, 1877-1913* (already cited), chaps. ii, iii, iv, ix; Frederic L. Paxson's *The New Nation* (Boston, 1915), especially chap. vi, Paul L. Haworth's *The United States in Our Own Times, 1865-1920* (New York, 1920), especially chap. x; and best of all in Charles Ramsdell Lingley's *Since the Civil War* (New York, 1920), chaps. iii, ix, xi, xiv, xxii.

The most extensive treatment of the modern period of American history to 1917 may be found in vols. 22-27 of *The American Nation: a History* (Albert Bushnell Hart, ed.; New York, 1905-1918), written by William Archibald Dunning, Edwin Erle Sparks, Davis R. Dewey, John H. Latané and Frederic Austin Ogg. These volumes give attention to social and economic factors as well as to political, constitutional and diplomatic developments.

The unity of the recent period is being clearly recognized by students of the cultural and intellectual history of the United States. Of such volumes the following are particularly valuable: Charles F. Thwing's *A History of Education in the United States Since the Civil War* (Boston, 1910); Fred Lewis Pattee's *A History of American Literature Since 1870* (New York, 1917); Ellwood P. Cubberley's *Public Education in the United States* (already cited), chaps. xi-xv; Charles Edward Merriam's *American Political Ideas, 1865-1917* (already cited); and James Melvin Lee's *History of American Journalism* (Boston, 1917), pp. 317-450.

CHAPTER XII

THE RIDDLE OF THE PARTIES

I

With the ratification of the nineteenth amendment shortly before the presidential election of 1920, several millions of women received the right to use the ballot for the first time. Gloomy predictions had been made, time and again, that this extension of the suffrage boded ill for the welfare of the nation because of the inability of the feminine mind to comprehend political matters. The election has receded far enough into the past for us to see now, with clearer vision, that the chief obstacle in the way of intelligent voting by the women was not their fancied mental inferiority in political matters but rather the incapacity of the political parties to make themselves intelligible to the women.

What was so dramatically revealed in the campaign of 1920 was not a new thing in our recent political history. Every year has witnessed the entry of a million or more new partners into our great democracy—young men newly attaining the age of twenty-one, and foreign-born citizens fresh from their final naturalization papers. These new voters have all been confronted with the same need to align themselves with parties that faced the huge battalions of women voters in 1920.

The importance of making a reasoned decision need not be argued in a country in which the motive power of government is generated by parties. Such a choice would not be, and should not be, the same for all voters; but it is supremely important that the selection, whatever it be, should be made upon the basis of unbiased information and of an independent judgment of the principles and policies for which each party stands. Hence if our government is to be motivated by the collective intelligence of the citizens, it follows that every facility should be afforded voters to discover the truth about the political parties through which they must act.

Whatever may have been true of certain periods of the past, every new voter who has sought to cast a conscientious ballot in recent elections will agree that our democratic methods of government have failed at this critical point. There seems to be a conspiracy, not of silence but of volubility, to conceal the real meaning of parties. Efforts of intelligent citizens to penetrate the darkness and confusion surrounding party meanings have too frequently caused them to react in disgust or in consequent indifference thereafter to the political life of the nation; or else the individual, in lieu of anything better, has allowed his party loyalty to be dictated by the social pressures of the community in which he lives or by the inherited prejudices of his clan.

One of the most alarming tendencies of contemporary times in the United States has been the steady decline in the proportion of citizens who perform their periodical functions at the polls. Not only is this true in state and local elections but in national elections as well. This tendency has been most marked since the McKinley-Bryan campaign of 1896; and its lowest point was reached in the last presidential contest (1920) when about half of the citizens entitled to vote went to the polls. Many factors have contributed to this phenomenon, but an important element has undoubtedly been the failure of the major parties to convince the voters that they represent clearly differentiated bodies of opinion.

The mental confusion of the average man is readily understood when many signs lead him to believe that there are, in fact, no essential differences between the major parties. Thus, prior to the national conventions of the presidential campaign of 1920, the *New York World,* a traditional Democratic organ of vast influence, announced its readiness to support Herbert Hoover for president regardless of which party might nominate him. And the *Saturday Evening Post* with its mammoth reading public called upon the great parties to join in making Mr. Hoover their presidential choice. Mr. Hoover at that time was engaged in sternly disavowing that he was a party man in any orthodox sense although he subsequently reached the conclusion that he was a member of the Republican party. The impression has undoubtedly won wide acceptance in the country that the great parties are like two armies that have been sitting opposite each other for so long a time that they have forgotten the original cause of their quarrel.

II

How, then, can one learn what the parties stand for? Party platforms originated back in Jackson's day for the express purpose of clarifying such matters for the voter in advance of the election; but since that time, they have tended to degenerate into collections of pleasant generalities that are more likely to bewilder than enlighten the inquiring voter. The popular attitude toward them has become one of indifference or cynicism, because of the proneness of a party to straddle the principal issues and its likelihood of disregarding its other pledges should it succeed in winning the election. Indeed it is not too much to say that the chief function of a party platform today is one of internal importance. For reasons that will be noted later, the typical platform is a treaty of amity designed to compose differences among discordant elements of the party for the duration of the campaign and to permit the party to present a united front against the common enemy.

One reads the platforms in vain for those statements of fundamental differences and tendencies which might constitute a clarion call to a citizen to identify the public welfare with the one party rather than the other.   When such attempts at definition are made, as in the platforms of 1908, the promise falls far short of fulfillment.   It may be helpful for the voter to learn from the Republican platform that "The trend of Democracy is toward socialism, while the Republican party stands for a wise and regulated individualism"; but what is he to think upon discovering from the Democratic platform that "The Democratic party is the champion of equal rights and opportunities to all; the Republican party is the party of privilege and private monopoly"?

Next to these official declarations of party belief, the voter is forced to turn to partisan newspapers and campaign orators for the information he seeks.   Here again he encounters difficulties: who would trust a lover for an unbiased and dispassionate opinion of his sweetheart?   A copy of the *London Chronicle* of May 8, 1766, yellowed with age, expresses a conviction that bears the fresh impress of truth today, so far as party liegemen are concerned: "Party is a fever that robs the wretch under its influence of common sense, common decency, and sometimes common honesty; it subjects reason to the caprices of fancy, and misrepresents objects; . . . we blame and pity bigotry and enthusiasm in religion; . . . are party principles less reprehensible, that, in a worse cause, are apt to intoxicate and disorder the brain, and pervert the understanding?"   The attitude of John Randolph of Roanoke toward the Whig party of his time may be taken to represent the viewpoint of the orthodox party man toward the opposition party.   The Whigs, declared Randolph, have exactly seven principles, "five loaves and two fishes." Better for the voter than one partisan organ are two newspapers representing opposite sides of the discussion; but the determination of the truth on the basis of such evidence would require the faculties of an expert in historical research and the wisdom of a Solomon.

Perhaps in particular cases there may be other and less obvious channels of information open to the diligent seeker; but in final analysis the conclusion is unavoidable that the only way to ascertain the truth about party principles is the thorny path of finding out how the party originated, what influences shaped its development, and what seem to be its present sympathies and impulses. In other words, if political parties are, in any degree at all, coherent and developing bodies of opinion, it is not wise to pass judgment on a party from the cross-section of its policies that is exposed to one's gaze in the heat and smoke of a particular political campaign. Only from an historical view, properly understood, can one arrive at a well-considered opinion concerning the present fitness and future development of parties.

III

The Republican party is the younger of the two major parties, having been founded within the memory of many men still living. It took form in the fall of 1854 as a fusion of the anti-slavery elements of the Whig and Democratic parties with the preëxisting Free Soilers or "Free Democrats." Its fundamental tenet was the non-extension of slavery beyond the southern states in which the institution was deeply rooted; but it waged battle with the "Slave Power" in all the efforts of the latter to dictate the policy of the government. The new party quickly attracted into its fold the wage-earners of the northern cities and most of the newly-arrived immigrants, not only because of the inherent opposition of slave labor and free labor but, more specifically, because of the plan of the "Slave Power" to discourage free settlement in the western territories by the establishment of the slavery system there. The issue was made unmistakably clear to the common people of the North when in June, 1860, President Buchanan, acting under southern influence, vetoed a homestead bill that had originated in the Republican House of Representatives. Through its generous idealism the party also won a wide support among the church-goers of the North as well.

The creed of the new Republican party was a radical, if not a revolutionary, one. Its great leaders, William H. Seward and Abraham Lincoln, had both been guilty of public utterances that were regarded at the time as little short of incendiary, Seward when he declared that there was "a higher law than the Constitution," and Lincoln when he charged the chief justice of the United States Supreme Court with having knowingly engaged in a great pro-slavery conspiracy to extend slavery into all the territories. The financial interests of the East viewed the growth of the new party with alarm; and on the eve of the Lincoln campaign of 1860, it was reported that William B. Astor had contributed one million dollars to encompass the defeat of the Republicans in New York.

The new party was successful in winning the presidency within six years of its birth, principally because the ranks of the opposition party were sundered in the campaign. By the time President Lincoln was inaugurated in 1861, most of the slaveholding states had already declared themselves outside of the Union; and this new party, inexperienced, heterogeneous and unaware of its own potential strength, was confronted with the most stupendous task that a political party has ever had to undertake in American history. How the Lincoln administration mobilized the spiritual and material resources of the North, preserved the Union and abolished slavery is part of a larger story than the history of a single party; but the consequences were pregnant with significance for the later development of the Republican party.

The very completeness of the success attained by the Republicans in carrying through their anti-slavery program became the party's greatest menace at the close of the war. With the destruction of slavery and the "Slave Power," there was no logical reason for the continuance of the party of Lincoln and Seward, unless new and vital issues of permanent importance should be added to the party creed. How was the party to insure self-preservation? The task of reconstructing the South and securing the rights of the freedmen was a direct consequence of the war policy of the Republicans; and for several years after the war their energies were largely absorbed in dealing with this complex and unprecedented problem. Meantime, mute powerful forces, set in motion by the economic revolution through which the country was then passing, were preparing to supply the party with the badly needed new policies.

Contrary to a widely held opinion today, no national Republican platform had ever declared for a protective tariff prior to 1872, save only the platform of 1860 when a deliberate political play was made to capture the support of the iron districts of Pennsylvania. Nevertheless, the Republicans had been forced to enact high protective tariffs as a war revenue measure; and under shelter of these enactments a new and mighty manufacturing class had come into existence. The manufacturers, the railroad enterprisers and the financial interests generally sought refuge in the dominant party, demanded that protection be continued as a permanent policy of the government and that other energetic measures be adopted to foster the material development of the nation. The nationalistic temper of the Republican party, born of the

Civil War, lent a certain idealistic tinge to all such demands; and from 1868 on, the party platforms began to reflect, pretty faithfully, the ideals and aims of the dominant economic interests of the age. The great tenets of Republicanism during the remaining years of the century became such questions as the protective tariff and "sound money," and in general a reluctance to cramp or curb the processes of business enterprise. The party had thus passed from a party of radical humanitarianism to a party of business conservatism.

But the almost uninterrupted success of the Republicans for many years following the war cannot be accounted for solely by the new economic affiliations of the party. The party had won a deep and abiding hold on the affections of the people of the North because, as it seemed to many, it had been the instrument of Providence in saving the nation in its time of trial and stress. The political thinking of the generation which had taken part in the war was dominated by that great crisis; and to the minds of many northerners it was nothing short of disloyalty to the flag to vote anything but the straight Republican ticket. For twenty-five years following the war, Republican platforms opened with impassioned reminders of the past glories of the party; and campaign orators of the party lost no chance to assail the opposition party as traitors in the late war. In political parlance such manoeuvres were called "waving the bloody shirt"; and the effectiveness of this practice was heightened by the generous bids for the soldier vote which the Republicans made through pension legislation. These emotional appeals furnished Republican leaders with a means of diverting public attention at times when the party was guilty of bad government and made it possible to develop almost undisturbed their new economic policies. James G. Blaine, one of the great party chieftains of the period, is an example of a man who never tired of "waving the bloody shirt," but his political integrity has been forever clouded in American history by his dubious, if not illicit, relations, while in public position, with railroad corporations.

IV

Let us now turn aside from the Republican party as that great organization had developed by the closing years of the nineteenth century and consider the record of its chief rival, the Democratic party. The history of the Democratic party may, in a sense, be said to be coëxtensive with that of the Constitution, although in its early years the party was as often called Republican as Democratic. It made its appearance in Washington's administration as a protest against the aristocratic and centralizing tendencies of the Federalist party then in power. Under the leadership of Thomas Jefferson it gathered to itself the support of the agricultural interest—northern farmers, southern planters and western pioneers—and in the fourth presidential election (1800) it swept the Federalists into a defeat from which they never recovered. For the first sixty years of the nineteenth century the party dominated the national political scene and was even more continuously in power than the Republicans have been since then. Under its second great leader, Andrew Jackson, the party received a new impulse toward democracy; so that it has been said that Jefferson stood for government "of the people and for the people" while Jackson added "by the people."

Shortly after Jackson's retirement, the party entered upon a new phase of its development when it fell under the control of its southern leaders and became devoted to the advancement of pro-slavery interests. Thus it happened that in the twenty-year period before the outbreak of the Civil War the Democrats insensibly came to lay less emphasis on popular rights and to stress increasingly doctrines and principles which would promote and entrench the prosperity of the cotton capitalists. The secession movement of 1860-1861 was engineered by southern Democratic leaders; and the outbreak of the war saw the northern Democracy sadly divided among those who frankly joined the Republicans in a wholehearted support of the Lincoln administration, those who continued the party organization on a program of criticism of the conduct of the war, and those who sought to commit the party to a policy of immediate peace at any cost. It was to the last group that the name "Copperheads" properly applied; but in the public mind the whole party became inseparably identified with the doctrine of disloyalty and disunionism.

If the close of the Civil War raised a problem of self-perpetuation for the Republicans, the situation of the Democrats was infinitely more difficult. Disorganized and leaderless, its *ante bellum* issues obsolete, discredited in the North by its war record, its southern supporters largely disfranchised, the party faced dissolution, or else must pin its faith to its ability to profit by the mistakes of the self-confident Republicans. The next twenty years constituted the most critical period in Democratic history. That picturesque Democrat Henry Watterson, who knew these times as an actor in them, wrote many years later of "the ancient label of a Democracy worn by a riffraff of opportunists, Jeffersonion principles having gone quite to seed." The remarkable thing is that the party managed to survive; and for this miracle the Republican party may, in very large degree, be held responsible.

In the first place, the reconstruction policy of the Republicans affronted and humiliated the southerners, who bitterly resented carpetbag misrule and negro ascendancy at a time when the natural leaders of the native white population were disfranchised by federal enactment. As the states one after the other recovered their full political rights, their *ante bellum* antipathy for the Republican party was unutterably deepened by angry memories of the reconstruction period. The southern whites promptly deprived the negroes of the suffrage; and the ex-Confederate states reëntered national politics as a solidly Democratic section. Hence the "Solid South" constituted a substantial nucleus about which the Democrats of the North might expect to rebuild their party. It meant, for instance, in the election of 1880 ninety-five electoral votes, out of a total of three hundred and sixty-nine, which the party could secure for its candidate without an effort and irrespective of the issues at stake.[1] To this irreducible minimum might ordinarily be added the electoral votes of the other ex-slave states, Missouri, Kentucky, Maryland and Delaware, amounting in 1880 to thirty-five.

Furthermore, the overconfidence of the Republicans in their national administration furnished excellent opportunities for the Democratic minority. The presidency of General Grant was marked by a series of scandals and revelations of corruption which involved many high officials of the government. Republican mistakes spelled Democratic opportunity. The Democrats took advantage of the situation to nominate Samuel J. Tilden, who had won a reputation for reform in New York politics; and supported by a widespread popular dissatisfaction, they almost succeeded in electing him in the campaign of 1876. Warned by this experience, the Republicans became more cautious in the type of candidates they nominated and in their conduct in office; and Democratic fortunes again ebbed until 1884 when the Republican organization, in defiance of the protests of Theodore Roosevelt and other young leaders of the party, offered James G. Blaine as their presidential nominee. The Demo-

[1] The first break in the Solid South came in 1920 when Tennessee gave its electoral vote to Harding.

crats gleefully revived their tactics of eight years before, and nominated Grover Cleveland, the reform governor of New York, on a platform which, save for its destructive criticism of the record of the Republicans, differed in no vital respect from the platform of the opposition party.

This time the Democrats were successful; and Cleveland found himself president of a party whose "cardinal principles," as he himself confessed, had in recent years been "relegated to the rear and expediency substituted as the hope of success." To Cleveland fell the choice of continuing this course of vacillation and opportunism, or of endowing the party with a constructive fighting program. To a man of Cleveland's uncompromising characteristics only the latter course was possible. Before his first term was completed, he had definitely committed the party to the principle of a revenue tariff although Democratic policy on the tariff had been ill-defined since the war or even inclined to protectionism. He had courted the enmity of the old-soldier element by his dogged determination to eliminate laxness and fraud in the granting of pensions; and in general he had stood for economy in governmental expenditures. Cleveland occupied the same relationship to the party after the Civil War that Jefferson and Jackson had, in turn, in the earlier history of the party. The Democrats entered the campaign of 1888 as a party regenerated, as indeed it was. Although Cleveland was defeated on the basis of the new issues, he was splendidly vindicated four years later when the people returned him and his party to the control of the government.

V

A new era—the present era—opened in the history of the Republican and Democratic parties about 1896 or 1900. Prior to that time neither party had shown any primary concern for the welfare of the wage-earners or the farmers or the small business men. Neither party had advocated policies that were designed, first and foremost, to better the conditions of those ordinary men and women who compose the great bulk of the people. Party politics had been largely shaped by the tugs and pressures of the transforming economic life of the nation. "In the encouragement of the investment of capital," so William Howard Taft tells us, "we nearly transferred complete political power to those who controlled corporate wealth, and we were in danger of a plutocracy." While these influences were chiefly felt by the party which was in almost continuous control during the period, the Democratic party by no means escaped them. Both parties ordinarily acted on the assumption that the welfare of the toiling masses would automatically follow from the prosperity of the manufacturers and financiers.

Although old party leaders constantly minimized the amount of economic distress and social discontent caused by the rapid industrial development, the less fortunate classes had sought, from time to time, to voice their protests through special parties organized for the purpose. These parties were invariably unpromising and short-lived until in 1892 when an upheaval of angry farmers created the People's party and polled more than one million votes in the presidential election, a greater number than the difference between the total votes of the Democratic and Republican candidates. The Populists declared in their platform that they were not to be deceived by "the struggles of the two great political parties for power and plunder" during the last quarter-century nor by their more recent "uproar of a sham battle over the tariff"; and they proclaimed that the well-being of the "plain people" was bottomed upon the adoption of the free and unlimited coinage of silver at the ratio of sixteen to one.

Now, "free silver" is a problem of higher economics whose

implications were no better understood in the nineties by the verbose controversialists of either side than they are by the average person today. Certainly the issue represented no reasoned conviction on the part of the untutored "plain people" who saw in it their great hope of economic redemption. For them it signified something infinitely more : it was a symbol, a Merlin's wand, with which to destroy the iniquitous power of "Wall Street" and "Big Business" in the national government. Thus, "free silver," however ill-conceived the issue may have been, represented the first stentorian demand for a consideration of homely and purely human interests in national politics.

Since the injection of this disturbing spirit into the political arena, party politics in this country has undergone a profound change. Fearful of the vote-getting strength of the new issue, the Democratic party under the leadership of William Jennings Bryan declared for "free silver" in their platform of 1896, although Cleveland and many other eastern Democrats temporarily left the party rather than lend their countenance to the doctrine. A mighty campaign followed ; and by the election of McKinley the issue in its temporary and exigent form was forever discredited. But its living spirit had found a lodging place in the national councils of both parties.

By Bryan the new impulses were transmuted and extended and enriched until they embraced all varieties of reforms that tended to a broader recognition of human rights in government. The Republican organization yielded more slowly to the new influences ; but by the accident of McKinley's death in 1901, a man came into the presidency whose instincts responded strongly to the need of ameliorating the conditions of the masses and who popularized the new gospel. Under the inspiration of Bryan and Roosevelt, a group of young leaders sprang up in each party, demanding the destruction of "Special Privilege" and a larger participation by the people in the control of government. These new tendencies were bitterly resisted by the older leadership. Cleveland and his friends denounced the "Bryanization" of the Democratic party. "Standpat" Republicans sneered at the "philosophy of failure" and fought the progressive tendencies at every turn. Both parties were plunged into destructive factional warfare, the progressive wings battling with the conservative elements for the direction of party policy, although the force of tradition has usually been strong enough to enable the party organization to maintain a united front on election day. These internal differences constitute the most striking characteristics of party politics today, and furnish the chief element of confusion in any attempt to arrive at the significance of the old parties.

The division between the progressives and conservatives within each party may be likened to a seesaw, one end being up at one time and the other at another; and when one end of the Republican seesaw is high, a train of influences is set in motion which usually causes the opposite end of the Democratic seesaw to rise, and *vice versa*. A hasty review of past elections will demonstrate the truth of this statement. In 1900 the conservative McKinley on the Republican ticket opposed the progressive Democratic candidate Bryan. In 1904 the progressive Republican Roosevelt was nominated against the conservative Democrat Parker. The conservative Republican Taft battled in 1908 with the progressive Bryan. Four years later the internecine quarrel in the Republican party reached the breaking-point, and the two factions were no longer willing to live under the same roof. The regular organization renominated their conservative standard-bearer Taft; and the bolting elements, adopting the name "Progressive party" and supported by sympathizers from outside the party, offered as their candidate the veteran progressive, Roosevelt. The Democrats nominated Woodrow Wilson, who described himself as a "progressive with the brakes on." Since Taft ran a bad third, it appeared for the moment that the progressive spirit had completed its conquest of the old parties. Four years later, however, the old ferment was at work again, with Wilson as the progressive Democratic candidate and Hughes supported by the conservative Republicans. In 1920 the voters were once more presented with the choice between a conservative Republican and a Democrat of progressive antecedents.

For the conscientious voter the situation has thus become sadly complicated, inasmuch as the progressive wings of the opposing parties have more points of similarity than the opposite wings of the same party. This baffling situation has tended to wear down old-time party distinctions and has made it easy for a Roosevelt Republican to become a Wilson Democrat or for a Cleveland Democrat to become a Taft Republican. The growth of the independent vote has been a significant development of recent campaigns. In a more important sense, this situation has served to impair the effectiveness of the old parties as agencies of the popular will. Many of the outstanding legislative measures of the contemporary era have been the product not of concerted party action but of temporary combinations of like-thinking groups of opposite parties in Congress. Such laws as the following cannot, with any degree of accuracy, be labeled "Republican" or "Democratic": the federal income tax amendment, popular election of senators, federal restriction of child labor, the literacy test for immigrants, conservation of natural resources, national prohibition, and the federal grant of woman suffrage. Although almost any of these measures might have furnished material for clearcut party cleavage, most of them were the product of the progressive members of the two parties acting in conjunction.

Is there, then, no residue of principles, policies or sympathies which belongs distinctively to the one party rather than to the other? A further examination of the record of the parties in recent years may shed some light upon this point. We used to be told that the Republicans stood for a broadly national policy based upon a liberal construction of the Constitution, whereas the Democrats were strict constructionists desiring to enhance the power of the states at the expense of the national government; but, as has been shown elsewhere in this volume, this distinction has broken down in practice.[1]

In the absence of fundamental constitutional differences, let us turn to a consideration of what are usually considered as party measures. In an effort to solve the trust question, the Democrats enacted the Federal Trade Commission Act of 1914. The basic principle of the law had, however, been urged upon Congress for adoption by President Roosevelt again and again, and the Republican platform of 1912 had pledged its adoption in case Taft should be reëlected. This difference between promise and fulfilment cannot rightly be laid to congenital party differences or be taken as a criterion of Republican bad faith and Democratic performance; but, rather, it represented a difference in the relative preparedness of the public mind for the accomplishment of the reform.

The organization of the federal reserve banking system in 1913 was another great law passed by the Democrats although the preliminary investigations for this measure had been made by a Republican commission during the Taft administration. In the details of the plan, a real difference of party principle emerged, for the Democrats in enacting the law conferred upon the government direct control over the banks whereas the Republicans had desired the central management to be directed by the banks themselves.

[1] See pp. 235-242.

The tariff is another question that has stirred both parties to legislative expression in recent years. The results present an interesting contrast between the theory and the practice of the Democrats in this matter. Measured by actual performance, the Democrats do not stand for a tariff for revenue only but merely for a less degree of protection than do their opponents. Both parties are agreed upon the desirability of an expert tariff commission as an aid in tariff legislation.

In the matter of labor legislation, a difference between the parties is to be found. The Democratic party has been more inclined to lend an ear to the demands of the workingmen than has been the Republican. Without going into detail, the best evidence of this is to be found in the fact that since 1908, when the practice originated, the officers of the American Federation of Labor have given their endorsement to the Democratic national ticket.

In foreign affairs the attitude of the parties is more difficult to define even though questions of foreign relations have bulked large in some recent campaigns. In 1900 the Republicans stood squarely for the acquisition of insular dependencies in distant parts of the globe, whereas the Democrats denounced Republican "imperialism" and protested against the United States becoming involved in "so-called world politics, including the diplomacy of Europe and the intrigue and land grabbing of Asia." But by the time of the campaign of 1916 the Democrats were fully alive to the necessity of "so-called world politics," in their own meaning of the term, and they endorsed President Wilson's proposal of a league of nations. Four years later they gave their support to the Covenant framed at the Paris Peace Conference; whereas the Republicans, divided in opinion among those who favored the Covenant, those who wanted a different covenant and those who wanted no league at all, framed a platform which contained crumbs of comfort for all three groups. The fact is that the league issue, which had one of its strongest supporters in ex-President Taft, was ill adapted to partisan uses. A careful review of the diplomatic practice of the two parties would show, I think, that, in general, Republican foreign policy has been firmer, being more conscious of the needs of our overseas trade and tending to become aggressive; whereas the international policy of the Democrats has been postulated on more idealistic grounds and has tended to be less practical in its results.

From such evidence as the foregoing, it is fair to conclude that there is today no basic disagreement between the old parties as to theory of government; nor does either party take issue with the existing economic organization of society. The difference between the parties is largely one of point of view, partly one of temperament. Both parties are opportunistic in their statesmanship, waiting for issues to arise and cry for attention before formulating a definite policy for dealing with them. But, as the foregoing examples suggest, the Republicans approach public problems with the predispositions of the successful financier and large business man, while the Democrats incline to consider public questions from the standpoint of the small business man and of the laboring man who is on the make. As a result the Republicans tend to cling to the concrete benefits and positive achievements of the past, whereas the Democrats are likely to respond more quickly to demands for social and economic reform through changes in the laws.

VI

This discussion has, for the most part, proceeded on the assumption that there are only two parties in American politics; and so far as the vast majority of the voters is concerned, the assumption is entirely valid since, save on two occasions, no third party has ever cast more than a negligible percentage of the total popular vote. Nevertheless, minor parties cannot be ignored since some unforeseen development might conceivably convert one of them into a major party, just as back in the fifties the Republican party crowded the Whig party out of existence.

Minor parties, in our modern sense, began to make their appearance with the election of 1872. They were the inevitable accompaniments of the maladjustments of society occasioned by the great economic revolution following the Civil War. The aggrieved classes regarded the old parties as defenders of the new capitalistic order, and they saw relief only in the establishment of their own political parties. The wage-earners of the cities were especially active in such movements although some of the most promising parties were launched by the western farmers. In rapid succession candidates were nominated and platforms adopted by such parties as the Labor Reformers, the Greenbackers, the United Laborites, the Union Laborites and the Populists; their platforms demanded such reforms as fiat money, the eight-hour day, prohibition of Chinese immigration, government control of railroads and corporations, the taxation of swollen incomes, and "free silver." All these parties suffered for lack of experienced political leadership and their inability to secure the funds necessary to sustain a continuous party organization.

In 1892 the ranks of the minor parties were enlarged by a political organization of a new type: the Socialist Labor party. This party and its subsequent embodiments have denounced the efforts of other minor parties to secure social amelioration as mere palliatives, and have offered instead a comprehensive program for the complete reorganization of society and government. Politically the chief asset of the Socialists has been the fact that they have visualized for the voter the ultimate goal toward which their philosophy tends. In a practical sense they have benefited from the fact that they have never been in power in the nation, and therefore their platform professions are unsullied by the mistakes, compromises and ineptitudes of a party that is responsible for the everyday conduct of the government. The Socialist vote exceeded nine hundred thousand in 1912 and again in 1920 but has not as yet won a single electoral vote. The Prohibition party founded in 1872, the Socialist Labor party established in 1892, and the American Socialist party organized in 1901 have enjoyed the longest continuous existence of any of the minor parties now in politics.

Despite the inferior vote-getting power of minor parties, they have undoubtedly performed a vital function in our political development. They have sometimes proved the means by which important new issues have been forced upon the reluctant attention of the old parties. This was the case in 1896 when the Democrats took over the great Populist issue of "free silver," and again in President Wilson's first administration when the Democrats undermined the strength of the Progressives by enacting most of their ideas into laws. Such pressure, however, is effective only when the strength of the third party has reached threatening proportions. In a more general way, minor parties have served a useful educational purpose in directing the attention of the people to great problems as yet unthought of and accustoming them to the consideration of novel ideas of public policy.

It is possible, however, that minor parties have played their most important rôle as a safeguard to the peaceful and orderly development of American society. Under our system of government any group of malcontents have the right to hold a convention, launch a new party in a fever heat of excitement and enthusiasm, and give full release to their repressed emotions in a glowing statement of their grievances. Where there is no occasion for secret conspiracy and underground plotting, minor parties become the safety-valve of social discontent.

The continual formation of new parties argues, on the whole, a healthful condition of the public mind. The eternal striving for improvement, the "divine discontent" of the poet, is the source of life in a progressive nation.

BIBLIOGRAPHICAL NOTE

Every important party in American history has had one or more eulogistic historians; but efforts at impartial characterization and description have been comparatively few. The new school of political scientists, represented by such men as James Bryce, M. Ostrogorski, Charles A. Beard, Henry Jones Ford, Frank J. Goodnow, A. Lawrence Lowell, Jesse Macy, Woodrow Wilson, James A. Woodburn and P. Orman Ray, have devoted careful study to the structure and functions of parties. But the historical significance of parties has not as yet received adequate treatment although illuminating brief discussions may occasionally be found in the general histories of the United States, in historical monographs and in treatises on American government. The discussion of James Bryce in *The American Commonwealth* (2 v.; New York, 1888, and many later editions), vol. ii, chaps. liii-lvi, is almost classic; and the summaries in Charles A. Beard's *American Government and Politics* (New York, 1910, and later editions), pp. 103-125, and Jesse Macy's *Political Parties in the United States, 1846-1861* (New York, 1900), chap. iii, are of much value. *Third Party Movements Since the Civil War* (Iowa City, 1916) by Fred E. Haynes is the only book on that subject, and it should be supplemented by Morris Hillquit's *History of Socialism in the United States* (New York, 1903).

INDEX

ADAMS, ABIGAIL, lacks early educational advantages, 130; on rebellion of women, 131-132.

Adams, Henry, on effects of economic revolution, 250; as author, 102.

Adams, John, as Harvard student, 73; on proportion of colonists opposed to independence, 161; explains term: American Revolution, 161-162; on religious cause for Revolution, 169; in First Continental Congress, 36; is complimented by horse-jockey, 178; on influences behind Federal Convention, 192; opposes manhood suffrage, 87; as author, 101.

Adams, John Quincy, presidential levees of, 88.

Adams, Samuel, as political organizer, 172-173, 176.

Agricultural revolution. See Economic revolution; Farmers' movements.

Aliens. See Immigration; Nativism.

Altschul, Charles, as author, 181.

Alvord, Clarence W., as author, 70, 183.

American Revolution, defined, 161-162, 179; misrepresented in text-books, 160; geographic factors in, 25, 37; influence of non-English frontier in, 6, 76; religious influences in, 169-170; divisions among colonists, 161, 180-181; British background of, 162-164; American setting of, 165-168; attitude of sections toward, 168-169, 176-177, 178; Grenville acts and colonial opposition, 170-172; Townshend acts and colonial opposition, 172-173; troubles with East India Company, 173-174; significance of Boston Tea Party, 174-175; acts of 1774, 175; First Continental Congress and results, 175-178; issue of independence, 178-179; not a contest over abstract rights, 179; the patriot-agitators, 114; loyalists of, 76-77, 180-181; rôle of women in, 130-131; bibliographical note, 181-183. *See also* War for Independence.

Ames, Herman V., as author, 244.

Andrews, Charles M., on English colonization, 51; as economic historian, 71; significance in historiography of colonial period, 181; as author, 181, 182.

Anthony, Susan B., wishes to learn long division, 135; agitates for immediate emancipation, 145; wants no cessation of suffrage agitation during Civil War, 146; author of nineteenth amendment, 154; on oligarchy of sex, 98; as author, 159.

Aristocracy, defined, 72; significance in American history, 72-

INDEX